Review and Expositor

A BAPTIST THEOLOGICAL JOURNAL

*Published by the Faculty of the Southern Baptist
Theological Seminary, Louisville, Kentucky*

VOL. LXXXIV, No. 3   **SUMMER, 1987**

Review and Expositor

A BAPTIST THEOLOGICAL JOURNAL

VOL. LXXXIV, No. 3   SUMMER, 1987

CONTENTS

Editorial Introduction

How does the Old Testament end? We have learned in recent years to pay more attention to the canonical order of the books of the Bible. Why, then, is it significant that the Old Testament ends with Malachi? This last of the Book of the Twelve minor prophets contains a series of controversies, or disputes, between the Lord and his people which expose God's hopes and expectations for the community of faith.

Those who lead Southern Baptist churches in the study of Malachi this year will find this issue to be a ready and valued resource. Thoughtfully designed by Thomas G. Smothers, Professor of Old Testament at Southern Seminary, this issue contains introductory articles; surveys of the content of Malachi; articles on special topics; and aids for preaching, teaching, and planning worship centered around the book of Malachi.

The introduction to the Book of Malachi, written by John D. W. Watts, not only surveys current critical positions regarding the authorship, date, and unity of the book but also situates Malachi in its canonical context and discusses the genre and shape of the book as literature. Joel F. Drinkard, Jr., amasses the archaeological evidence to provide a fascinating look at the socio-historical setting of Malachi in the early period of restoration (539-450 B.C.). These articles provide the information that those who teach Malachi will need in order to place the book in its social setting and bring it to life for contemporary Christians.

The content of the book is surveyed in two articles. The term *questions* appears in both titles because Malachi is structured around a series of six disputations or questions and answers. The messenger of the Lord raises the people's questions for them and then reports the Lord's answers, or announces the Lord's questions and repeats Judah's answers. Marvin E. Tate comments on the first three disputes: Yahweh's love for Israel (1:2-5), indictment of the priests and the people (1:6-2:9), and profaning the covenant with the fathers (2:10-16). The last three disputes, which are interpreted by Pamela J. Scalise, are concerned with judging the guilty and rewarding the faithful: wearying the Lord with doubts about divine justice (2:17-3:5), apostasy and repentance (3:6-12), and assurance for God-fearers (3:13-4:3).

The next three articles deal with topics which command a great deal of current interest: divorce, stewardship, and messianism. At points in the study of Malachi discussion will inevitably turn to these topics. David E. Garland, who recently co-authored *Beyond Companionship: Christians in Marriage* with Diana Garland, compactly surveys the biblical teachings on marriage, divorce, and remarriage, dealing with the difficult issues that these subjects raise for contemporary Christians.

W. Clyde Tilley, Professor of Religion and Philosophy at Union University, has given us an engaging essay which provides a fresh, biblical approach to stewardship. The potential importance of the article can be sensed from the topics it addresses: New Testament stewardship, human dominion and Christian stewardship, a perspectival interpretation of stewardship, Christian stewardship and tithing, and the concept of the graduated tithe. This eloquent call for a fresh understanding of Christian stewardship concludes: "We must live simply that others may simply live."

Interest in the development of Israel's messianic expectations has focused attention on three passages in Malachi: the messenger who comes to prepare the way of the Lord (3:1), Elijah's coming (4:5a), and the Day of the Lord (4:5b). Gerald L. Keown interprets each of these references and traces the history of their interpretation in ancient Jewish literature and the New Testament.

The next set of three articles provides immediate, practical suggestions and resources for ministers who will be planning worship, preaching, and teaching Malachi this year. W. Hulitt Gloer's article on preaching from Malachi outlines a procedure and suggests specific themes that can lead to appealing, solidly constructed sermons. Gloer is an Associate Professor of New Testament Interpretation at Midwestern Baptist Theological Seminary. In the creative and provocative article entitled " 'You Say': Confrontational Dialogue in Malachi" John D. Hendrix introduces the concept of *recursiveness* and develops a method for teaching the confrontations in Malachi recursively. Those who are searching for creative, new ways of doing Bible study will find this article exciting. Likewise, all who plan worship will find valuable assistance from Paul A. Richardson's "Worship Resources for Malachi." Richardson has conveniently gathered scripture readings, prayers, and hymns related to Malachi.

R. Michael Harton's faculty address, which analyses the history and influence of the early Chautauqua Institution as a model lifelong learning enterprise, concludes this issue.

Future issues of the *Review and Expositor* will be devoted to the following themes:

Fall, 1987 — The Baptist Heritage
Winter, 1988 — Worship
Spring, 1988 — Church Social Work
Summer, 1988 — John

Introduction to the Book of Malachi
J. D. W. Watts

Current students of Malachi are fortunate to have a number of recent commentaries that are accurate, provocative of thought, and readable. Ralph L. Smith of Southwestern Baptist Seminary wrote a full-scaled commentary including notes on the Hebrew text in 1984.[1] The translation, comments, and explanation section can be useful to all readers with or without skills in Hebrew. Page H. Kelley of Southern Baptist Seminary produced a readable and informative commentary in the same year.[2] Walter C. Kaiser, Jr., has written a detailed and helpful exposition of the book which preachers and teachers alike will find invaluable.[3] Elizabeth Achtemeier has continued her inspired interpretation of Old Testament books for preachers and teachers in 1986.[4] All of these are exceptionally competent and helpful works.

This introduction will take three forms. The significance of Malachi for the Canon of Scripture as well as the canonical position of the book will be discussed first. The usual issues of historical criticism, date, authorship, and unity will be treated. A literary introduction will deal with the context, genre, and shape of the book.

The Canonical Position

Malachi appears last in the Book of the Twelve (Minor) Prophets in virtually all collections, last in the Hebrew Latter Prophets, and last in the Old Testament in most Greek collections[5] and in the English Bible without Apocrypha. The canonical order is of considerable importance in assessing the meaning and significance of this little book.

For Jews the Pentateuch preserved the sacred traditions on which their faith and very existence were based. The Prophets helped them come to terms with the loss of their national identity and homeland. These prophetic books called for recognition that God continued to have a purpose for them, a life in covenant with them, and a faith for them in a day when they were scattered over the entire Persian empire. They focused attention on the possibility for Jerusalem and its Temple to be again the focus of Jewish worship as they applied the teachings of the Torah to a life-style in dispersed communities. The prophetic books turned their eyes toward a present and a future in which God had meaning and purpose for them.

The last of the prophetic books is Malachi. It epitomizes the prophetic insistence on God's continued love for this chosen people. It is very practical in demanding faith and faithfulness in the realistic situations in which priest and people find themselves. It insists on the reality of God, his presence, his purpose, and his love. It also knows that he distinguishes sharply between true worship and false, between genuine dedication and sham, and between a quality of life consistent with the Torah and one that is not. He will tolerate no lowering of these standards. Malachi proclaims the importance of God's will as revealed through the Torah (4:4). It also calls for a look to the future when God's intervention will come. And it promises a prophetic figure, Elijah, to intercede with the people in calling them to faith. It relates the Law and the Prophets to each other and binds the people to observance of both. These verses tie the Latter Prophets with the Pentateuch (Moses) and with the Former Prophets (Elijah).

Within the Christian Bible, containing Old and New Testaments, Malachi provides a bridge by summarizing the prophetic exhortations which the New Testament proclaims have been fulfilled in Jesus Christ (3:1) and by implying the prophetic character of his ministry and the preparation for it. The Gospels identify John the Baptist with the prophecy and 4:5-6 (Mark 9:12-13; Matt. 17:9-13).[6] They also use Malachi 3:1 and Isaiah 40:3 to describe John the Baptist as the one who will prepare the way of the Lord[7] (See Matt. 11:10 and John 1:21). The narratives of the Transfiguration (Mark 9:4 and Matt. 17:3) also build on the references to Moses and Elijah in the conclusion to Malachi.[8] Revelation 11:3-7 draws on the prophecy of Malachi 4:5-6 in speaking of two witnesses who are sent to warn of the judgment to come.

Apocryphal literature follows Malachi's picture of Elijah's mission. Sirach 48:1-11 has a forerunner who calms the wrath of God, turns the heart of the father to the child, and restores the tribes of Jacob.[9] The Coptic Apocalypse of Elijah (4:7-15 and 5:32) presents both Elijah and Enoch in such a role.[10] The Apocalypse of Daniel (14:1-3) pictures Elijah as one who fights against the anti-Christ.

The Historical-Critical Approach

Historical-literary criticism traces the origins of literature. It seeks critical answers to questions of date, authorship, and unity.

Otto Eissfeldt[11] summarized the critical position in the '40s. E. J. Young[12] presented a conservative position at about the same time. There is very little disagreement between them, nor has there been in books on Old Testament Introduction since then.

The superscription of the book (1:1) is of no help in finding answers to these questions. The term *oracle* or *burden* is identical to that over Zechariah 9:1 and 12:1. "The Word of Yahweh to Israel" identifies the book as intentionally canonical, i.e., an authoritative presentation of the word of God, and identifies the intended readers to be "Israel."

Malachi means "My Messenger." He is not identified further. Such a prophet is otherwise unknown, and many scholars think this may be a contrived name taken from the same word in 3:1. The Greek version translates it "by the hand of his angel." The Jewish custom was to personalize the name, and many scribes thought of Malachi as one alongside Haggai and Zechariah. The Targum of Jonathan adds "who is called the scribe Ezra." Jerome and Rashi also thought Ezra wrote the book, and Calvin agreed. Other early writers developed views that Malachi was a Levite who came from Sopha (or Sophira) in Zebulun.[13]

The book has three chapters in Hebrew. The Greek and English versions divided the same verses into four chapters. The Hebrew 3:19-24 becomes the English 4:1-16. The unity of the book has been rarely challenged except for the last three verses (4:4 and 5-6), which are broadly thought to be additions intended to interpret 3:1 by suggesting that Elijah will be "my messenger" and also intended to be a fitting end for the Latter Prophets or the Old Testament (see the paragraphs on "the Canonical Position" above).

The date of Malachi is to be set after the Exile, and the references to the Temple imply that it is written after Haggai-Zechariah (about 520-515 B.C.). But the lack of a clearly ordered priestly service suggests that the work of Ezra-Nehemiah (about 445 B.C.) had not yet taken place. There is little variation from these positions in the majority of introductions to the Old Testament.

The author of Malachi is unknown, therefore, apart from this mention in the superscription. The date is to be set in the fifth century B.C. The conditions mentioned and issues raised are similar to those found in Joel and in Isaiah 55-65. There is a Temple and worship in Jerusalem, but conditions are chaotic with no discernible leadership apparent. The literary structure of the book is reasonably clear with little reason to think of earlier sources or much later redaction. But 4:4 and 4:5-6 are thought to be editorial additions related to Malachi's position in the larger canon.

A Literary Introduction

Recent trends in biblical interpretation have exploited the methods used in secular literary interpretation to make old and familiar texts "come alive" for modern readers in fresh ways.[13] These methods read the Bible as literary texts, that is, they look at books as whole works, asking about their literary character (poetry or prose, narrative, speech, letter, etc.). They analyze what actually happens when a person reads a book and seek to increase a reader's competence to understand. Attention is focused on the text and the reader rather than on the author and the editors as in earlier methods.

A major trend in this method turns to the response which a reader gives to reading. It may look on the reading as an event or act which has a certain result. Both the text read and the reader bring certain elements to that encounter.

What results depends upon the dynamics in the text and the capacities and competences which the reader brings to the reading.

While the text of Malachi is the same for all readers, the meaning that readers draw from reading Malachi will not be the same. As readers decide upon how they relate to the text, they open or close doors of meaning and application to themselves. One way of applying new literary criticism is to see the book as a series of "speech acts" which happen to the reader. The reader is invited by the text to enter into the process of reading/understanding/responding. As the reader responds to each teasing gap in the text which has to be filled, the reader is prepared to continue the process in the next act.

Malachi as a Series of Speech Acts

A significant branch of modern literary theory views the reading of a text as engaging in a series of "speech acts" between the text and the reader.[14] Texts can be classified according to their nature. They assert a fact which is intended to elicit a response from the reader, or they express a wish or argument that is intended to convince a reader. Also, the intended response can be recognized.

Texts draw the reader into the act by intentionally leaving some things unsaid, creating gaps which the reader must fill.[15] The reader or interpreter becomes a part of the process of achieving meaning by filling in the gaps and thus steering the effect of the text in a direction that is relevant.

When Malachi is read with this in mind, what happens?

An Analysis

Speech Acts	Types	Effect
1:2a "I have loved you."	Assertive	Assurance
1:2b-5 "How have you loved us?"	Dialogical	To convince
1:6-14 "If I am a Father"	Dialogical/ Expressive	Persuade
2:1-9 "If you do not honor"	Dialogical/ Expressive	Threaten/Warn
2:10-12 "Why do you break covenant"	Dialogical/ Expressive	Persuade
2:13-16 "I hate divorce and violence"	Assertive	Assurance
2:17 "You have wearied the Lord"	Assertive	Assurance
3:1 "I will send and come"	Assertive	Assurance
3:2-5 "Who can endure the day"	Expressive	Threat/ Assurance
3:6-12 "I do not change" "Return to me and I to you"	Assertive	Assure/ Persuade
3:3-15 "You have said harsh things"	Assertive/ Accusation	Persuade

3:16 "Then they talked"	Narrative Report	Response
3:17-18 "They will be mine" "I will spare" "I will distinguish"	Assertive	Assurance
4:1-3 "The day is coming" "For you who revere . . . the sun of Righteousness"	Assertive	Warning/ Assurance
4:4 "Remember the Law of Moses"	Expressive	Evoke Obedience
4:5 "I will send Elijah"	Assertive	Assurance

When read in this way, the "gaps" which the reader must "fill in" become apparent immediately. In the first "act" the speaker is identified as Yahweh, the Lord. The reader who has read the Book of the Twelve Prophets (sometimes called the Minor Prophets) will be alerted to a return to the theme with which Hosea began. The gap lies in identifying the person addressed, the "you." The title helps. The implied reader is "Israel." But that, too, needs definition. The Israel that Moses led out of Egypt is known. The twelve tribes in Canaan are known. The Northern Kingdom of Israel is known. But who is the Israel addressed here? The text implies a group probably in Jerusalem in the fifth-century B.C. Kaiser understands this to address the "real reader" of the Christian Scriptures. Whether a reader can follow Kaiser, depends upon his or her willingness to fill the gap of the addressee with one's own person or group, that is, to identify oneself with the Israel addressed here. To do so is to open oneself in faith to hearing the Lord remind us (as well as fifth-century Jews) of all the ways that he has loved us.

The second speech-act (1:2b-5) recognizes a potential gap: "How have you loved us? The Lord chooses to answer by tracing the line of election back to his choice of Jacob over Esau, a line with relevance to the Jews because of the role of Edom in the destruction of Jerusalem in 587 B.C. and in even more recent history (cf. Amos and Obadiah). But the Lord insists that his elective love for Israel has not varied.

The third speech act (1:6-14) begins with a simple truth: "A son honors his father, and a servant his master." Then God puts personal equivalents into the equation: "If I am father, or master, where is the honor due me? Priests are identified as culprits. They are addressed. They ask for explanation, which is furnished. The quality of sacrifice shows disrespect for God. The word to the priests is continued (2:1-9) to show why they have been despised by the people. They have failed in sacrifice and in teaching, and God's curse is on them. The reader also knows that his worship and doctrine are under scrutiny and test. The passage picks up the theme of false worship begun in Hosea and in Amos 4:4-5.

Three short speeches respond to God's accusation. The first (2:10-12) acknowledges that their covenant with God binds them to one another and asks why they "break faith" with each other. Judah is accused of "desecrating the sanctuary by marrying the daughter of a foreign god" and calls for such a person to be excommunicated even if he brings offerings. A gap exists because the sin is not more closely identified. But the implication is clear. Under the pressure of God's accusation and warnings Israelites begin accusing each other of unfaithfulness to the covenant. Perhaps these are priests that try to turn the pressure on someone else.

A second speech (2:13-16) suggests that the reason God does not respond to offerings is that God is standing as judge over a divorce action. God acknowledges that he hates divorce and violence against his wife.

A third speech (2:17) accuses the hearers of "wearying the Lord with their words" (cf. Isa. 43:22 and Micah 6:3). Their words imply that he really does not care whether one does right or wrong.

The next speech (3:1) puts an end to the accusations and counter accusations. The Lord will send his messenger, and then he will suddenly appear in the Temple. This messenger of God's covenant, who of course they all desire, will come in person. The speech changes the entire climate of the dialogue. A gap is clear: what would it be like for God to come in person? And is that what they really want?

The next speech (3:2-5) fills those gaps with the anxiety that one feels about such a close encounter with God. It sees him as a "refiner," "a purifier" to deal with the Levites' problems. He will then have men to bring acceptable sacrifices. It does not say whether these are Levites or not. Then the offerings of Judah and Jerusalem will be acceptable. Then the Lord fills the gap: he will testify against those who break his laws and who do not fear God.

God seizes the initiative again. He insists that he is dealing with them just as he has in the past. He has not changed (3:6-12). He has always been ready to receive them and return to them, even when they have sinned, if they will turn to him. The address is now not to priests but to all Israel. In feigned innocence they asked, "How shall we return?" God gives a practical suggestion: change your actions. You are now robbing God of his tithes, and you are under the curse because of it: change. Begin bringing your tithes to God, who will lift the curse.

God charges them with slanderous talk (3:13-15). The only narrative in the book recounts how they responded (3:16). They are "those who feared God." They talked about the issues. And "the Lord listened and heard." And they wrote a scroll in his presence with their names on it. The Lord recognizes their sincere act (3:17-18), promises to spare them, and notes that now one will again be able to recognize the righteous, that is those who fear and honor God, and distinguish them from the wicked who do not.

Again the Lord announces the coming day (4:1-3). Note the theme picks up that of the Day of the Lord from Joel, Amos, and Zephaniah. The previous separation of the righteous from the wicked is important, for the wicked are to be destroyed. But the day promises hope and assurance for the believers who "revere God's name." "The sun of righteousness will rise with healing in his wings." There is no preparation for this announcement. It is a true gap that needs to be filled. The Christian will think in canonical perspective of Christ. The implied reader of the fifth century B.C. could hardly have thought of anyone but God himself or God's chosen one. But the joy to follow is unmistakable. The triumph of the righteous in that day is clearly promised.

The final speeches emphasize the foundations of post-exilic faith: attention to the Torah of Moses (4:4) as God's law for all Israel, and the role of the prophet (Elijah) to call the people to reconciliation under the threat of judgment. These translate to the Christian reader as exhortations to heed the Bible as God's word and to heed prophetic preaching that calls on them to be reconciled with each other.

Malachi as the Last Book of the Twelve

The Minor Prophets are generally thought of as separate books. But they function in the Hebrew Latter Prophets as one book to balance the large prophetic books. This calls for more attention than we have usually given. The twelve books together present a more coherent and powerful message than they do separately, especially if they are viewed as their readers have to view them, that is as a complete collection.

Malachi is placed last in virtually all collections. Hosea is first in almost all collections. The two books have much in common, especially the first three chapters of Hosea. They both stress the unchanging elective and covenant love of God for a people who have dishonored and abandoned him. They both picture him as unchanging in this relationship. Both see it in terms of a marriage which God is unwilling to recognize as broken.

Micah is undeniably the central book of the Twelve, and chapter four is its central chapter. Its picture of the raised and restored Temple Mount to which all peoples may come is the ideal against which fifth-century B.C. worship practices are to be measured. Malachi shows how far short the worship in the second Temple fell from that goal. In Isaiah 2 the same passage becomes the central theme for the book,[16] which is then fulfilled in chapter 66.[17] The Book of the Twelve uses the same theme but exalts it by putting it at the center of the book, whereas Isaiah put it at the beginning and the end. The Book of the Twelve chooses to put the theme of God's unchanging love through election and covenant at the beginning and the end.

The theme of "the Day of the Lord" is developed in the Book of the Twelve Prophets as in no other part of the Old Testament. In Joel, Amos, and Zephaniah "the Day" is announced and described. It reoccurs in Malachi, a reminder that the day was not to be seen as fulfilled in the terrible destruction of Jerusalem of 587 B.C. The readers of the entire collection still look forward to it with fear and trembling.

Like Isaiah, the Twelve finally come to recognize that promises and threats cannot always apply to the entire people and nation. Finally there must be a division, even in Israel, between the believing, reverent worshipers and the unbelieving and idolatrous wicked. In Isaiah it comes in chapter 65.[18] In the Book of the Twelve it is recognized in Malachi 3:18.

The hope of a future deliverer for Jews is held high by Malachi 4:2-3. While there are passages that imply a hope for this one to be a king of the line of David, such as Amos 9:11-12 and Micah 5:2, it is significant that this hope is not held consistently. The full thrust of the book gives no support to Judean monarchs of the fifth century B.C. Rather, hope centers in a restored temple that will be open to all (Micah 4 and Isaiah 2). The same trend is clear in Isaiah. The high hopes for a successor to the throne of Ahaz in Isaiah 7-11 are fulfilled in Hezekiah. But this is finally a disappointment, and the rest of the prophecy sees hope in a restored temple with no reference to a Davidic ruler (see Isaiah 66).[19]

The Book of the Twelve is filled with hope, based on the constancy of God's love for Israel and the assurance of salvation for those who revere and honor him. The assurance of "the sun of righteousness" who will rise is supported by the commitment to Moses' Torah and the Elijah's preparation.

Some primary themes bind the Book of Malachi together. When these are recognized, the purpose and direction of the book are much clearer.

The overriding theme is the constancy and permanency of God's elective love for Israel.[20] It is explicit in 1:2 and 3:6, but it undergirds the entire book. The problem for this theme is to show how God's justice can punish breech of covenant while still exercising his election-love. The book answers by showing how he will distinguish the righteous ones from the covenant breakers in the days of judgment (3:17-18).

A second theme is the reconciliation of fathers and children. It sometimes refers to God, the father, and Israel, his children (1:2-5; 1:6; 2:10). It sometimes refers to intergenerational conflict among the Jews (4:6).

A third theme is the anticipation of the coming day of judgment (3:2-5; 4:1-3). This coming day is related to judgments past (1:3-5) and to present curses in retribution for dishonor (2:2), and the promise of a messenger to come before, and in relation to, the Lord's appearance for judgment (3:1 and 4:5). These all make significant contributions to the Bible's teachings on these issues.

---

[1] Ralph L. Smith, *Micah-Malachi*, Word Biblical Commentary, 32 (Waco, Texas: Word Books, 1984), pp. 296-342.

[2] Page H. Kelley, *Micah, . . . Malachi,* Layman's Bible Book Commentary, 14 (Nashville: Broadman Press, 1984), pp. 147-163.

[3] Walter C. Kaiser, *Malachi: God's Unchanging Love* (Grand Rapids: Baker Book House, 1984).

[4] Elizabeth Achtemeier, *Nahum-Malachi,* Interpretation (Atlanta: John Knox Press, 1986), pp. 171-198.

[5] See Roger Beckwith, *The Old Testament Canon of the New Testament Church* (Grand Rapids: Wm. B. Eerdmans, 1986), pp. 450-451.

[6] See W. Wink, *John the Baptist in the Gospel Tradition* (Cambridge: University Press, 1968), pp. 28-29, *et passim.*

[7] See John A. T. Robinson, "Elijah, John and Jesus: An Essay in Detection," *New Testament Studies,* 4 (1957-58), 268, and references in the commentaries.

[8] See M. Pannent, "Moses and Elijah in the Story of the Transfiguration," *The Expository Times,* 92 (1981), 338.

[9] See relevant passages in D. R. James, "The Elijah/Elisha Motif in Luke" (Dissertation, Southern Baptist Theological Seminary, 1984).

[10] See M. M. Faierstein, "Why Do the Scribes Say Elijah Must Come First?" *Journal of Biblical Literature,* 100 (1981), 78.

[11] Otto Eissfeldt, *The Old Testament: An Introduction,* trans. by P. R. Ackroyd (New York: Harper and Row, 1965), pp. 441-443.

[12] Edward J. Young, *An Introduction to the Old Testament* (Grand Rapids: Wm. B. Eerdmans, 1949), pp. 275-277.

[13] See J. M. P. Smith, *Book of Malachi,* International Critical Commentary (Edinburgh: T.&T. Clark, 1912), p. 10.

[14] See Edgar V. McKnight, *The Bible and the Reader: An Introduction to Literary Criticism* (Philadelphia: Fortress Press, 1985), and David Robertson, *The Old Testament and the Literary Critic* (Philadelphia: Fortress Press, 1977).

[15] See Seymour Chatman, *Story and Discourse* (Ithaca, N.Y.: Cornell University Press, 1978), pp. 161-165; John Austin, *How to Do Things with Words* (New York: Oxford University Press, 1962); Wolfgang Iser, *The Act of Reading* (London: Routledge & Kegan Paul, 1978); John R. Searle, *Expression and Meaning: Studies in the Meaning of Speech Acts* (Cambridge: University Press, 1979).

[16] John D. W. Watts, *Isaiah 1-33,* Word Biblical Commentary, 24 (Waco, Texas: Word Books, 1985), pp. xliv, 26-29.

[17] John D. Watts, *Isaiah 34-66,* Word Biblical Commentary, 25 (Waco, Texas: Word Books, 1987), commentary on chapter 66.

[18] Ibid., commentary on chapter 65.

[19] Ibid., commentary on chapter 66.

[20] See Walter Kaiser, *Malachi,* pp. 11-13.

The Socio-Historical Setting of Malachi
Joel F. Drinkard, Jr.

The time frame for Malachi is that of post-exilic Judah, or better, restoration Judah.[1] As such it was certainly not a very auspicious era for Judah and a far cry from the "golden age" of the monarchy, even in the years of its decline. Just as Judah tended to look back nostalgically to what had been, so we today tend to look at the restoration period as a sort of appendage to Judah's history, a dark age that lay between the period of the monarchy and the beginning of the New Testament era. Often our stereotypical view sees from this era only the rise of "legalistic Judaism" with its emphasis on perfunctory performance of ritual over against the high ethical demands and living faith called for by pre-exilic prophets. Even in the field of Biblical Archaeology, major textbooks either omit entirely[2] or treat only in the most cursory fashion[3] the restoration period. Therefore, a look at the social and historical context of restoration Judah is needed to understand the milieu out of which Malachi arose.

The Period of Dispersion-Exile, 586-539 B.C.

The year was 586 B.C. Catastrophe of greatest proportions had struck Judah. An abortive attempt to revolt against Babylonian rule, spurred by promises of aid from Egypt and encouraged by some prophets and a pro-Egyptian element in the royal court, had resulted in a full invasion of Judah by Nebuchadnezzar to quell the revolt. And quell it, Nebuchadnezzar did. The land was occupied and the fortified cities, including Jerusalem, were destroyed. The monarchy was officially terminated;[4] some leading royal, cultic, military, and probably commercial, personnel were deported to Babylon.[5] Others fled Judah to resettle in Phoenicia, Transjordan, and Egypt. The Temple, that symbol of God's presence in the midst of his people, was destroyed. Thus every major stackpole of Judah's culture was gone.

Rather than focusing on the situations of those Judeans who were deported, a better view of restoration Judah can be gained by looking at the situation of those remaining in the land. Albright and Bright have estimated that Judah's population dropped from over 250,000 in the eighth century B.C. to less than 20,000[6] as a result of the wars with Assyria and Babylon and the collapse of the monarchy. In contrast to this estimate of the catastrophe, Gottwald has estimated that no more than five percent of the inhabitants were deported.[7] In all likelihood, the true state of affairs lies between these two extreme estimates. Probably the bulk of the population remained in the land —

though it was bereft of its leadership. As is so often the case those who did not flee, who could not flee, were the peasants, the unskilled and the semi-skilled. They are called "the poorest people of the land."[8]

In addition to the disruption caused by the deportation of the leadership, the economy of the land was in shambles due to the war. And whatever agriculture and economy survived would have faced taxation at the hand of the Babylonian conquerors. The devastation and famine of the last days of Judah before the fall and the early part of the exilic period are described in Lamentations.[9] There are even some indications that the economy was so ravaged that Judah had to import food,[10] putting even more strain on the economy. Care must be taken, however, in using stylized poetical laments to depict precisely the condition in Jerusalem and Judah after the fall of the monarchy.

A closer examination of the archaeological evidence shows that all of Judah did not suffer the same destruction and disruption as did Jerusalem and her fortified cities. In recent years, excavations from northern Judah and especially in the region of Benjamin have indicated that city life continued to exist after the fall of Jerusalem and throughout the Babylonian period.[11] Cities such as Tell en-Nasbeh (Mizpah?), Gibeon, Bethel, and Tell el-Ful (Gibeah?), no more than ten miles from Jerusalem, not only existed but prospered in the late sixth century.[12] At Tell el-Ful, the size of the town actually increased in mid-sixth century, and peaceful conditions permitted the building of houses outside the Iron Age city wall.[13]

Furthermore, a survey of smaller settlements, probably villages, of the central hill country of Judah revealed unwalled sites that continued to exist after the destruction of Jerusalem.[14] The implication of these finds is that in the rural areas daily life continued much as before the destruction. One can guess that after the initial disruption caused by the destruction of Jerusalem and the shift of power entirely to Babylon, the peasant's life returned to semi-normal — a subsistence life with heavy taxes due to the state, only now the state was Babylon and not Judah. And even in Jerusalem, life continued. Houses were rebuilt, and some semblance of city life remained. Even Lamentations at its bleakest does indicate that people still inhabited Jerusalem (see esp. Lam. 5).

So the community in Palestine survived. Surely the conditions were difficult, but life continued. No evidence exists for a resettlement of foreign populace into Judah of the sort the Assyrians practiced in Israel and elsewhere. Thus the population remained intact and maintained its cultural identity. Furthermore, we should not assume a total absence of contact between those in Babylon and the remaining population in Judah. Jeremiah sent at least two letters to the deportees and received a letter in return (Jer. 29). Likewise at the time of Nehemiah, communication between Jews in Persia and those in Palestine took place (Neh. 1). No reason exists to doubt a regular contact between the deportees and the Judeans in Palestine throughout this period.

Apparently some form of worship continued among the ruins of the Temple (Jer. 41:4-5, assuming "the house of the Lord" referred to the Temple). Even worshipers from Israelite cities such as Samaria, Shechem, and Shiloh brought offerings and incense to the Temple ruins (Jer. 41:4-5). Some priests remained, probably of lesser ranks, but the worship patterns and festivals were virtually abandoned (Lam. 1:4). Yet the religion itself was not abandoned. Although severely tested, the faith of those remaining in Judah also survived. The book of Lamentations, while bemoaning the sorry state of affairs in Jerusalem and Judah following the fall, still holds to a faith in God. The fall is described as God's judgment on Judah's sins, a judgment which was correct (Lam. 4:6; 1:17-18). Yet Lamentations closes with a call for God to remember, restore, and renew his people (Lam. 5:1, 21). Out of despair came the hope and faith that God might still show mercy to his people.

The political situation in Judah following 586 B.C. is unclear. It is certain that the monarchy was ended. Gedaliah, probably a member of Zedekiah's court, was chosen as governor by the Babylonians. After serving for a short period of time, he was murdered by Ishmael, a member of the royal Davidic family (Jer. 40-41).[15] It seems likely that Babylon then placed Judah under the control of the province of Samaria.[16] Judah thus would have lost both its independence and its separate identity. (And incidentally such annexation of Judah to Samaria during this period could partially explain the bitterness of the Jews to the Samaritans evident from the subsequent period of Ezra and Nehemiah.)[17]

The Early Period of Restoration, 539-450 B.C.

Less than fifty years after Babylon reached the peak of her power, she had ceased to exist as a nation. The last king, Nabonidus, brought about a great deal of internal dissension within Babylon. He was a devotee of the moon god Sin and apparently sought to replace Marduk as chief god with Sin.[18] For a ten-year period Nabonidus transferred his official resident to Teima in North Arabia, not even returning to Babylon for the New Year Festival, Babylon's most important religious festival. Thus he was hated by the priests of the major religion, and many of the people of Babylon were not loyal to him because of his long absence. Babylon was ripe for conquest, and her conqueror was at hand.

Cyrus began as prince of Anshan, a province of Media. He revolted against Media and conquered it in 550 B.C. He then moved across the northern part of Mesopotamia and into Asia Minor, conquering Lydia and its proverbial king Croesus in 547/546 B.C. Apparently Cyrus then moved back eastward, and conquered Parthia before moving against Babylon. In the summer of 539 B.C. Babylon's army was defeated soundly by the Persians under Cyrus. A Babylonian general Gobyras, who had previously switched allegiance to Cyrus, entered Babylon without resistance. Soon Cyrus was welcomed into the city as a liberator; he publicly took part in the worship of Marduk and claimed the throne of Babylon.

Cyrus inaugurated a new policy of permitting certain captive peoples to return to their homelands. With a massive empire now twice as large as any previous empire in the region, Cyrus chose to permit more local autonomy in order to gain support of his subject peoples. Thus the Edict of Cyrus (Ezra 1:2-4; 6:3-5) that permitted Jews to return to their homeland was part of a broader Persian policy.

The actual number of exiles who returned to Judah in the first group in 538 B.C. is unknown. Sheshbazzar, a prince of Judah (Ezra 1:5-11), was the leader of this first group of returnees. The account in Ezra specifies that a part of Sheshbazzar's mission was to rebuild the Temple and that he did indeed get the foundation laid, but little more (Ezra 1:5; 5:13-15). Apparently, few of the exiles were willing to return. They were satisfied with their new lives in Babylon. Judah seemingly had little to offer. Josephus puts it plainly: they were "not willing to leave their possessions."[19]

What little work was accomplished by this first group of returnees soon ended. Eighteen years later, at the beginning of Haggai's prophecies, the Temple still had not been rebuilt (Hag. 1:2). The grand vision in Isaiah 40 of the return of the exiles with God at their head was a far cry from the reality of 538 B.C. The glorious restored Temple vision of Ezekiel 40-44 was a far cry from the pathetic attempts of Sheshbazzar.

Ultimately the Temple was rebuilt during the time of Zerubbabel and Joshua from 520-515 B.C. The preaching of Haggai and Zechariah seems to have had a major role in influencing the leadership and the people to the task of rebuilding. More exiles had returned to Judah during this period, but apparently most remained in their new land (Ezra 4:1-6, 23-24). Ezra reports that the Samaritans delayed the building work with accusations of rebellion against the Jews.[20] But when the charges were proven unfounded, the work continued and the Temple was completed in 515 B.C. (Ezra 6).

But the restored Temple did not inaugurate the golden age for the restored community in Judah. The second Temple was no match for the Solomonic one. Even at the laying of the foundation for this second Temple, many of the elders who remembered the first Temple wept (Ezra 3:12). Furthermore this second Temple was not a national shrine as the first Temple had been. Samaria was not permitted to be a part of the rebuilding process. Samaria and the Samaritans would go their own way. Even Judah was nothing like the Judah of old. No longer a nation and not even a province until the time of Nehemiah, Judah now only covered an area of about ten to fifteen miles around Jerusalem. So the actual, restored community and Temple were unlike the hoped for new age, unlike the prophecies of second Isaiah and Ezekiel, and a bitter disappointment to many whose expectations had been raised by the prophecies.

The socio-economic situation in Judah did not change drastically with the restoration. Jerusalem probably saw more rebuilding following the return, as one would expect these families of aristocracy, priests, and skilled craftsman to locate there. In the rural areas, life probably continued unchanged. The archaeological evidence indicates a continuity of life in the villages and smaller cities from before the fall of Judah through this period.[21] Some evidence for the economic situation of the early period of restoration can be drawn from Haggai. There are several references to drought, poor harvests, and famine (Hag. 1:5-11). These disasters are interpreted as God's response to the people's unfaithfulness. Probably indicated by the prophecies are a couple of seasons of poor harvest immediately prior to Haggai's ministry. More relevant is Haggai's mention of the way the people of Jerusalem were then living:

> "This people say the time has not yet come to rebuild the house of the Lord . . . . Is it a time for you yourselves to dwell in your paneled houses, while this house lies in ruins?" (Hag. 1:2, 4).

Certainly Haggai is not addressing all the people of Jerusalem with his charge. But since the word is issued directly to Zerubbabel and Joshua (Hag. 1:1), undoubtedly they and others of the aristocracy who had returned had built fine homes for themselves. The remaining citizens of Jerusalem might not have had such grand homes, but they had busied themselves with their own homes while the Temple lay in ruins (Hag. 1:9). Thus in Haggai's time (520-525 B.C.), Jerusalem shows evidence of rebuilding and restoration. It was considerably smaller than it had been a century earlier and certainly not nearly so grand, but it was being rebuilt. Apparently this restored city had no defensive wall until the time of Nehemiah in 444 B.C. (Neh. 2-7). This lack of a defensive wall may not have been the result of economics, nor even of the small size of Jerusalem's population, but more a consequence of its relative unimportance. Judah was apparently governed from Samaria during this time. To indicate Samaria's dominance, officials there would refuse to allow Jerusalem to become a walled city again.[22] The displeasure of Sanballat at Nehemiah's building of the wall would be obvious (Neh. 2:19; 4:1, 2, 7-8). Sanballat feared he was losing Judah from his control, which is apparently what happened. Judah became a separate province of Persia under Nehemiah.[23]

Dating Malachi

The precise date of Malachi is much disputed, thus creating difficulty in understanding its historical setting. Adam C. Welch, on the one extreme, dated Malachi to the period before the restoration of the Temple.[24] On the other extreme, H. Winckler[25] and A. Spoer[26] proposed a date in the Maccabean era. But the general consensus of scholarship[27] places Malachi somewhere in the period between the completion of the second Temple in 515 B.C. and the work of Ezra and Nehemiah.[28]

The general economic picture is a continuation of that depicted above for the period following the destruction of Judah and the restoration.

In turning to the book of Malachi itself for historical points of contact, one finds few definite historical references. The book opens with a word of contrast between God's love of Israel and God's hatred of Edom. This reference describes Edom as being laid waste, shattered, and in ruins (Mal. 1:3-4). Apparently the great enmity between Israel and Edom began after the fall of Judah (e.g., Ps. 137:7-9) and replaced an earlier more fraternal relationship (Gen. 36). While earlier writings build on the Genesis identification of Esau with Edom, the later writings without exception emphasize the hatred toward Edom because of Edom's seizure of part of the Negeb (southern Judah) after 586 B.C. (Ezek. 35; 36:5; Lam. 4:21-22; Obad.). It is possible that the devastation of Edom mentioned in Malachi 1:3-4 refers to the expulsion of the Edomites from their homeland at the hand of the Nabateans, but even this possibility does not provide an exact date. It is not known precisely when the Nabateans displaced the Edomites.

More helpful are the references to offerings presented on the altar (Mal. 1:7), to the sanctuary of the Lord (Mal. 2:11), and to the Lord's temple (Mal. 3:1). These references certainly imply a rebuilt temple.[29] The reference to the altar alone may not be conclusive. But the additional references to both sanctuary and temple imply a rebuilt structure as opposed to a ruin where worship might continue. Furthermore, the concern of Malachi is not about the rebuilding but about the offerings and worship in the Temple and the practice of the people. The Temple itself is presupposed. Thus the earliest date possible for Malachi would be the restoration of the Temple, 515 B.C.

The use of the term *governor* (Mal. 1:8) does tend to relate the book to the Persian period; however, the use of this word is not confined to that period and it does not help limit the date of Malachi any further.

Malachi does refer to the matter of marrying foreign wives (Mal. 2:10-12). This suggests that Malachi was addressing the same problem as did Ezra (Ezra 9-10). The fact that the matter of foreign wives was dealt with so decisively by Ezra strongly suggests that Malachi's concern is either antecedent to or contemporary with Ezra. In the same way, Malachi's strong statement against divorce (Mal. 2:13-16) also seems to be antecedent to or contemporary with Ezra's call to divorce foreign wives. After Ezra's legislation was enacted, it would have been very difficult for Malachi's position to be held. These two factors taken together suggest the latest possible date for writing Malachi was the enactment of Ezra's legislation, variously dated to 458 B.C., 428 B.C., or 398 B.C.[30] Additional references to mixed marriage occur in Nehemiah (10:30 and 13:23-30). While these references denounce mixed marriages and require an oath not to permit one's children to enter a mixed marriage, Nehemiah's oaths do not demand divorce from mixed marriage. Nehemiah apparently served two terms as governor. His ministry and message is usually dated to 444 B.C. and 432 B.C. It is possible that Nehemiah's message is later than Ezra's legislation and thus Nehemiah does not mention divorce because it is presupposed by

Ezra's legislation. Most scholars feel, however, that the ministry and message of Nehemiah is earlier than Ezra.[31]

The message of Malachi seems closer to that of Nehemiah since neither Malachi nor Nehemiah demand divorce from mixed marriages. Malachi's strong statement against divorce stands in direct contrast to Ezra's legislation and would thus seem to represent an earlier position or a competing contemporary position. Indeed, in Malachi the denunciation of mixed marriages stands juxtaposed with the statement abhorring divorce with no apparent contradiction. Malachi thus does not call for divorce as a possible solution to mixed marriages. The juxtaposition would seem to rule out divorce as a way of dealing with mixed marriages. The result of these comparisons is the suggestion that Malachi is no later than Ezra and seems closer to Nehemiah. So a date of 458 B.C. to 398 B.C. seems reasonable for the latest possible date for Malachi.

In addition, no distinction is made between priests and Levites in Malachi (Mal. 2:1-9; 3:3-4). But a distinction appears already in Nehemiah (Neh. 10:35-39) between the Levites and the priests who are specified as "son of Aaron" (Neh. 10:38). Some period of time seems to have passed between Malachi's message and Nehemiah for these distinctions to arrive and be implemented.

The combination of these factors places Malachi between 515 B.C. and 458-398 B.C. Especially due to the lack of distinction between priests and Levites, I would place Malachi earlier in that time frame, to approximately 500 B.C.

---

[1] The terms *Exile* and *post-exilic* do not reflect the broad dispersion of the Hebrews during this period to Egypt, Phoenicia, Syria and Ammonite, Moabite, and Edomite areas (Jer. 40:11). They also focus primarily on the relatively small group deported to Babylon (though granted they were much of the leadership) and omits the majority who remained in the land. The terms also fail to recognize that most of the "exiles" chose not to return at the period of restoration.

[2] Yohanan Aharoni, *The Archaeology of the Land of Israel*, trans. Anson F. Rainey (Philadelphia: Westminster, 1982). The major text on Biblical Archaeolgy by an Israeli archaeologist ends with the fall of Jerusalem and end of the Monarchy.

[3] Kathleen Kenyon, *Archaeology in the Holy Land*, 5th ed. (Nashville: Thomas Nelson, 1985), has a total of 7 pages out of 312 devoted to the exilic and post-exilic periods.

[4] Following an earlier revolt, the Babylonians had deported King Jehoiachin and had put Zedekiah on the throne. Thus the Babylonians had hoped to control a rebellious vassal state with a ruler who would be loyal to Babylon rather than having to disrupt the society. A deportation of many leading citizens occurred at this earlier date (597 B.C.). See John Bright, *A History of Israel*, 3rd ed. (Philadelphia: Westminster, 1981), p. 328.

[5] The figure Jeremiah gives (52:29) of 832 persons may only represent adult males and then only those from within the city of Jerusalem itself (see Bright, *History*, p. 330, n. 61).

[6] W. F. Albright, *The Biblical Period from Abraham to Ezra* (New York: Harper, 1963), pp. 87, 115-111; Bright, *History*, p. 344.

[7] Norman Gottwald, *The Hebrew Bible — A Socio-Literary Introduction* (Philadelphia: Fortress, 1985), p. 423.

[8] Literally, "the poor of the people of the land," 2 Kgs. 24:14; 25:12; cp. Jer. 40:7; 52:15, 16.

[9] See esp. Lam. 1:3, 11; 2:11; 4:4, 8-9; 5:4, 6, 9, 11.

[10] Lam. 5:6, literally "we gave hand (submitted) to Egypt and Assyria to have enough food."

Reference to paying for other essentials in Lam. 5:4 makes it possible that the same is true here.

[11] Ephraim Stern, *Material Culture of the Land of the Bible in the Persian Period 538-332 B.C.* (Warminster: Aris and Phillips, 1982), p. 48.

[12] Paul Lapp, "Tell el-Ful," *Biblical Archaeologist,* 28 (1965), 6.

[13] Stern, *Material Culture,* p. 34.

[14] Ibid, p. 40.

[15] The date 458 B.C. is entirely arbitrary—it follows the traditional date for the beginning of Ezra's ministry (Shemaryahu Talmon, "Ezra and Nehemiah," *Interpreter's Dictionary of the Bible,* supp. vol. (Nashville: Abingdon, 1976), pp. 317-328. No suggestion is being made that restoration ended at 458 B.C., only that Malachi had probably been written by that date and our historical survey need not extend beyond that date.

[16] Albrecht Alt, "Die Rolle Samarias bei der Entstehung des Judentums," *Kleine Schriften,* Vol. 2 (Munich: C.H. Beck'sche, 1953), pp. 317-337.

[17] Neh. 2:19-20; 4:1-5, 7-9, etc.; Neh. 13:28-29. Sean McEvenue, "The Political Structure in Judah from Cyrus to Nehemiah," *Catholic Biblical Quarterly,* 43 (1981), 364, draws attention to this possible cause for the later bitterness and schism.

[18] Bright, *History,* p. 353.

[19] Josephus, *Antiquities of the Jews,* XI.1.3.

[20] The census list in Ezra 2 (cp. Neh. 7) probably gives returnees down to the time of Ezra. Note that this list includes ones returning with Zerubbabel (before 520 B.C.) and Nehemiah (444 B.C.) and others (Ezra 2:2).

[21] See above notes 11 and 14.

[22] Such enforced humiliation could also be part of the Jewish bitterness toward the Samaritans already alluded to earlier (p. 385 and note 17).

[23] Gottwald, *The Hebrew Bible,* p. 432.

[24] Adam C. Welch, *Post-Exilic Judaism* (Edinburgh: William Blackwood, 1935), pp. 113-115.

[25] H. Winckler, *Altorientalische Forschungen,* vol. 2 (Leipzig: E. Pfeiffer, 1899), pp. 531-539.

[26] A. Spoer, "Some New Considerations Towards the Dating of the Book of Malachi," *Jewish Quarterly Review,* 20 (1908), 167-186.

[27] Bright, *History,* p. 373; Gottwald, *The Hebrew Bible,* p. 510; Eissfeldt, *The Old Testament: An Introduction,* trans. Peter R. Ackroyd (New York: Harper & Row, 1965), p. 443.

[28] The dating of Ezra and Nehemiah is itself a much debated issue. See the brief discussion in Gottwald, *The Hebrew Bible,* pp. 434-437.

[29] Contra Welch, *Post-Exilic,* pp.113-115.

[30] For a discussion of the dates for Ezra, see Bright, *History,* pp. 391-402, and S. Talmon, "Ezra and Nehemiah," *Interpreter's Dictionary of the Bible,* supp. vol. (Nashville: Abingdon, 1976), pp. 320-321.

[31] Following Bright, *History,* pp. 391-402; contra Talmon, "Ezra," pp. 320-321.

Questions for Priests and People in Malachi 1:2-2:16.
Marvin E. Tate

This article is concerned with the exposition of the first half of the Book of Malachi. Introductory and contextual matters are dealt with in the first two articles found in this issue of the *Review and Expositor,* and I will not give them any major attention in the discussion which follows. The speaker/narrator in the book is not identified beyond the brief superscription in 1:1 which refers to him as Malachi ("My Messenger"), which is probably a literary construct derived from the "messenger of Yahweh of Hosts" in 2:7 and "my messenger" in 3:1. The "messenger" in 2:7 refers to the function of a priest, and the functioning of priests is a major concern in this book. The perspective on the priesthood in Malachi seems clearly to be that of the Deuteronomistic materials, which project all Levites as priests (cf. Deut. 17:9; 18:1-8; Jer. 33:21; Neh. 13:29; note the covenant with Levi in Malachi 2:7; also 3:3), rather than emphasizing the role of the sons of Aaron or Zadokites as priests (e.g., Num. 16:40; Ezek. 44:15). Thus it seems appropriate to consider the speaker in Malachi to be a Levitical priest/prophet (cf. 1 Chr. 25:1; 2 Chr. 15:1; 20:14-17) who speaks as a messenger of Yahweh.[1]

The dominant literary feature of the book is the question-and-answer format. The question-and-answer style of discourse is found elsewhere in the prophetic literature (e.g., Haggai 1:4-6, 7-11, 2:3-5, 15-16; Zech. 1-8; Micah 2:6-11; Isa. 40:12-17). The style is frequently called that of the "disputation oracle" or "prophetic disputation" (cf. Jer. 2:29-37; 3:1-5; 15:18).[2] *Disputation* is a general term for a dispute or controversy between two or more parties in which differing points of view are expressed in rather formal manner. In prophetic literature, this form is used to answer implied or stated charges made against God.[3] The genre is flexible and varies in the ways in which it is expressed. In Malachi, the disputation has a literary formation which begins with some sort of basic statement, or a rhetorical question which expects an affirmative answer (as in 1:6). The question (e.g., "How have you loved us?" in 1:2) is followed by a response from God (and the prophetic speaker) which may include a pronouncement of judgment (e.g., 1:14; 2:3, 9). The disputation is ultimately derived from real life, from situations such as conversation, street speaking or preaching, teaching, and legal proceedings. One can think of a priest/prophet called Malachi (or one who thought of himself or herself under this rubric) carrying on a disputative type of preaching or teaching in the Temple (cf. the disputations of Jesus with various groups in the Temple according to the Gospels) sometime during the period of 520-450 B.C.[4] A rather large body of Old Testament literature seems to reflect this period (Isa. 55-66 — and the Book of Isaiah as such — Haggai, Zechariah, Ezra, and Nehemiah). This literature bears the marks of having emerged from troubled, factious communities in which the polemic language of controversy between groups was common. Clearly, the communities were struggling for faith and a godly way of life in difficult times.[5]

The reader's understanding of the book may be enhanced by the use of historical imagination to contextualize the written material in appropriate life situations. In fact, in a way the book invites the reader to do so in the short narrative section in 3:16-18.[6] The material in the book, however, is primarily literary in nature and should be read as such. The reader should build interpretation on the text as we have it rather than on attempted historical reconstructions. The message of Malachi lives in the interaction of readers with the text of the book.

The disputations in Malachi are usually considered to be incorporated into six major sections of the book:

Yahweh's love for Israel (1:2-5)
Indictment of the priests and the people (1:6-2:9)
Profaning the covenant with the fathers (2:10-16)
Wearying Yahweh with doubts about divine justice (2:17-3:5)
Apostasy and repentance (3:6-12)
Assurance for God-fearers (3:13-21; English: 3:13-4:3)

Two short additions conclude the book (4:4; 4:5-6). It seems to me, however, that 2:10-12 is a separate section from 2:13-16, and it is so treated in this article. The expository section of this article, which follows, is concerned with the first three of the major sections (including 2:10-12).

Yahweh's Love for Israel (1:2-5)

This section begins with a general affirmation by Yahweh, "I have loved you." The love which was effective in the past is effective still (cf. Hos. 11:1; Deut. 7:7; 10:18; Ezek. 16). The concept of *love* (*'ahabh*) is a broad one in biblical language, in ways parallel to the meaning of *love* in English.[7] In general, it is the strong desire to be intensely associated with a person in a full range of relationships. Parallel ideas and expressions in biblical texts help toward understanding the meaning of love. To love is to cleave or cling to someone (Deut. 11:22; 30:20; Prov. 18:14), to go (or even to run) after someone (Jer. 2:25b; Isa. 1:12), or to seek or to choose another (Prov. 8:17; Deut. 7:7-8; 10:15; Isa 41:8; Ps. 78:60). Love has an enduring, everlasting quality (e.g., Jer. 31:3; 1 Cor. 13:8; cf. Hos. 11:4). Internally, love knits soul to soul (1 Sam. 18:1) and produces strong desire (Ps. 34:12; Song of Sol. 5:8). Love, however, is not solely an inner disposition because it involves conscious action on behalf of the beloved (see the accounts of Saul and David in 1 Sam. 18:1-4; 20:17-23; of Jacob serving many years for

Rachel in Gen. 29:18, 30 and making a long garment for Joseph in Gen. 37:3-4; also Ex. 21:5; Prov. 10:12; 17:9). Silent love is love which does not express itself in appropriate behavior (Prov. 27:5). Love is not a passive emotional state, but it is active in things that are consciously done on behalf of the person loved. Indeed, "Love is as strong as death" (Song of Sol. 8:6):

> Many waters cannot quench love,
> Neither can floods drown it.
> If a man offered for love
> All the wealth of his house,
> it would be utterly scorned. (Song of Sol. 8:6, 7)

The strong language of human love is applied to Yahweh's relationship with Israel:

> When Israel was a child, I loved him,
> and out of Egypt I called my son.
> . . .
> I led them with cords of compassion
> with bands of love,
> And I became to them as one
> who eases the yoke on their jaws,
> and I bent down to them and fed them. (Hos. 11:1, 4)

Yahweh's love for Israel is also said to be like a man's love for a woman (see Hos. 3; Ezek. 16:23; Isa. 63:4-5) In the early days, Israel responded with love to Yahweh with a bride-like devotion (Jer. 2:2; also Isa. 63:9), but in time Israel went after other lovers (Jer. 2:20, 23, 25; 30:14; Hos. 9:15) and broke faith with Yahweh. But Yahweh's love was an enduring love which continued in faithful devotion despite Israel's failures (Jer. 31:3-6; cf. Hos. 11:8-9; Zeph. 3:17).

The question of the people follows the statement of Yahweh's love in verse 2: "How have you loved us?" The question seeks for concrete affirmation of Yahweh's love. The reader can hardly doubt that this question reflects a period of disappointment and frustration, "a time of small things," not a time when great acts of God were being perceived (cf. Zech. 1:7-12). The question voices both complaint and doubt, and asks for the needed reassurance of love. Elizabeth Achtemeier has gathered up the force of the question in the following statements:

> It does little to hear, in the midst of our suffering, the tales of God's love in the past. A vanquished Israel knew all about God's mighty past deeds of grace and that made her defeat more painful (cf. Ps. 44:1, 9; 80:8, 12). Job remembered the love of God and that rendered his suffering more incomprehensible (cf. Job 10:8-9) — just as our Lord on the Cross must have remembered those words he had heard at the beginning of his ministry: "Thou are my beloved son; with thee I am well pleased" (Mark 1:11). The truth is that the love of God in

the past makes the taste of present suffering more bitter, because it contradicts what we have previously had from the hands of our Lord. It gives little comfort to remember past mercy when one is experiencing present agony.[8]

It seems that love requires constant renewal; without renewal it dies. American politicians have a saying (which I first heard voiced by Alben Barkley, former United States Senator and Vice-President) that in any election campaign their constituents do not want to hear about what the office holder did for them in the past; their question is "What have you done for us lately?" Love requires continual reaffirmation in word and deed.

The response of Yahweh in 1:2-4 is one which recalls the past and focuses on the present and the future. Esau is used here in the sense of Edom (cf. Gen. 36:1), "Jacob's [Israel's] brother." Ethnic ties related the two peoples (cf. Deut. 23:7-8), but in time a long history of hostility between them emerged. After the Exile (following 587 B.C.), the hostility between the two became very bitter (see Obadiah, Ps. 60:9-12; 137:7). The exact nature and sequence of events which led to the increased animosity between the Israelites and the Edomites cannot be recovered at the present time. It is probable that they cooperated with the Babylonians at the time of the destruction of Jerusalem (note Ps. 137:7; Obad. 12; Jer. 49:7-22) and exploited the misfortunes of an overrun people. In any case, in the later prophetic literature the Edomites become an archetypical enemy of Israel and representative of the hostile and often treacherous world in which the Israelites lived (see Ezek. 35; Isa. 63; Lam. 4:21-22).[9]

A better understanding of Edomite history might let us clear up the difficulty with verse 3. Should the laying waste of the hill country (of Edom; see maps in a biblical atlas) be understood as a recent event (as in RSV, "I have laid waste his hill country"), should it be future, "I will lay waste his hill country," or is it fully past tense, "I laid waste [at some time is the past] his hill country"? The context seems to favor the recent past (note v. 4), and the ransacking of Edom by the Nabatean Arabs sometime between 550 and 312 B.C. may lie behind the language in Malachi.[10]

In response to the question of "How have you loved us?" Yahweh replies that he had loved Jacob but that he had hated Esau (Edom). The love-hate language is troublesome, but not confined to this context. *Love* is used fairly often with *hate* as an antonymic word pair (e.g., Gen. 29:31; Deut. 7:9-10; 21:15; 2 Sam. 19:6 [Heb. 19:7]; Micah 3:2; Prov. 8:36). Two matters are especially important in understanding this language. First, references to man-woman relationships in Genesis 39:30-31; Deuteronomy 21:15; 22:13; 24:3 show that the word for love-hate can be used in the sense of prefer or like more. Rachel and Leah were not equally loved, but it would be a mistake to assume that Leah was "hated." (as also in Deut. 21:15-17; note that RSV translates "hated" as "disliked" in these verses.)

To put the matter bluntly, the "hated" wife in both these relationships was the *less* loved one. This same nuance of meaning has carried over in the Semitism found in the Greek antonymic use of *agapan/misein* in Matthew 6:24 and Luke 16:13. "To love" is, in effect, *to prefer* or to be faithful to one while "to hate" is to slight or *think less* of another.[11]

Thus we should be cautious about thinking of the elective love of God expressed in his choice of Jacob as anything like a set and psychologically intense dislike. It was, however, a deliberate act on the part of God.

Further, specialists in ancient Near Eastern political treaty texts have discovered that the verb *to love* can be used to describe the loyalty and commitment of treaty obligations relating kings to kings and kings to vassals and subjects. Such language occurs in the Old Testament in several places. For example, we read that Hiram of Tyre was ready to deal with the new king, Solomon, because "Hiram always loved David" (1 Kgs. 5:1; 5:15; cf. 2 Sam. 5:11-12; and 2 Chr. 2). While we need not assume that Hiram was totally unattracted to David, there can be little doubt that his "love" was primarily political (thus NIV translates, "he had always been on friendly terms with David"). See also Ezekiel 23:5, 9, where the Assyrians are named as "lovers"; also Hosea 8:8-9; Jeremiah 22:20-23; Lamentations 1:2-3, 19. The book of Deuteronomy reflects the use of the language of political treaties in such terms as "to love," "to cleave," "to fear," "to serve . . . others," and "to act in truth." Unlike the expression "to love," the term "to hate" does not seem to occur in political language outside the Old Testament.[12] In the Old Testament itself, however, the term appears in contexts with strong political overtones (see 2 Sam. 19:6-7; Ezek. 16:36, 37; 2 Sam. 5:8; 2 Chr. 1:11; Ezek. 23:28; Lev. 26:17; Ps. 44:8). The allies (good and bad) of the Israelites were "lovers," and their enemies were "haters."

Thus the terms *love* and *hate* may occur with reduced personal intensity. The usage may be primarily political or simply conventional language for like and dislike, preference and non-preference. Such language, however, should not be reduced to *mere* conventional talk. Even in highly political contexts, the personal and emotional intensity may be quite high. The range of meaning in the biblical *love* and *hate* is similar to that in contemporary English. We may use *love* or *hate* casually, without a great deal of personal emotional involvement, or we may use the words with very high levels of feeling — and at all degrees of meaning between. The context is of prime importance.

Thus Yahweh affirms that he has shown love for Israel by his choice of Jacob/Israel rather than of Esau/Edom. He has demonstrated his love more recently by devastating the Edomite hill country. Further, any Edomite hopes of rebuilding their ruined strongholds (like Petra, an inaccessible town cut out of rock) are only illusions because Yahweh will tear them down again (v. 4) — a process which will be repeated, if necessary, until their territory is known as the "Wicked Country" or the Territory of Guilt; "wicked" or "guilty" because the stricken state of the Edomites would indicate to others that the land had received great punishment for evil ways and sins. Edom will become "a standing witness to the abiding wrath of God."[13]

The result will be that the Israelites will be able to see with their own eyes that Yahweh is "great . . . beyond the border of Israel."[14] They will be able to affirm that Yahweh's action is not confined to Israel's territory. Thus preoccupation with internal and immediate difficulties should not be allowed to obscure his actions in world history or in his larger domain. "If Israel were more outward-looking she would come closer to a knowledge of God's love, and see, by contrast with the experiences of other nations, how wonderfully God had dealt with her."[15]

Indictment of the Priests and the People (1:6-2:9)

This large section may be divided into three parts. In the first, the priests are charged with despising the name of Yahweh by allowing unsuitable animals to be sacrificed (1:6-10). This section closes with the assertion of Yahweh that he will not accept an offering from the hands of the priests (v. 10). The second part (1:11-14) may be a second condemnation of the priests for profaning the worship of Yahweh, but I think it is a rebuke of the people for their unacceptable attitude toward worship. The third part (2:1-9) returns to the indictment of the priests, who have beome contemptible and discredited before the people (v. 9).[16]

Priests Who Despise the Name of Yahweh (1:6-10)

This sections begins with a proverb-like saying:
A son honors a father;
A servant [fears] his master.
To "honor" means "to give weight to," "to pay attention to," "to treat as important" (e.g., Ex. 20:14; Deut. 5:16; Prov. 4:8; Ps. 91:15) and is closely related to "glorify" (e.g., Ex. 14:4, 17, 18; 24:16-17; 33:18; Isa. 24:15; 49:5; Hag. 1:8). The saying in verse 6 expresses the respect and commitment commonly expected from a son to a father and from a servant or a slave to a master. As father and master/lord of Israel, Yahweh should receive honor and fear from his people — and especially from his priests. But, instead, the priests "despise" his name and corrupt his worship. The questions which activate the discourse which follows come from the priests to Yahweh: "How have we despised (*bzh*) your name?" The answer is that they have offered "polluted food" and held the "table" of Yahweh in contempt ("despised" it, a form of *bzh*). The "food" recalls the idea of sacrifices and offerings as food for the deity (see Gen. 8:20-21; Ezek. 44:7; Lev. 3:11; 21:6-8, 8, 21; 22:25; Num. 28:2) — of course, the word had long since lost any literal, physical sense. The nature of the "polluted food" is made clear in verses 8 and 13-14. Defective, lame, sick, and stolen animals[17] are

brought and offered to Yahweh; animals specifically prohibited in various worship stipulations (Lev. 22:18-25; Deut. 15:21; cf. Ex. 12:5; 29:1; Lev. 1:3, 10, etc.). Yahweh, the Great King, whose name will be dreaded among the nations (v. 14), is offered sacrifices which would be rejected with displeasure by a Persian governor! And they are offered with no sense of shame or contrition — for them "it is no evil" (2 times in v. 8), which in ordinary street English may be translated as "No problem!" or "It's okay."[18]

Verse 9 is probably best read as ironic, even sarcastic. The "and be gracious to us" (*vichannenu*) is probably an ironic reference to the Priestly Blessing in Numbers 6:25: "May Yahweh . . . grant you favor/grace" (*vichunnekka*). The "Will he show favor to you" is literally, "will he lift up faces from you," and is probably an inversion of the prayer in Numbers 6:26, "May Yahweh lift up his face toward you" (cf. Mal. 2:3, 9). [19] The paraphrase in the *Jerusalem Bible* matches the ironic tone of verse 9:

> Now try pleading with God to take pity on us (this is your own fault);
> do you think he will receive you graciously?

The meaning of 1:10-11 has been the subject of much attention, but there is no consensus among interpreters.[12] Verse 10 seems clear enough, however, as an extension of the ironic language in verse 9 and continues the denunciation of the priests. Rather than open the doors of the Temple for entry to the sacrificial tables (cf. Ezek. 40:39-41) for the people to bring their bad sacrifices and for the priests accept them, it would be better for someone among the priests to close the doors and accept no sacrifice at all, not even lighting a fire on the altar. The priests are responsible for allowing corrupt worship in the Temple (note the "this is from your hand" in v. 9), and so Yahweh declares that no offering will be accepted from their hands: "I have no pleasure in you." (Cf. 2:17; 2 Sam. 15:26; Isa. 62:4; 65:12; Jer. 9:24).

People Who Profane the Name of Yahweh (1:11-14).

It is usually assumed that the charges against the priests continue in verses 11-13, and even in verse 14. Verse 11, however, belongs with verses 12-14 to form a separate unit dealing with the behavior of the worshipers who bring defective sacrifices. Of course, the language in verses 12-13 can be understood of the priests — the antecedent of the plural pronouns is not given. But verse 14 must refer to laypersons who cheat on their vows to God.[21] There are literary features which link verses 11-14 together. The "it" in verse 12 refers to "my name" in verse 11. The use of "great" twice in verse 11 and once in verse 14 links these verses and indicates that they may form the opening and closing of a unit. This is supported by the interlocking parallelism in verses 11 and 14. The endings of the verses are as follows:

> For great is my name among the nations,
> says Yahweh of Hosts (v. 11).

For I am a great king,
　　says Yahweh of Hosts
And my name is feared (dreaded) among the nations (v. 14).

An X-pattern of ABB'A' with a pivotal statement links verse 11 and verse 14 as the beginning and end of a unit. In addition, the domain of a "great king" is well described in verse 11 by the "From the rising of the sun to its setting my name is great among the nations."[22]

The interpretation of 1:11 is uncertain. The explanations given for the verse vary widely. What is meant by the greatness of the name of Yahweh among the nations? Who makes the offerings referred to in the verse? A traditional Jewish interpretation reads the verse as referring to offerings made by non-Jews in the names of their gods; but indirectly and in reality they are made to God (Yahweh) because they are made with pure spirits, contrasting with the corrupt sacrifices offered by the worshipers in the Temple at Jerusalem. The major objection to this interpretation is that it does not seem to fit well with the emphasis on Yahweh's special relation with Israel (1:2-5; however, cf. Deut. 4:19b; 29:26; 32:8-9) and the rejection of intermarriage with foreigners as well as the focus on the future purified worship in the Temple in 3:1-4. The explicit statement in 1:11 that the offerings are made "to my name" (i.e., Yahweh's name) does not support the idea of Gentiles sacrificing in the names of other gods.

A second line of approach is that of understanding the offerings in 1:11 as made by Israelite exiles in their far-flung places of residence in the post-exilic period. This approach takes varied forms. One could think of the possibility of animal sacrifices in Israelite temples outside of Palestine, such as the temple at Elephantine in Egypt near Syrene (sixth and fifth centuries B.C.). An option along this line is to understand the offerings in 1:11 as references to incense and gifts in general rather than to animal sacrifices.[23] The argument is that "pure" offerings (non-animal offerings) are being made by Jewish exiles in contrast to the corrupt animal sacrifices in Jerusalem. More probable is the understanding that 1:11 refers to the interpretation established in later Judaism that the regular Temple sacrifices could be replaced by prayer and the study of the Law (*Torah*) until proper Temple worship was restored.[24] According to this interpretation, the offerings in 1:11 should be understood as study of the Torah, prayer, fasting, and other actions of piety. Thus, the argument is that the verse affirms that the worship of Jews in their synagogues "retains its value in relation to temple sacrifices even when the temple sacrifices themselves are offered unworthily in Jerusalem."[25] This is an attractive interpretation, but unfortunately it depends on sources much later than Malachi and seems to lack any support in the text.

A third line of approach is to assume that verse 11 continues the hyperbole and irony of verses 8-10 and that the statements are rhetorical and not to be read with historical precision. In this interpretation the verse should not be read as setting forth a liberal theological agenda of some sort. The point is that the worship in Jerusalem is so bad that worship anywhere is pure in comparison to it. The weakness of this approach is that verse 11 seems specific, and reading it as only ironic hyperbole seems forced.

A fourth line of approach is to read 1:11 as eschatological, referring to the future. The participle "caused to be offered" in verse 11 is read as having the sense of "is about to be offered," referring to an action expected in the near future.[26] This view relates the verse to the messenger passage in 3:1-4 and the anticipated purification of the Temple, followed by the reestablishment of acceptable worship of Yahweh. The purification and renewal of worship would bring in a new era in which the Gentiles would offer pure offerings to the great name of Yahweh (cf. Isa. 2:2-4; 11:10; 19:16-25; 42:6; 49:6; 55:3-5; 66:10-21; Ezek. 36:23; 37:28; 38:23; 39:7). I think that this approach is most likely to be correct. The participle in verse 11 could, of course, refer to contemporary action, but the near future idea fits the eschatological outlook of the book as a whole. The "great" name of Yahweh which is to be beyond the borders of Israel in 1:5 links well with his "great" name to be among the nations in verse 11. The participle "feared" in verse 14 may also be understood as referring to the imminent future. Pushing this interpretation into a prophecy of the sacrifice of Christ or of the Lord's Supper/Eucharist is, of course, unacceptable. Equally incorrect is the tendency of Roman Catholic interpretation to read the verse as a prophecy of the Mass. Such detailed fulfillment is foreign to the prophetic literature.

In any case, the offerings to the great name of Yahweh among the nations will be pure, but the worshipers in Jerusalem who cheat on the sacrificial regulations (v. 14) and regard them as wearisome hardships (v. 13) profane the name of Yahweh. They do this by saying to themselves in expression of their intentions that Yahweh's table is polluted and its "food" (sacrifices) is despised. So they sniff at the worship requirements and bring lame or sick animals, and those which are stolen (v. 13). Even in the case of thanksgiving sacrifices (cf. Jonah 2:9; Deut. 28:20-22; Num. 20:2), the vow-makers cheat and substitute a blemished and less valuable animal (v. 14; Lev. 22:18-19; cf. Ps. 76:11). Thus if the interpretation above is correct, the people have become as corrupt as the priests.

The Corruption of the Covenant with Levi (2:1-9)

The priests are the subject of the long pronouncement of punishment in this section. According to the RSV, verse 2 opens with the language of a condition, but it ends with a positive statement of judgment: "I have already cursed them." This could be a stylistic device to emphasize that time is running out and action is imperative. It is better, however, to hold the future tense in the last part of the verse: "I will curse it (the command in v. 1) because you are not laying it to heart." The blessings turned into a curse can be either the blessings pronounced by the priests or the blessings received by the priests, but it is probably the former, since this section seems to be a kind of negated exegesis of the priestly act of blessing in Numbers 6:23-27.[27] The curse will be a twofold one (v. 3). (1) The arms of the priests will be "rebuked" — made powerless to officiate as priests, especially in lifting their arms over the people to bless them (cf. Num. 9:22).[28] (2) The dung and offal from sacrifices will be flung in their faces — a humiliating experience. The last expression in verse 3 is most likely a pun on the "May Yahweh lift up (*nasa*) his face to you and give you *shalom* (peace)." The only "lifting" up which will result from the worship led by these priests will be lifting up their faces to get splattered by the dung and offal from the sacrifices! "A more violent condemnation of the priests can hardly be imagined."[29] The emphasis on the name of Yahweh in 1:6-2:9 should be noted. The name of Yahweh represents his effective presence, especially in worship. Yahweh's power to bless and curse is activated when his people use his name. The Levitical priests in Deuteronomy are said to have been chosen by Yahweh to minister in his name and "to bless in the name of Yahweh" (Deut. 18:5; 21:5). At the end of the Priestly Blessing in Numbers 6:27 it is said of the priests (Aaronites) that "they shall set (or "establish") my name on (or "over") the Israelites and will bless them." According to Malachi, however, the priests are "despisers" of Yahweh's name (1:16), and their blessings will become curses (2:2). The people also are "profaners" (1:12) of Yahweh's name by their behavior.

The "covenant with Levi" (2:4, 8; cf. 3:3) is not known in the Pentateuch. According to Numbers 25:12, a "covenant of peace" and perpetual priesthood was made with Phinehas after he demonstrated his zeal for Yahweh. Phinehas, however, is described as an Aaronite, and there is no indication of a covenant with the Levites as a whole. Deuteronomy 33:8-10 describes the role of Levi among the tribes of Israel, but nothing is said of a covenant. A covenant with priests is mentioned in Numbers 18:19 and Leviticus 2:13, but these passages refer to Aaronites rather than to Levites (Note Num. 18:21-24). On the other hand, a covenant with the Levitical priests is referred to in Jeremiah 33:20-26 and Nehemiah 13:29 ("covenant of the priesthood and the Levites"). These verses serve to show that the idea of a covenant with the Levitical priests was known apart from Malachi, though it is possible that both the references in Jeremiah 33 and that in Nehemiah 13 are dependent on Malachi. It is probable that all the references to a levitical covenant stem from an exegetical construct derived from the study and expository coordination of passages in the Pentateuch.[30]

Most interpreters think that Malachi's references relate best to Moses' blessing of Levi in Deuteronomy 33:8-11, where the duties of the Levites are described as those of teaching *torah*, officiating at the altar, and of being responsible for the Thummim and Urim.[31] In Malachi the covenant is described as one of "life and peace (*shalom*, "wholeness/well-being")."[32] Levi is described as an ideal priest in 2:5-6, who feared God and stood in awe before the presence of the Divine name (cf. 1:11, 14; 2:1). "True instruction" (reliable and undiluted *torah*) came forth from his mouth; no wrong or misleading teaching was given
400

(v. 6). His manner of life was healthy (*shalom*) and upright, and many were turned away from sinful behavior because of his ministry (cf. 4:6; Dan. 12:2-4, 10; Isa. 53:11). Verse 7 sets forth the ideal demeanor of priests, who should have lips which "guard knowledge" so that people seek reliable interpretations of *torah* from them. For the priests are to be "messengers of Yahweh of Hosts" (cf. 3:1; Haggai 1:13). Priests as well as prophets are messengers of Yahweh.

The point of all this is, of course, the contrast with the reality of priestly behavior indicated in Malachi 2:8-9. The priests have corrupted the covenant with Levi, turned aside from the ways of Yahweh, and caused many to stumble in *torah*. They "lift up face" in *torah* (v. 9; RSV, "shown partiality in instruction"). Apparently this means that they have allowed their priestly decisions and interpretations to be influenced by the people and have connived with worshipers to offer unsuitable sacrifices. Fishbane notes the irony in relation to the Priestly Blessing in Numbers 6:26:

> Indeed the priests' perversion of their sacred office is such that they who asked YHWH to raise his countenance . . . in boon for the people now "raise the countenance" (theirs and others) in overt partiality and misuse of the Torah and its laws. . . ."[33]

Indeed, because of their behavior the priests are already under God's punishment, being held in contempt by the people with whom they have connived (v. 9a). They have lost the respect of the people whom they tried to please.

Profaning the Covenant with the Fathers (2:10-12)

Commentators usually include verses 13-16 in this section. The disputative question in verse 14 seems to indicate a new unit, however. The text in this section and in verses 13-16 is very difficult to read in several places, and all interpretations are open to question. Verse 10 begins with a rhetorical question which expects an affirmative answer (and so equals a positive statement): "Have we not all one father?" The parallel question follows: "Did not God create us?" — and indicates that God should be understood as the "one father," rather than Abraham or Jacob, as is sometimes argued. We should not read this verse, however, in the sense of a universal fatherhood of God and a brotherhood of mankind, as true as that may be. The point here is that *all Israelites* have one father-creator God (on God as creator and father, see Deut. 32:6; Isa. 62:16; 64:8).

The question in this section is put by an unidentified voice speaking as one of the people (v. 10): "Why are we faithless (*bgd*) to one another, profaning (cf. 1:12) the covenant of our fathers?" The form of the question is odd, since it seems to carry an affirmative judgment about the condition of breaking faith and profaning the covenant; whereas the questions in 1:2, 6; 2:16, 17; 3:7; 3:8; 3:13-14 convey a challenge to the charge being made.[34] Also, verses 11-13 follow poorly in the context, so much so that some commentators have argued that

401

verses 11-13 are an intrusion. The best solution seems to me to be either (1) to treat the question as ironic with the force of "How are we being faithless . . .," or perhaps implying "Why do you say that we are . . .," or (2) to assume that there is a deliberate breaking of the form at this crucial point in the book in which the prophetic speaker identifies with the people in their unfaithful behavior.[35] The prophetic speaker would be expressing the question which the priests and people should be asking. If this interpretation is correct, the disputative question becomes one of ironic lament.

Verse 11 puts the charge against Judah, who has acted in a faithless (*bgd*) and abominable manner, profaning the "holiness" which is loved by Yahweh. The word *holiness* is frequently taken to mean "sanctuary" (i.e., the Temple) as in RSV. It can equally well refer to Israel, however, the holy people loved by Yahweh (Jer. 2:3; Ezra 9:2; Ex. 19:6; Isa. 6:13; Deut. 32:9).

The last statement of verse 12 sets forth the profaning and covenant-breaking act of Judah: he has "married the daughter of a foreign god." The basic nature of this offense is a matter of debate. Most commentators think that the terms are collective and that they refer to men of Judah marrying foreign women who worship foreign gods. Those who hold this view assume that the situation is the same or very similar to that in Ezra 9-10 and Nehemiah 13:23-27. From a minority viewpoint, some interpreters have argued that "daughter of a foreign god" means a goddess and that the problem here is that of idolatry.[36] According to this interpretation, the figurative language for marrying a goddess refers to the unfaithfulness of the people in their participation in a foreign religion, which threatens the ancient covenant made by Yahweh with the forefathers of Israel (v. 10). The general context of Malachi and verses 13-16, however, favors the view of intermarriage with foreign women. [37] Nevertheless, it is doubtful that there is any reason to separate sharply between the two interpretations. Intermarriage with foreign women would have gone hand in hand with the worship of foreign gods (see Deut. 7:3; cf. 1 Kgs. 11:1-13; Jer. 44). Foreign women, like Solomon's wives, would probably have practiced their native worship even while living in Israel (Ruth the Moabitess was an exceptional case). The objection to intermarriage with foreigners was primarily religious rather than racial or nationalistic. The covenant with the fathers would have been threatened on both counts.

Verse 12 is a petition for God's judgment, but the translation is uncertain in some details. The RSV is one possibility. Another would go something like this:

> May Yahweh cut off from the tents of Jacob any man who would act this way — anybody who is alive — even one who is bringing an offering to Yahweh of Hosts! (cf. NIV)

Breaking Faith with Covenant Wives (2:13-16)

A further charge is made in verse 13. The people weep and groan at the altar of Yahweh, covering it with tears, because he has refused to accept their offerings with favor. The disappointed worshipers ask "Why is it?" The reason given is that of faithlessness to wives, who are described in three ways: (1) "the wife of your youth," a wife of many years; (2) as a "companion," a word not elsewhere used of a wife, but which is used several times in the masculine for close friends who share mutual interests, good or bad (Ps. 119:63; Prov. 28:24; Song of Sol. 1:7; 8:13; Isa. 1:23; Ezek. 37:16; Dan. 2:13, 17, 18) — "Malachi is a quiet witness to a mutually satisfying marriage relationship which, though begun in youth, does not become jaded with the passing of time";[38] and (3) as "the wife of your covenant." The covenant here may refer to the covenant of Yahweh with Israel, in which every individual Israelite participated. In this interpretation, a wife could not be considered outside the covenant relationship which bound all Israelites to treat one another faithfully. *Covenant* is used of marriage in Proverbs 2:17 and Ezekiel 16:8, however, and it seems better to assume that the marriage itself is the primary focus of "your covenant."[39] Also, it seems forced to say that Yahweh was a "witness" to his own covenant with Israel, but it strengthens the significance of the obligation assumed in marriage if Yahweh were the witness to the marriage relationship. In covenant language, the role of the witness was to guarantee that the obligations and stipulations of a covenant could not be evaded or forgotten. Whatever the exact meaning of "your covenant" in verse 14, marriage is not presented as a matter of personal arrangement or right. It is a solemn obligation undertaken before God as members of a people bound together in a common bond.

The meaning of the first sections of verse 15 is very uncertain. The last sentence is fairly clear: "So guard yourself in your spirit, and do not break faith with the wife of your youth" (NIV, cf. RSV). The first parts of the verse are generally considered beyond any convincing explanation by commentators (and the Greek text is equally as difficult). The RSV represents one set of informed guesses. It seems to me that the emphasis is on the "one" and that the general idea is close to that of the "one flesh" of man and woman in Genesis 2:24 (cf. Matt. 19:4-6; Mark 10:7-8).[40] The following is a possible translation:

Did he [God] not make them one [being]? — [in] flesh and spirit? —
And what is The One [God] seeking? Godly offspring. So guard your
spirit, and let none break faith with the wife of his youth.

Compare major translations for variations. None should be used as the basis for any important theological conclusion because the verse is too uncertain.

Unfortunately the difficulty of meaning continues in verse 16. The most popular reading of the first part of the verse among modern commentators and translations is "I [God] hate divorce (sending away)." This may be correct, and it is strongly defended. As such, however, this is an unparalleled statement in the Old Testament and in tension with the acceptance of divorce in Deuteronomy 24:1. Other readings have been preferred by a long line of interpreters.[41] In the first place, the text is not very clear because it can be read "He hates divorce,"[42] or it could be read as "If he hates (her) — send away." It is possible that the text itself was altered so that it could be harmonized with Deuteronomy 24:1, and this could be an argument of some weight for an original strong affirmative statement regarding God's displeasure with divorce.

The difficulty in the verse continues in the third section: "And violence covers over his garment." The meaning of "his garment" is uncertain, but it has been widely accepted as an expression for marriage (related to the idea that a woman was claimed as a wife by a man spreading his garment over her; cf. Ruth 3:9; Ezek. 16:8). "Violence" as a descriptive term for divorce seems odd, but it is possible as a reference to the painfully traumatic process (see below). In this sense, divorce would be compared to violent acts which harm and threaten life. This section, however, does not relate easily to the foregoing even with this meaning. The Greek text reads the passage in a more integrated way, and I think may be more nearly correct than the "I hate *divorce*" translation, viz., "But if hating, you should send away [divorce], . . . then ungodliness will cover over your thoughts. . . ." The Greek "ungodliness" (*asebeia*) seems to reflect the fact that the Hebrew *chamas* may be figurative, meaning "wrong action," or "injury," or "action intended to hurt" (cf. Gen. 16:5; Ex. 23:1; Deut. 19:16; Ps. 35:11; Job 21:27), and that the use of physical violence may not be directly involved. The New English Bible's translation lies close to the Greek text and may represent the thrust of the Hebrew text (modified to follow the order of the Hebrew text).

> If a man divorces or puts away his spouse, says the Lord of Hosts the God of Israel, he overwhelms her with cruelty [says the Lord of Hosts]. Keep watch on your spirit, and do not be unfaithful.

I think this fits the context as well as the "I hate divorce" reading. If the latter is retained, however, it is well to remember the discussion of the love-hate word pair earlier in this article and to understand "hate" as strong displeasure or preference rather than virulent animosity. Also, God may "hate" divorce, but he does not hate divorcees.

---

[1] For the prophetic messenger role, see James F. Ross, "The Prophets as Yahweh's Messenger," in *Israel's Prophetic Heritage*, ed. Bernhard W. Anderson and Walter Harrelson (New York: Harper and Brothers, 1962), pp. 98-107.

[2] For treatment of disputation in Second Isaiah, see Roy F. Melugin, *The Formation of Isaiah 40-55* (New York: Walter de Gruyter, 1976), pp. 28-44.

[3] W. Eugene March, "Prophecy," in *Old Testament Form Criticism*, ed. John H. Hayes (San Antonio: Trinity University Press, 1974), p. 168.

[4] Michael Fishbane, "Form and Reformulation of the Biblical Priestly Blessing," *Journal of the American Oriental Society*, 103 (1983), 119, says that "One may even wonder whether Malachi's diatribe [against the priests in 1:6-2:9] has its very *Sitz im Leben* in an antiphonal outcry in the gates of the Temple — one that corresponded to, perhaps was even simultaneous with, the recital of the Priestly Blessing in the shrine by the priests." Cf. Jeremiah's sermon in the Temple area in Jer. 7 and 26.

⁵ For treatments of the post-exilic situation which seems to be reflected in Malachi, see Peter R. Ackroyd, *Exile and Restoration* (Philadelphia: Westminster Press, 1968), pp. 218-231; Paul D. Hanson, *The People Called: The Growth of Community in the Bible* (San Francisco: Harper & Row, 1986), pp. 253-290, especially, pp. 277-290 for Malachi. Hanson thinks that Malachi emerged from groups who were opposed to the growing control of the Zadokite priestly party in the reconstituted community of Judah. He thinks the "disenfranchised Levitical elements making common cause with the disciples of Second Isaiah" (p. 281) were behind both the material in Isa. 56-66 and the book of Malachi. The group behind Malachi would have been very close to the Temple cult.

⁶ See Brevard S. Childs, *Introduction to the Old Testament as Scripture* (Philadelphia: Fortress Press, 1979), p. 496.

⁷ For a treatment of the word, see Jan Bergman, A. O. Haldar, and Gerhard Wallis, " *'ahabh,"* *Theological Dictionary of the Old Testament,* ed. G. J. Botterweck and H. Ringgren, trans. John T. Willis (Grand Rapids: Wm. B. Eerdman, 1974), pp. 99-118.

⁸ Elizabeth Achtemeier, *Nahum-Malachi,* Interpretation (Atlanta: John Knox Press, 1986), pp. 173-174.

⁹ See Bruce C. Cresson, "The Condemnation of Edom," in *The Use of the Old Testament in the New: Festschrift for W. F. Stinespring,* ed. J. M. Efird (Durham: Duke University Press, 1972), pp. 125-148.

¹⁰ For more details, see commentaries on Malachi; e.g., Ralph L. Smith, *Micah-Malachi,* Word Biblical Commentary, 32 (Waco: Word Books, 1984), pp. 298, 306, for brief discussion and references.

¹¹ Walter C. Kaiser, Jr., *Malachi: God's Unchanging Love* (Grand Rapids: Baker Book House, 1984), p. 27.

¹² See J. A. Thompson, "Israel's 'Haters,' " *Vetus Testamentum,* 29 (1979), 200-205; also on "love," see his "Israel's 'Lovers,' " *Vetus Testamentum,* 27 (1977), 425-481.

¹³ J. M. P. Smith, in H. G. Mitchell, J. M. P. Smith, and J. A. Bewer, *A Critical and Exegetical Commentary on Haggai, Zechariah, Malachi and Jonah,* The International Critical Commentary (Edinburgh: T. & T. Clark, 1912), p. 22.

¹⁴ "Great beyond" is the translation usually adopted by modern translations for the prepositional construction *meᶜal le,* and I think it is correct. This construction, however, usually means "over" or "above" in the Old Testament. Some commentators argue that this is the only meaning of *meᶜal le* and that the statement should be read as "Yahweh is great above the territory ("border" can mean "area," "territory," or "country") of Israel" in the sense that Yahweh is "enthroned over Israel in majesty and power and attracting the wonder and reverence of the world at large" (J. M. P. Smith, *Critical and Exegetical Commentary,* p. 23; also Wilhelm Rudolph, *Haggai — Sacharja 1-8 — Sacharja 9-14 — Malachi,* Kommentar zum Alten Testament, Band XIII/4 (Gütersloh: Gerd Mohn, 1976), p. 254, n. 5; Rene Vuilleumier, *Malachie,* Commentarie de l'Ancien Testament, 9 (Paris: Delachaux Niestle, 1981), p. 226. Three examples of *meᶜah le* besides Mal. 1:5 in the sense of "beyond" or "outside" may be argued for in 1 Sam. 17:39 ("And David girded his sword over his armor/garment" — "over" is good English idiom, but must mean "on the outside of") and Neh. 12:37, 38 where the topographical descriptions are too vague for certainty, but where NEB translates "past the house David" and "past the Tower of the Ovens"; sustained by H. G. M. Williamson, *Ezra, Nehmiah,* Word Biblical Commentary, 16 (Waco: Word Books, 1985), pp. 368, 375.

¹⁵ Joyce D. Baldwin, *Haggai, Zechariah, Malachi,* The Tyndale Old Testament Commentaries (London: Tyndale Press, 1972), p. 224.

¹⁶ Fishbane (see no. 4 above) has argued for the stimulating thesis that Mal. 1:6-2:9 is a polemically constructed exegetical oration based on the Priestly Blessing in Num. 6:23-27. This section is described as "at once, a systematic utilization of the language of the Priestly Blessing and an exegetical transformation of it" (118). The transformation, of course, is ironic and negates the positive aspects of Num. 6:23-27. Fishbane's proposal is found more recently in his *Biblical Interpretation in Ancient Israel* (Oxford: Clarendon Press, 1985), pp. 332-334.

¹⁷ RSV translates the Heb. *gazul* in 1:13 as "taken by violence, " i.e., caught and mauled by a wild

animal. Such animals were supposed to be discarded (see Ex. 22:31 [H. 30]; Lev. 17:15). The meaning of *gazul*, however, seems more likely to be "taken by robbery" or "plundered." (See Deut. 28:29, 31; Jer. 21:72; 22:3; cf. Isa. 61:8; Kaiser, *Malachi*, p. 49.

[18] The common translation of the Heb. expression in v. 8 is as in RSV, "Is that no evil?" — expecting the answer, "Yes, that is evil." I suspect, however, that the expression is an ironic treatment of the judgment which priests made regarding the acceptability or nonacceptability of a sacrifice. See Lev. 27:10-12, 33, where the priest is specifically charged with making a "good" or "evil" judgment with regard to unclean (unacceptable) sacrificial animals. In Malachi the priests are charged with indifference to their "good" and "evil" responsibilities, probably acting to please the people and consolidate their positions in power.

[19] Fishbane, "Form and Reformulation," p. 119.

[20] The suggestion that the priests are referred to on the basis of the provision for levitical cities (Num. 35:3; Jos. 21:2) with pasture lands for their own livestock (so Baldwin, *Haggai*, p. 231) is not very persuasive for the limited situation of post-exilic Judah. Cf. Rudolph, *Haggai*, p. 264.

[21] Dr. Tom Willett has suggested to me that the two questions in close proximity in 1:6 and 1:7 ("How have we despised your name" and "How have we polluted you"), which breaks the pattern elsewhere in the book, may indicate a double address in this section (v. 6 of the priests; v. 7 of the people). The verb "polluted" (*g'l*) is found in Malachi, only in vv. 7 and 12, while "despised" (*bzh*) is found in the same form in vv. 7 and 12; elsewhere only in 1:6 and 2:9, verses which form the limits of the larger unit.

[22] See major commentaries for review of the exegetical attempts; e.g., Ralph Smith, *Malachi*, pp. 312-316.

[23] The word for "offering" in this verse (*minchah*) can refer to any kind of sacrificial gift, animal or non-animal. See, conveniently, Gerhard von Rad, *Old Testament Theology*, Vol. 1, trans. D. M. G. Stalker (New York: Harper & Row, 1962), p. 256.

[24] An interpretation argued by James Swetman, "Malachi 1:11: An Interpretation," *Catholic Biblical Quarterly,* 31 (1969), 200-209.

[25] Ibid., p. 207.

[26] This verse has the unusual formation of two hophal participles used together. The first is usually taken as a substantive, translated as "incense" in RSV. The lit. "that which is made to smoke/burn" (*muqtar*) — a form not used elsewhere in the Old Testament — could be the burnt-offering, but because of the closely related form *miqtar* in Ex. 30:1 it is assumed to mean "incense," which is supported by the Greek text. The second participle, treated as a verb, means "that which is caused to be presented/brought (offering)." See Baldwin, *Haggai, Zechariah, Malachi*, pp. 228-230, who argues for the imminent future action of the participle. Also, see the discussion in Ralph Smith, *Malachi*, pp. 315-316.

[27] See references to Fishbane above.

[28] The reading "arms" in 2:3 involves a slight change in the spelling of the word in the Masoretic text, which is "seed." If "seed" is retained, it can be understood in the sense of (1) poor harvests, or (2) more probably in the sense of offspring (RSV). Sometimes the verb "rebuke" (*g^c r*) is read as *gd^c* in the sense of "to cut off"; thus, NEB, "I will cut off your arm." This receives some support from the Greek text which translates with a verb which means "to mark off" and "to separate," thus "to cut off." "Rebuke" may be retained without difficulty; its meaning is the stopping of effective action of someone or thing (e.g., 3:11; Ps. 9:5 [H. 6]; 119:21; 106:9; Nah. 1:4). Cf. Rudolph, *Haggai*, p. 260, n. 3.

[29] Fishbane, "Form and Reformulation," p. 333. The last part of v. 3 is difficult to understand. The translations usually read "will take you away with it" (KJV) or "you will be carried off with it" (NAB, NIV). RSV paraphrases, "I will put you out of my presence" (similarly, NEB). These translations represent the interpretation that the priests will be taken from the altar with the dung and waste material to the dump for refuse. But it seems more natural in the context to understand it as the expression as "And he will raise you up to/for it (the dung)." See Fishbane, "Form and Reformulation," pp. 118-119. Baldwin, *Haggai*, p. 233, who supports the "carry away" idea, notes that the Targum reads "I will make visible on your faces the shame of your crimes." Both Syriac and

Greek texts read first person ("I will . . .") rather than third person ("He will . . ." or "One will . . .").

[30] Steven L. McKenzie and Howard N. Wallace, "Covenant Themes in Malachi," *Catholic Biblical Quarterly,* 45 (1983), 550-551. Verse 4 is treated in NEB and JB as a negative statement: "It is I who have given you this warning of my intention to abolish my covenant" (JB) and "my covenant with Levi falls to the ground" (NEB). These readings are based on alteration of the present text (see Baldwin, *Haggai,* pp. 233-234; Ralph Smith, *Malachi,* p. 310, n. 40). But it seems better to keep the sense of maintaining the covenant with Levi as in RSV, NIV, etc. The "command" (2:1, 4) going out to the priests is a necessary consequence of the binding covenant with Levi (Rudolph, *Haggai,* p. 265).

[31] Sacred lots by which the Divine will could be known in cases lacking basis for a clear decision. Cf. 1 Sam. 23:9-12.

[32] Cf. Num. 25:12.

[33] Fishbane, "Form and Reformulation," p. 119.

[34] Cf. Walter A. Brueggemann, "Jeremiah's Use of Rhetorical Questions," *Journal of Biblical Literature,* 92 (1973), 369-370. The Greek text makes the question a charge against the people: "Why have you forsaken every man his brother, to profane the covenant of your fathers."

[35] Cf. Rudolph, *Haggai,* p. 272, n. 4.

[36] See Abel Isaksson, *Marriage and Ministry in the New Temple* (Lund: C. W. K. Gleerup, 1965), pp. 27-34, for summary and refutation of Isaksson, see Ralph Smith, *Malachi,* p. 323.

[37] See also, McKenzie and Wallace, "Covenant Themes," p. 552, n. 13.

[38] Baldwin, *Haggai,* p. 240.

[39] The meaning of Prov. 2:17 as relating to marriage is disputed by William McKane, *Proverbs* (Philadelphia: Westminster Press, 1970), p. 286. On Ezek. 16:8, see Walther Zimmerli, *Ezekiel 1,* Hermeneia, trans. R. E. Clements (Philadelphia: Fortress Press, 1979), p. 340.

[40] See Kaiser, *Malachi,* pp. 69-72.

[41] See Ralph Smith, *Malachi,* pp. 322-324, for some discussion and references.

[42] The "I hate divorce" (RSV) results from (1) changing the simple third masc. perfect to a first person perfect (see BHS) or (2) agreeing with Rudolph (*Haggai,* p. 270, n. 16) that the word is a verbal adjective used with meaning of a participle and assuming the pronoun "I" — "I am hating." Also, Ralph Smith, *Malachi,* pp. 320, n.16a, 324.

A BAPTIST THEOLOGICAL JOURNAL
*Published by the Faculty of the Southern Baptist
Theological Seminary, Louisville, Kentucky*

AVAILABLE BACK ISSUES

THE NEW TESTAMENT AND JUDAISM

PROCLAMATION

THE MINISTER

JAMES

CHURCH AND STATE

WOMEN IN MINISTRY

THE PHILOSOPHY OF RELIGION

HEBREWS

MISSIONS IN A GLOBAL CONTEXT

ISSUES IN THEOLOGICAL EDUCATION: A SOUTHERN SEMINARY SOURCEBOOK

SOUTHERN SEMINARY: 125th ANNIVERSARY

PSALMS

CHRISTIANITY AND ECONOMIC RESPONSIBILITY

THE CHURCH AND THE MEDIA

THE URBAN CHURCH

FIRST CORINTHIANS

RELIGIOUS DEVELOPMENT OF CHILDREN

WORSHIP

PEACEMAKING AND THE CHURCH

FIRST PETER

ISSUES IN SOUTHERN BAPTIST—ROMAN CATHOLIC DIALOGUE

FUNDAMENTALISM AND THE SOUTHERN BAPTIST CONVENTION

ORDINATION FOR CHRISTIAN MINISTRY

JEREMIAH

May be ordered by sending $3.50 for each copy to:
REVIEW AND EXPOSITOR
2825 Lexington Road
Louisville, Kentucky 40280

To Fear or Not to Fear: Questions of Reward and Punishment in Malachi 2:17-4:3[1]

Pamela J. Scalise

The last three disputes or discussions in the book of Malachi are concerned with judging the guilty and rewarding the faithful. In preparation for the LORD's coming to judge, the people are invited to return and live in worshipful obedience to God. Whether or not they will fear God is the ultimate question for their lives.

Malachi 2:17-3:5

The opening statement of this dispute is an indictment: "You have wearied the LORD with your words."[2] This word, *weary,* most often refers to physical labor and the tiredness resulting from it (Josh. 24:13; Eccl. 10:15; 2 Sam. 23:10), but it is also used to name mental, emotional, and spiritual fatigue (Isa. 43:23f.; Jer. 45:3). It is in this figurative sense that the term is used here, anthropomorphically, to describe God's response to the people's complaints. The implication is that their doubts regarding God's justness were a continuing attitude, frequently expressed. The judgment oracle which follows in 3:1-5 reveals that the actions of the people corresponded to their attitude. The priests were in need of purification, and the rest of the people failed to live in reverent obedience to God. Their experience had shown them no benefit from fearing God and living rightly, and their lives and their words both gave expression to their doubts.

The tone of voice in which the people's question is to be heard is not obvious: "How have we wearied him?" Is this a defensive, self-justifying response, demanding to hear evidence supporting the charge against them; or is it the question of surprised ignorance, desiring to know what they have done to deserve such an indictment? It is probably best to understand this question as a technique of the speaker's art, formulating the listeners' response to this opening statement in order to engage their attention and direct their thinking about the main message which follows.[3]

Examples of the people's God-wearying words are given in 2:17b, and these quotations do give clear expression to their attitude. "Everyone who does evil is good in the sight of the LORD" is the assertion of an appalling contradiction, the moral and theological equivalent of saying that black is white, for the things which God approves are by definition good and right. The expression, "good in the sight of the LORD," is almost always used in the Old Testament to indicate God's pleasure in and approval of actions rather than persons (e.g., Deut. 6:18; 1

Kgs. 3:10). The form of the statement in Malachi 2:17 is, therefore, somewhat unusual, but not totally removed from customary usage. It indicates divine approval of persons identified by their actions ("doers of evil") rather than of the actions themselves. "Evil" is the opposite of "good."[4] It is the term used in the expression which renders the antithetical judgment, "evil in the sight of the LORD" (Deut. 4:25). The people's claim denies morality and the true nature of God.

The second part of the statement reinforces the first: God "delights in" the evildoers. This verb denotes pleasure in and desire for its object. When God is the subject of this verb, it describes God's will and designates people chosen by God (1 Sam. 2:25; Ps. 115:3; Isa. 1:11; Jer. 9:23; and Num. 14:8; 1 Kgs. 10:9; Isa. 62:4). The Psalms testify that the LORD "establishes him in whose way he delights" (37:23) and, "By this I know that thou art pleased with me, in that my enemy has not triumphed over me" (41:11). According to this biblical logic, the prosperous evildoers apparently enjoyed God's favor. But this reasoning was faulty and denied the truth of Scripture: "For thou art not a God who delights in wickedness . . . thou hatest all evildoers" (Ps. 5:4). The people's ironic assertion turned out to be blasphemy.

The second example of the people's wearisome words is a question, "Where is the God of justice?" This is a unique title for God,[5] but it aptly summarizes the people's expectation that God ought to punish the wicked and vindicate the righteous. (This belief is sometimes called the "doctrine of retribution.") Once again the words themselves do not reveal their tone. This could be an earnest inquiry, as in Isaiah 63:11ff. or Jeremiah 2:6, 8, or the people could be taking the part of the taunting adversary, as in Psalms 42:3, 10; 79:10; 115:2. The despairing cynicism expressed in the previous statement is probably also behind this question. Whatever their attitude, Malachi's audience did not expect God's judgment to fall on them.

The oracle which follows in 3:1-5 answers the people's question by announcing the advent of the LORD, who will indeed judge the guilty. An explicit connection is established between the question in 2:17b and the judgment oracle by the description, "the Lord whom you seek" (3:1), and by the announcement, "I will draw near to you in judgment" (3:5).[6] There is also an ironic echo in 3:5, "the messenger of the covenant in whom you delight," of the people's claim in 2:17, "he delights in them."[7]

This oracle introduces a new eschatological figure, a messenger who prepares the way for the LORD's coming.[8] There are four statements announcing the coming ones: (1) "I send my messenger" (3:1); (2) "the Lord[9] whom you seek will suddenly come to his temple" (3:1); (3) "the messenger of the covenant in whom you delight . . . is coming" (3:1); (4) "I will draw near to you" (3:5). To how many individuals do these statements refer? The "I" in (1) and (4) is God, who is speaking throughout 3:1-5. Because of their close proximity in this context, the messengers in (1) and (3) may be understood as the same individual. The description in 3:2-4 of the messenger's function provides the details absent from the general statement in 3:1. The identity of "the Lord" in (2) is not immediately obvious. In the rest of the passage God is the first-person speaker,[10] but in (2) "the Lord" is referred to in the third person, just as the messenger is throughout the passage. Furthermore, statements (2) and (3) are closely parallel in form and content.[11] Nevertheless, it would be difficult to maintain that "his temple" could belong to anyone but God.[12] This observation leads to the conclusion that (2) and (4) both refer to God. The remainder of the oracle announces the distinct activities of the messenger, who will purify the priests (3:2-4), and God, who judges those who do not fear him (3:5).[13]

"The messenger of the covenant" is a unique title. In the Old Testament messengers are almost always identified by the person who sends them (e.g., "the messenger of Saul" in 1 Sam. 19:20). When the messenger is from the LORD, the word is usually translated "angel."[14] In this case the designation "of the covenant" seems to refer instead to the content of the messenger's commission.[15] But what does the purification of the priesthood have to do with making or keeping the covenant? An answer can be found in Malachi 2:1-9, in which the priests of that day are criticized by comparing them to the ideal minister, "the messenger of the LORD of hosts," described in verses 5-7. The priests had to return to fearing God in order to restore the covenant God had made with Levi, the eponymous ancestor of the Israelite priests (2:4). This "covenant of life and peace" (2:5) may refer to the "covenant of peace" made with Phinehas which promised a perpetual priesthood to him and to his descendants (Num. 25:10-13).[16] The description of the priest as the LORD's messenger in Malachi 2 emphasizes his responsibility to give instruction, i.e. Torah. Leviticus 10:11 and Deuteronomy 33:8-11, which stand within the larger context of God's covenant with Israel, made and renewed in the wilderness, also give the priests the commission to teach Torah as well as preside over the cult. The LORD's messenger is like a priest who must see that offerings are made according to the specifications of God's law.[17]

There are also indications in the book of Malachi that the messenger is like a prophet. The superscription (1:1) attributes the prophecy to one called Malachi, meaning "my messenger," which is the same word found in 3:1.[18] The designation of the prophet as a messenger of the LORD is an apt description of his commission to deliver God's word to the people.[19] The message of Malachi, like that of earlier prophets, is punctuated by the messenger formula, "says the LORD." The comparison of the messenger with a refiner of precious metals (3:2f.) makes use of another typically prophetic image.[20]

Furthermore, Malachi 4:5 identifies the forerunner in 3:1 with Elijah the prophet.[21] Elijah and his time had several features in common with Malachi: both addressed all Israel, but an Israel divided religiously and suffering under a curse on its land; both forced a decision for or against God; right offerings were involved in both cases, and fire from God was decisive.[22] Elijah was also a prophet like Moses, who met God at Mount Horeb and whose ministry was to eliminate false and foreign worship from Israel. Moses was both a descendant of Levi (Ex. 6:16-20) and a prophet (Deut. 18:15-18), and the law of Moses is the norm of obedience to God throughout Malachi, climaxing in 4:2. The effect of these final verses in the book is to show that the ministry of the LORD's eschatological messenger will be based upon and consistent with the law of Moses and the words of the prophets. Those waiting for the LORD's return are assured of the continuing relevance of the law and the prophets. In the absence of the messenger they can look to Scripture in order to hear God's word.

God's messenger is also like the angel in Exodus 23:20-33.[23] This passage is located in a covenant context, between the laws of the Book of the Covenant in chapters 20-23 and the narrative of the covenant ceremony in chapter 24. The Exodus angel guards the people's way to the land of promise, while the messenger in Malachi prepares the way for God. Both figures, however, usher in a new age in the life of Israel in which divine blessings are offered to those who will abandon false worship and obey God.

Since the messenger is an eschatological figure, he is not presented in a sharply focused picture. The evidence in Malachi suggests that he will be like a priest, a prophet, and even a guardian angel.

Traditional Christian interpretation finds prophecies about Christ in Malachi. One can hardly read 3:1-3 without hearing the words sung to the music of George F. Handel's *Messiah*. Calvin, for example, identifies the four figures in 3:1 and 5 as follows:[24] (1) "my messenger" (3:1) is John the Baptist, according to Matthew 11:10, and "I" is Christ.[25] (2) "The Lord" and (3) "the messenger of the covenant" are both Christ, who is both king and reconciler of the people.[26] (4) God is the one who will come as judge and witness against the wicked. The multiplicity of titles has made room for this christological interpretation of Malachi's oracle.

The similes used to describe the messenger's work are images of purification rather than destruction. The heat of a refiner's fire melts down silver and gold so that the dross may be removed from the molten metal.[27] The suds made by a fuller's soap loosen soil on fabric so that water can rinse it away.[28] In both cases the material itself is improved and made better suited for use.

The LORD's return to the Temple will fulfill promises found in Ezekiel 43:1ff., Haggai 2:7, and Zechariah 8:3. The preparation of the priests and people is an ancient requirement. Moses prepared Israel for the theophany at Sinai (Ex. 19), and he consecrated Aaron as priest, erected the Tabernacle, and made offerings on the altar before the glory of the LORD filled the Tabernacle (Ex. 40). Israel's wilderness period may be "the days of old" and "former years" of verse 4.

The people's question in 2:17b receives an answer in 3:5—the God of justice is coming to them! In the LORD's court, God will be both judge and witness. The list of defendants includes those who violate the basic value of life as God's people. Participles are used throughout the verse to indicate that their sinning is habitual. "Sorcerers" may include practitioners of all types of magic, such as those named in Deuteronomy 18:10f. Adultery and false swearing are forbidden by the Ten Commandments (Ex. 20:7, 14, 16; cf. Lev. 6:1-5). The law protects hired laborers, requiring that they be paid daily (Deut. 24:14f.), and provides for the economically powerless widows, orphans, and resident aliens (Deut. 24:19-22). "Those who . . . do not fear me" describes every offender on this list as well as others not specified here.

In this discussion with the prophet the people who ask to see God establish justice hear that they themselves must stand under judgment on "the great and terrible day of the LORD." At least two questions remain unanswered, however. There is no word directed to their present life except by implication; they are reminded of what the LORD requires and what is forbidden. There is also no promise in verse 5 parallel to verses 3-4, telling what will become of the ones who survive or escape God's judgment. The final two disputes address these concerns.

Malachi 3:6-12

The next unit consists of a dispute within a dispute. The response following the opening statement and echoing question ("How shall we return?") is another round of opening statement, question, and response. The second response is a command with a promise of reward ("showers of blessing"). Verse 6 introduces the unit with a word of assurance about God which serves as a further answer to the people's complaint in 2:17: the evildoers, who include both priests and people, have not yet been consumed because of God's unchanging fidelity to Israel.[29] Like the verses which follow, this verse accounts for the current situation rather than describing the future day of the LORD. God has faithfully preserved them even though all the generations since Abraham, Isaac, and Jacob have been disobedient. The principle of reward for the righteous and punishment for sinners has been overridden in the case of sinful Israel by God's forbearance. Malachi's audience still has the opportunity to repent. The indictment in verse 7 is followed by an invitation, "Return to me and I will return to you." God's promise of reconciliation provides another answer to the question in 2:17: The God of justice comes to those who repent and walk in God's way.[30] Returning to the LORD is rewarded with blessing (3:10, 12; cf. Deut. 30:8-10; Jer. 3:12-14; Hos. 5:15-6:3), but the converse is not true; those who receive blessings are not necessarily righteous. The real test of righteousness is obedience to the law of God, not the enjoyment of success and prosperity.

The people's echo question, "How shall we return?" is given a specific practical answer in the remainder of this unit (vv. 8-12). A second opening statement charges that they are guilty of the unthinkable: They rob God by withholding their tithes and offerings.[31] The particular "offerings" named here are contributions to God for the support of the priests and Levites (e.g., Num. 5:9; 18:8, 11, 19).[32] The practice of tithing is reported in Genesis.[33] The laws requiring the gift of the tenth are scattered throughout the Pentateuch, and they do not reflect a uniform requirement. Deuteronomy requires that tithes of crops be brought each year to Jerusalem and eaten as a feast to the LORD (12:6f., 11f.; 14:22-27), except that every third year they should be kept at home to feed the landless people who could not raise their own food: the widows, orphans, sojourners, and Levites (14:28f.; 26:12-15). Leviticus 18 assigns every tithe to the Levites as their heritage from the LORD, in lieu of land and in payment for their service in the cult (vv. 21-24). The tithe was taken from the produce of grain, wine, and oil (Deut. 14:23; Lev. 18:27; Neh. 10:37) and, according to Leviticus 27:32, from the flock and herd. In Nehemiah 10:28-39, the people of the restored Jerusalem community take an oath to observe God's law, including the payment of tithes.[34]

Malachi 3:6-12 does not mention priests or Levites. The question of their worthiness to receive support is not an issue here. The reason for tithing is "that there may be food in my house." Sacrifices are called "food" in 1:12.[35] This is a rare concept in the Old Testament, and it should not be understood as a claim that God needs sacrifices and offerings as nourishment.[36] Tithes were paid (and the priests were fed) from the basic necessities for life, the grain and oil used to make daily bread. These provisions were God's gifts.

This salvation oracle moves from curse (3:9) to blessing (3:10, 12). The consequence of the curse under which they were suffering must have included the very things the blessing promised to remove: drought and "devourers."[37] This curse was not God's petty revenge ("You're robbing me so I'll deprive you."); nor was it an example of God's neglect to do justice. The people were suffering under this curse because of their failure to serve God no matter what their circumstances. The practical solution called for here—the full payment of tithes—is a concrete action of repentance.[38] This entire transaction stands within the larger context of the covenant, according to which reward and punishment resulted from the people's faithfulness or disobedience to the LORD (cf. Deut. 28 and Lev. 26). Rain and abundant food crops were among the primary blessings promised by God to obedient Israel.

An invitation from God to "put me to the test" is rare in the Old Testament.[39] Malachi 3:15 recognizes it as a dangerous act, as it indeed was when Israel tested God in the wilderness (Ps. 95:9). God invites this examination of divine integrity only here, in 3:10, and in Isaiah 7:12, where Ahaz is encouraged to ask for a sign to confirm the prophet's word.[40] The wording of this invitation to put God to the test is a reminder that the truth of the covenant depended on the character of God, whose integrity is questioned throughout Malachi.

414

Two unusual expressions describe the blessings offered by God in verses 10-12. Through "the windows of heaven" the waters above the firmament poured as rain to make the great flood in Noah's day (Gen. 7:11), but this picture of destruction has become an image of abundance with a positive effect (2 Kgs. 7:2, 19). God's rebuke turned back other kinds of enemies and left Israel secure (e.g., attacking nations in Isa. 17:13 and Satan in Zech. 3:2).[41] The other nations will pronounce a beatitude about Israel because such agricultural productivity will make it a land to be desired and enjoyed.[42] Fame among the nations and the fertility of the land are both important elements in the Old Testament portrayal of the blessings of the end-time (e.g., Isa. 62:1-5; Amos 9:13-15).

Malachi 3:13-4:3

The final dispute begins with an indictment very similar in content to 2:17. The people are accused of slandering God by declaring that it is of no use to serve God; there is nothing to be gained for themselves[43] by observing God's commands or by living a life of repentance.[44] The people's statements in verse 15 use the language of the previous oracle but contradict the promises made there. They, too, pronounce a beatitude, but theirs is "blessed are the arrogant," who stand in opposition to God (Ps. 119:21; Jer. 43:2).[45] The wicked put God to test, without an invitation, as Israel did when they murmured in the wilderness (Ps. 95:9), but remain unpunished. The response to this complaint is found in 4:1. Like God's answer to the similar complaint in 2:17, this verse announces eschatological judgment on the "arrogant" and "evildoers" (cf. 3:3-5). As in the earlier passage, fire is the means, but in this oracle it appears in an image of total destruction. Stubble is worthless to begin with and highly flammable (cf. Isa. 47:14). Like plants consumed by the fire both above and below ground, only ashes will remain (4:3).[46]

This unit is different from all others in the book because it is interrupted by a short narrative in 3:16 describing the actions of those who fear the LORD. Some interpreters, following the Septuagint and other ancient versions, understand the first word in the verse as a conjunction, so that the speakers in verses 14f. are the people in verse 16.[47] Others retain the present Hebrew text and identify the God-fearers of verse 16 as a subgroup of the speakers in verses 14f.[48] or as an entirely separate group.[49] The unique shift from quotation to narrative introduces a time sequence into the book.[50] It is reported that part of Malachi's audience responded to the prophetic word by setting themselves apart and speaking together.[51] What they said remains unspecified, but, as a result of their action, their names were recorded as "those who feared the LORD and thought on his name." The passive form of the verb does not reveal who did the writing, God or the people. "Book of remembrance" is a unique term in the Old Testament, but there are several other references to records kept by God of people's deeds (Neh. 13:14; Dan. 7:10; 10:21) or the names of persons loyal to God (Ex. 32:32-34; Ps. 69:28; Ezek. 13:9). The former correspond to chronicles such as those kept by the Persian king (Esth. 2:23; 6:1-3), and the latter are analogous to census lists (Ezra 2; 8; Neh. 7) or the list of officials who set their seals to the renewed covenant in post-exilic Jerusalem (Neh. 10). The "book of remembrance" may be a metaphor for God's commitment to remember and save them at the time of judgment (cf. Isa. 4:3; Dan. 12:1). On the other hand, given the importance in the post-exilic community of recording the names of individuals who chose to serve God by returning to Jerusalem or by entering into the covenant, the "book of remembrance" may have been an actual document drawn up by the God-fearers to record their commitment.[52]

The promise to the God-fearers in 3:17-4:3 encompasses the judgment on the evildoers. God's justice will be accomplished not merely by punishing the guilty but also by making the difference between "the righteous" and "the wicked" obvious again (3:18). The best that the people seem to be able to imagine is prosperity and the avoidance of punishment (3:15), but the righteous are promised much more than a just reward. As a gift of grace, God announces a special relationship with them. They will be God's "special possession," a term which signals the election of Israel in Exodus 19:5, and they will be God's son (cf. Ex. 4:22).

The metaphors from nature in 4:2 complement the images of personal relationship in 3:17. The picture of the sun rising like a bird and administering healing to the people[53] stands in stark contrast to the day which dawns "burning like an oven" and consumes the guilty (4:1). The calf set loose from the stall experiences the joy of life, for the threat of an early death has been removed.[54]

In 4:3 God acknowledges the utter seriousness of the people's original complaint. It is not just for the wicked to remain unpunished, so God will act to rectify the situation and vindicate the God-fearers. The survival and prosperity of evildoers will no longer stand as evidence against the justice of God.

Malachi's audience, then and now, doubts the justice and integrity of God because, in their experience, wickedness seems to earn reward rather than punishment. God's word given through the prophet reveals four important truths: (1) You, too, are among the guilty. (2) The LORD, preceded by the messenger of the covenant, will come to purify and judge the guilty. (3) In the meantime you may still repent and enjoy the blessings which come from obeying God. (4) If you choose to fear God, you will survive the day of judgment to come because you are God's special child and treasure.

---

[1] In Hebrew, Mal. 2:17-3:21. Subsequent chapter and verse numbers will also follow the English translation.

[2] Quotations from the Bible are from the Revised Standard Version.

[3] The same may be said about the questions in 1:2, 6, 7, 8, 14; 3:7, 13, which have a similar form and function. Each asks for an explanation of the statement just made by God or by the prophet and echoes the language of that statement without tendentious additions. One often hears the same

technique employed in the pulpit today.

[4] 'Evil" translates *ra'* and "good" translate *tov*.

[5] "The LORD is a God of justice" (Isa. 30:18) is nearly identical, and Ps. 4:2, "O God of my right *tsidhki*," expresses a similar thought. In the Old Testament, the phrase, "the God of . . .," is most often completed by the name of a person or nation which is in a relationship of worship and service to God, as in "the God of Israel" or "the God of Abraham." The title, "the God of my/our/your/his salvation" occurs frequently in the Psalms and prophets. It emphasizes experience with God rather than an abstract attribute. ("God of my right" in Ps. 4:2 should probably also be thought of in this way.) "The God of truth" in Isa. 65:16 is the closest analogy to Mal. 2:17, although it lacks the definite article.

[6] The same word, *mishpat* is used in both 2:17 and 3:5.

[7] Forms of the root *hpts* are used in both places.

[8] A hint of such a one is also found in Isa. 40:3, "In the wilderness prepare the way of the LORD." This picture is of one who clears the obstacles from the route to be traveled by a dignitary.

[9] This is the noun, *'adhon*, not the personal name of God, *YHWH*.

[10] The messenger formula, "says the LORD of hosts," in vv. 1 and 5 is, of course, an exception.

[11] Note the repetition of the root *bo'*, and the use of relative clauses with nearly synonymous participles (*shbq* and *hpts*) to modify "Lord" and "messenger."

[12] *Ha'adhon*, with the definite article but without a modifier, is unique here. Elsewhere in the Old Testament unmodified *'adhon* refers to human superiors.

[13] Bruce V. Malchow, "The Messenger of the Covenant in Mal. 3:1," *Journal of Biblical Literature*, 103 (1984), 252-255, reviews various contemporary proposals for identifying the figures in 3:1. His own conclusion is that "the messenger of the covenant" is a priestly messiah. For the traditional identifications of the messengers, see below.

[14] A single Hebrew word, *ml'k*, may mean "messenger" or "angel."

[15] Cf., for example, "the envoys of peace" in Isa. 33:7 and "a messenger of death" in Prov. 16:14.

[16] This covenant was offered to Phinehas as a reward for his zealousness in purging Israel by killing an Israelite man and his Midianite wife. Apparently the priests of Malachi's time had not displayed the same zeal in this matter (2:11)! Neh. 13:29 also mentions a covenant of priesthood.

[17] Cf. Malchow, "Messenger," pp. 253-255.

[18] Cf. the article in this volume by John D. W. Watts for a discussion of the question whether "Malachi" is a proper name or a title. This prophet cannot be *the* promised messenger, but the fact remains that he is called God's messenger too.

[19] Cf. 1 Kgs. 22:5-28; 2 Chr. 36:15f.; Isa. 6:1-13; Jer. 23:18; Hag. 1:13.

[20] Cf. Isa. 1:25; 48:9-11; Jer. 6:27-30; 9:6; Dan. 11:34f.; 12:10; Zech. 13:9; Steven L. McKenzie and Howard N. Wallace, "Covenant Themes in Malachi," *Catholic Biblical Quarterly*, 45 (1983), 554.

[21] Many modern interpreters consider 4:5f. to be a late interpretive addition—e.g., Wilhelm Rudolph, *Haggai— Sacharja 1-8—Sacharja 9-14)—Maleachi*, Kommentar zum Alten Testament, Band XIII/4 (Gütersloh: Gerd Mohn, 1976), pp. 291-293. Whether or not this is true, these verses are essential to the message of the book.

[22] Brevard S. Childs, *Introduction to the Old Testament as Scripture* (Philadelphia: Fortress Press, 1979), pp. 495f.

[23] David L. Peterson, *Late Israelite Prophecy* (Missoula: Scholars Press, 1977), p. 43.

[24] John Calvin, "Malachi," *Commentaries on the Twelve Minor Prophets*, vol. 5 (Grand Rapids: Wm. B. Eerdmans, 1950), pp. 567-570, 576.

[25] Calvin finds in the messenger "a striking allusion to Moses," whose intercessory role was taken up by John the Baptist (Calvin, "Malachi," p. 567).

[26] Ibid., p. 569. This interpretation accords with the particular literary features of this verse, noted above, i.e., the parallelism between these two lines and the use of the unusual title, *'adhon*.

[27] P. L. Garber, "Refining," *The Interpreter's Dictionary of the Bible* (Nashville: Abingdon, 1962), 4:23f.

[28] H. N. Richardson, "Soap," *The Interpreter's Dictionary of the Bible*, 4:394f.

²⁹ In spite of this link with 2:17-3:5, v. 6 belongs with the following section. Its mention of Jacob is connected to the reference to the patriarchs ("your fathers") in v. 7. Furthermore, the first dispute in the book also begins with a positive statement about God (1:2).

³⁰ Cf. Zech. 1:2f.

³¹ Verse 9, "you are robbing me," is another participle (cf. 3:5), the form which suggests continuous practice. The key verb in vv. 8f. is *kb* (cf. Prov. 22:23, the only other occurrence of this verb in the OT), but the Septuagint seems to be translating *'kb* "cheat," an even more obvious play on the name Jacob, *y'kb* (v. 6).

³² The term may also refer to the tithe of the Levite's portion given to the priests (Num. 18:25ff.). Since the book of Malachi does not acknowledge separate categories of priest and Levite, it is unlikely that this second usage applies here.

³³ Abraham paid a tithe of the spoils of war to Melchizedek, priest of Salem (14:17-24), and Jacob made a vow at Bethel to pay God a tithe of his possessions if God would bring him safely back home (28:18-22).

³⁴ Neh. 10:39 is the only other OT mention of the "storehouse" for tithes and offerings at the Temple.

³⁵ Two different words are used. *'kl*-1:12; *toph*-3:10.

³⁶ Cf. Ps. 50:12f. Roland de Vaux, *Ancient Israel*, vol. 2 (New York: McGraw-Hill, 1965), pp. 449f.

³⁷ The participle of *'kl* stands alone here. Since the victims are crops, the culprit was very likely the locust (cf. Joel 2:25; 2 Chr. 7:13). If "the devourer" was also responsible for the vine's failure to produce, then the term may be meant to include the worm (cf. Deut. 28:39).

³⁸ "In our temptation to see in this a purely legal spirit, let us remember that the neglect to pay the tithes was due to a religious cause, unbelief in Jehovah, and that the return to belief in Him could not therefore be shown in a more practical way than by the payment of tithes. This is not prophecy subject to the Law, but prophecy employing the means and vehicles of grace with which the Law at that time provided the people." George Adam Smith, "Malachi," *The Book of the Twelve Prophets*, vol. 2 (London: Hodder and Stoughton, n.d.), p. 367.

³⁹ The word, *bhn*, has God as its object only here and in Mal. 3:15 and Ps. 95:9. Its synonym, *nsh*, with one exception, of Israel's testing God by murmuring and rebelling in the wilderness.

⁴⁰ Ralph L. Smith interprets 3:10ff. by analogy to Isa. 7 as a one-time offer to Malachi's generation in *Micah-Malachi*, Word Biblical Commentary, 32 (Waco: Word Books, 1984), p. 334. This interpretation seems unlikely, however, since promises of blessing for obedience to God's law are found throughout the OT.

⁴¹ In Mal. 2:3 God's rebuke of the priests' seed will result in sterility.

⁴² Cf. the discussion of *hpts* above.

⁴³ The "good," *bts'*, in v. 14b most often refers to plunder or unjust gain.

⁴⁴ "Walking as in mourning" refers not only to a life characterized by humility and self-denial but to the gestures of repentance which resembled the demeanor of those in mourning; cf. Ps. 35:13f.; 38:5-8.

⁴⁵ Their attitude is the opposite of "mourning."

⁴⁶ Trampling on ashes is the opposite of putting them on one's head as a gesture of mourning.

⁴⁷ E.g., Rudoph, *Maleachi*, p. 288.

⁴⁸ E.g., Calvin, "Malachi," p. 602.

⁴⁹ E.g., Smith, *Micah-Malachi*, p. 338.

⁵⁰ Calvin, "Malachi," p. 602.

⁵¹ This is a Niph'al form of *dbr*, as in v.13, but it is not followed by a prepositional phrase.

⁵² "Before Him" might then mean "in the Temple"; cf. Ex. 16:33f.

⁵³ Traditional Christian interpretation identifies "the sun of righteousness" as a prophecy of Christ; e.g., Calvin, "Malachi," pp. 617-620.

⁵⁴ Calves were kept in stalls to be fattened before slaughtering.

A Biblical View of Divorce

David E. Garland

A rabbi was once asked what God did to while away the hours since finishing the creation; he answered, "He brings marriage partners together."[1] Marriages may well be made in heaven, but they must be lived out here on earth where fallen humans are wont to separate. Divorce has been around almost as long as marriage. In our culture the divorce rate is approaching fifty percent, and in some states it is even higher. Therefore, treating the subject of divorce requires sensitivity since there is a good chance that a number of people in our congregation or readership have been touched in some way by divorce. It also requires an exegetical sensitivity since the passages in the Bible related to divorce are notoriously difficult.

Deuteronomy 24:1-4

When we think of divorce, we think in terms of a judgment decided by a court of law. In biblical times it was an independent action taken by a husband against his wife. The legal stipulations in Deuteronomy 24:1-4 take for granted the practice of putting away a wife. It was a time-honored way of disposing of an unwanted wife. Divorce was so accepted as a regular part of life that it is used as an image to describe the broken relationship between Israel and God. Even God divorces: "Thus says the Lord: 'Where is your mother's bill of divorce with which I put her away?' " (Isa. 50:1, see Jer. 3:8).

Deuteronomy 24:1-4 was intended to regulate the practice of putting away a wife. It requires the husband to give his wife a bill of divorce if he puts her away and forbids him from ever remarrying her after she becomes the wife of another man who later divorces her or dies. The abomination is not divorce but remarrying the first wife.[2] The law is primarily aimed at preventing this abomination from occurring in Israel.

One could put the Mosaic law in a better light by arguing that it was also intended to allay the potential injustice that a discarded wife might suffer. With a written certificate of divorce the wife could not be charged later with adultery if she were to live with another man. It also may have caused the husband to think twice before putting his wife away since she would forever be forbidden to him, and it would certainly forestall any interference on his part if she should remarry.

Deuteronomy 24:1-4 does not explicitly define the grounds for divorce. It

419

rather impassively notes that if the wife finds no favor in her husband's eyes because she is guilty of some indecency (literally, "the nakedness of a thing," 24:1), or if he simply dislikes her (24:3), he gives her a bill of divorce and may never remarry her after she becomes the wife of another man. It makes no explicit judgment as to whether the husband ought to divorce his wife in these situations or not. It does not sanction divorce; it simply places restrictions on the husband if he should decide to put his wife away.

A Prophetic Protest: Malachi 2:10-16

Malachi 2:13-16 contains the only protest in the Old Testament against putting away a wife. It is also a passage riddled with exegetical difficulties which are best reflected in the translation of the King James Version. W. Rudolf offers a helpful outline of the structure of the passage.[3] Verse 10 forms the introduction and is followed by a condemnation of mixed marriage in verses 11-12 and a condemnation of divorce in verses 13-16.

To Malachi, divorce was a treachery. The word "breaking faith" runs through the entire passage (vv. 10, 11, 14, 15, 16). Just as marriage with idolatrous foreigners is a treachery that violates the covenant with God (vv. 11-12), so divorce is a treachery that breaks the covenant established with the wife, of which God was a witness. Therefore, the prophet believes that disloyalty to God goes hand in hand with disloyalty to one's wife; and covenants may not be broken without dire consequences (see Gen. 31:49-50). It is another reason why God refuses to accept their offerings (2:10).[4]

Marriage is conceived as a covenant between a husband and wife (see also Prov. 2:17; Ezek. 16:8). The wife is described as "the wife of your covenant" (v. 14). She is also identified as your "partner" (v. 14). This is the only time that the term appears in the feminine form in the Old Testament. It is normally used of men to designate their equality with one another. To use this term for a wife suggests that she is not a piece of property that may be discarded at will; she is an equal and is to be treated as such — as a covenant partner. The wife is also identified as "the wife of your youth" (vv. 14, 15). Some have taken this to refer to the youthful beauty of a wife that fades with the passing of the years. She has endured the hardships and struggles and has shared the joys with her husband over the years, but now she is cast aside. The father and mother whom she left to marry her husband are now dead, and she is all alone in the world. To whom can she turn for care and support?[5]

Given the prophet's view that the wife is a companion and a covenant partner, one can see why divorce was portrayed as a treachery when she is cruelly jettisoned by the husband of her youth. It is even worse if he divorced his Hebrew wife to marry a pagan woman. The prophet goes further to say that divorce is an act of violence.[6] W. C. Kaiser claims that the phrase "covering one's garment with violence" in verse 16 utilizes the image of spreading a garment over a woman, which is a euphemism for conjugal relations and refers to claiming her as a wife (see Ruth 3:9; Deut. 22:30; Ezek. 16:8). Kaiser concludes that the "sign of wedded trust" has become "an agent of violence toward the wife."[7] Rudolf contends, however, that the phrase suggests that divorce is compared to an act of murder. The husband's garment is flecked with the bloody traces of his misdeed.[8] God hates the putting away of a wife because it violates the covenant relationship both with God and with the wife, because it is a cruel act of violence, and because it negatively affects the rearing of godly offspring.[9]

The Divorce Debate

The protest of Malachi had little effect on the general acceptance of divorce. *Targum Jonathan,* for example, radically refashions Malachi 2:16 by rendering it: "If you hate her, divorce her." This reveals that for the majority of early Judaism, divorce was an accepted part of life that was not condemned. The disapproving lament of Rabbi Eliezer, who interpreted Malachi 2:13 to mean that the whole altar sheds tears when a man divorces, is a minority view.[10] The pious who cared about such things did not believe that God hated divorce but that God wanted it to be controlled by due process. The tractate *Gittin* ("bills of divorce") in the Mishnah addresses every conceivable issue concerning how a husband is to give his wife her marital pink slip in accordance with the provisions of Deuteronomy 24:1. It outlines the procedures to be followed in securing witnesses, the contents of the bill, how it is to be delivered (for example, the husband is not to slip it in her hands at night while she is asleep), and what to do if he should want to withdraw it.

But this is not to say that there were not some who, like Malachi, rejected divorce. According to Mark 10:2, the Pharisees attempted to trap Jesus with the question, "Is it lawful for a man to divorce his wife?" A number of commentators have argued that this question is a Marcan formulation because it is assumed that no Jew would have doubted the legality of divorce and, therefore, no Jew would have ever raised the question. They contend that the question has been framed to fit the situation in the Greco-Roman world where divorce was epidemic.[11] All Jews, however, were not unanimous that it was permissible to divorce a wife. The Damascus Document (4:21) and the recently published Temple Scroll (11Q Temple 57:11-19) indicate that the covenanters at Qumran rejected divorce. Therefore, one should be cautious before dismissing the question as it is recorded in Mark 10:2 as unhistorical. The questioners may have known or suspected Jesus' opposition to divorce.

Matthew's version of this incident has the Pharisees ask: "Is it lawful to divorce one's wife for any cause?" (Matt. 19:3). The phrase "for any cause" was a catchword in a raging debate in Jesus' day.[12] According to *m. Gittin* 9:10, there were two schools of thought on the grounds of divorce. The debate concerned how one was to interpret the ambiguous phrase in Deuteronomy 24:1, "a matter of indecency." The school of Rabbi Hillel placed stress on the word *matter;* any matter that provoked the husband's displeasure with his wife, such as ruining a dish or finding a prettier woman, was grounds for divorce.[13] The school of Rabbi Shammai emphasized the word *indecency;* one could divorce his wife if he found some indecency in her. One should not take this to refer only to adultery, which would normally lead to automatic divorce. Most believed that the husband should not continue to cohabit with his wife after she had defiled herself in an adulterous relationship.[14] Instead, "some indecency" refers to other violations of sexual propriety such as conversing with men, spinning in the streets with bare arms (*m. Ketub.* 7:6), loosening the hair in public (*b. Git.* 90b), as well as deliberate transgressions of the law.

We can assume, then, that most Jews in Jesus' day were of the opinion that husbands had an inalienable right to put away their wives, although they may have differed over the permissible grounds for doing this.[15] The only real obstacle to divorce — and it was substantial — was the development of the marriage contract, the *ketubah.* This was a sum settled on before the marriage which was to be paid to the wife should her husband divorce her. It was not a large sum and would hardly provide a lifetime income; it usually would tide a wife over for only a year or so. Nevertheless, the cost of making this payment to an unwanted wife prevented many in economic straits from following through with a divorce.[16]

The Question for Jesus

In Mark 10:2 and Matthew 19:3, the opponents attempted to ensnare Jesus in some way with a test question on divorce. The territorial note in Mark 10:1 that has puzzled many commentators can best be explained in light of this. The question about divorce was asked within the jurisdiction of Herod Antipas where the issue of divorce and remarriage had become a politically touchy subject since John the Baptist had rebuked Herod Antipas for divorcing his wife and marrying Herodias, the former wife of his brother whom she had divorced. This all too public denunciation, from Herod's point of view, led to John's arrest and eventual execution (Mark 6:14-29). It is possible that the opponents of Jesus, who are seen collaborating with the Herodians in Mark 3:6 and 12:13, intended to trap him by getting him to denounce divorce and Herod Antipas' remarriage with the same stridor that John had. This, they may have hoped, would ultimately lead to Jesus' undoing.

Jesus ignored the human controversy, however, and raised the question to the level of the unconditional will of God. God's intention for marriage from the beginning was that it be a lifelong commitment (Mark 10:6-9; Matt. 19:4-6). It was to take precedence over all other relationships, including the relationship to parents. It was designed by God to be indissoluble. Jesus punctuated this with the familiar saying: "What God has joined together let not a man put asunder" (Mark 10:9; Matt. 19:6).

If one takes the question of the opponents as a serious question, one can see that it was based on a false premise. The opponents began with Deuteronomy 24:1-4 and assumed, as nearly everyone did, that God endorses divorce. They only thought in terms of the commands concerning the dissolution of a marriage and ignored the fact that God "originated and purposed the couple's union."[17] From Jesus' perspective, the law in Deuteronomy 24:1-4 did not make divorce acceptable. He started instead with God's commands at the beginning. What God intends for marriage is not to be found in Deuteronomy 24:1-4 but in Genesis 1-2. The opponents have therefore misunderstood both the Scripture and God's will for marriage.

In Mark 10:3, Jesus asked his interrogators, "What did Moses *command*?" They responded, "Moses *permitted* a man to write a bill of divorcement and put her away" (Mark 10:4). Jesus then countered by citing texts combined from the first book of Moses, Genesis 1:27 and 2:24, and implied that these are the verses that contain Moses' real command as well as the unadulterated will of God for marriage. In Matthew 19:7, it is the Pharisees who asked Jesus, "Why did Moses *command* one to give a certificate of divorce, and to put her away?" Jesus countered by saying that Moses did *not* command this; he *permitted* this because of human hardness of heart. The stipulations in Deuteronomy 24:1-4 were only a concession to the willful obstinacy of humans.[18] Jesus went on to condemn any attempt by the husband to break up the marriage union.

Even though it seems to have a biblical warrant because of the legal provisions found in Deuteronomy 24:1-4, Jesus rejected divorce as contrary to the will of God.[19] According to Jesus, God had joined the couple together; and God is therefore the Lord of the marriage. Consequently, the husband may not dispose of his wife as if he were the lord of the marriage.[20] This undercut all those who thought that a husband could consider himself righteous before God if he put away his wife according to the proper procedures. Jesus, in effect, regarded these legal procedures as nothing more than a "self-legitimation and legalization of sin"[21] that attempts to make an end run around the will of God. With the breaking in of the kingdom of God in Jesus' ministry, one can no longer deal with God on the basis of what Moses may have "permitted" and where the pettifoggers might find loopholes. God's will as it is revealed by Jesus invades all areas of life, including what is culturally accepted and legally permitted.

The Exception Clause

Matthew's gospel includes an exception to the absolute prohibition of divorce. Matthew 5:32 reads, "everyone who puts away his wife except on the ground of *porneia* (*parektos logou porneias*) and marries another commits adultery"; and 19:9 reads "whoever puts away his wife except for *porneia* (*mē epi porneias*) and marries another commits adultery." This so-called exception clause has been the occasion of much debate for centuries, and a number of explanations have been offered.

Some have claimed that Jesus forbade divorce for anything less than adultery. Matthew added the exception clause as a parenthetical remark to make explicit what would have been assumed by Jesus — namely, that adultery broke the marriage bond.[22] Another twist to this view contends that Jesus maintained that not only was divorce followed by remarriage adulterous, but that divorce itself was adulterous (Matt. 19:9). Matthew added the exception clause to free some divorces from this charge. If a wife is guilty of fornication, the husband who divorces her is not guilty of adultery because he divorced her.[23]

Others have argued that this does not reflect the intention of Jesus but that of a church which was uncomfortable with Jesus' absolute rejection of divorce for any cause. Therefore, an escape clause was added either by the Evangelist or in the earlier tradition that allowed for divorce in the case of fornication. The exception could have originated in a community with strong ties to a Jewish tradition that considered adultery to be not only sufficient grounds for divorce but something that necessitated it.[24] But this was also the case in the Greco-Roman world. According to Demosthenes, a citizen who failed to divorce a wife taken in adultery was deprived of his civil rights;[25] and according to the Julian law in Rome, a man who failed to divorce a wife caught in adultery was guilty of the offense of condoning (*lenocinium*).[26] One can see how the early community might have wanted to modify the severity of Jesus' teaching to safeguard the obligation to divorce an adulterous wife.

A strong case can be made for the fact that the exception clause does not go back to Jesus. First, the parallel sayings in Mark 10:11-12 and Luke 16:18 do not contain it; nor does Paul betray any awareness of an exception as the word of the Lord (1 Cor. 7:10-11). Second, the exception would seem to run counter to Jesus' argument that God intended for the marital union between husband and wife to be permanent. It seems to say that the bond is permanent only until *the wife* does something to break that permanence, and it allows divorce on demand for the husband (only) as long as the wife has committed some sexual sin. This is essentially the same view as that of the House of Shammai. Third, the shocked reaction of the disciples in Matthew 19:10, "if such is the case of a man with his wife, it is expedient not to marry," would seem to indicate that the disciples understood Jesus to forbid divorce, period. They were worried about marrying and getting stuck for life with a lemon. For them, marriage was only reasonable if one could easily unload a wife who might turn out to be a disappointment. The evidence of the gospels points to the fact that Jesus consistently made radical demands that challenged societal norms; and it is not unreasonable to believe that Jesus disallowed divorce for any reason, including adultery. Jesus expected his disciples to love and forgive without limit (see Matt. 6:14-15; 18:21-35), and there is no reason to believe that this did not also include the spouse. But if it is the case that the exception clause was a later addition, would the church or the Evangelist have felt free to modify the teaching of Jesus so drastically as to permit divorce in cases of adultery when Jesus did not?[27]

Another view interprets the phrase in an inclusive sense, no divorce *even in the case of adultery;*[28] but this runs afoul of Greek syntax that makes it highly improbable. Others have argued that it refers to the discovery of premarital fornication during the betrothal period, as Joseph may have suspected was the case with Mary (Matt. 1:18-25).[29] In Jesus' day the betrothal was a binding agreement that could only be broken by formal divorce even though the marriage had not yet been consummated. But one might ask why it is not stated more clearly, and why this would not apply to adultery after consummation of the marriage as well?

An ever increasing number of scholars have argued that the Greek word *porneia* can refer to sexual sins in general and does not mean, in this instance, unchastity or fornication. Instead, it refers to marriage within the forbidden degrees found in Leviticus 18:6-18; 20:11-12, 14, 17, 19-21 and Deuteronomy 22:30; 27:20, 22-23. It refers to what Jews would consider an unlawful union. The marriage of Herod Antipas and Herodias, the former wife of his brother would be such an unlawful union. It could not be considered a levirate marriage, (Deut. 25:5-10) since she had a child by her former husband, who was also still alive.

Four arguments can be mustered to support this interpretation. First, the word that specifies adultery (*moicheia*, verb forms, *moicheuō, moicheaomai*) is used in 5:27-28 and 32 but not in the exception clause. The two words are distinguished from one another by the Evangelist since they appear together in the same list of vices in Matthew 15:19 (see also 1 Cor. 6:9; Heb. 14:4). Second, the Jerusalem Council ruled that if Gentile converts wanted to have fellowship with Jewish Christians, they need not become circumcised but were to abstain from "pollution of idols, what is strangled, blood, and *porneia*" (Acts 15:29; also 21:25). *Porneia* is usually translated "unchastity," but why specify that Gentiles need to refrain from unchastity as a minimal requirement for fellowship with Jewish Christians? This is not something that was or is optional for Christians. Since the other requirements in the list refer to restrictions found in Leviticus 12-18 (meat offered to idols, 17:8-9; blood, 17:10-12; strangled meat, 17:15), it would seem likely that *porneia* refers to sexual contact with a partner prohibited in Leviticus 18:6-18. Third, in 1 Corinthians 5:1, Paul expressed his shock that a man is living with his father's wife and the Corinthians have done nothing about it. The word he uses to describe this relationship is *porneia,* or incest, marriage within forbidden degrees (Lev. 18:6-8; see also T. Reub. 1:6; 4:8; *T. Jud.* 13:3; Jub. 16:5; 20:5). Fourth, the Damascus Document explicitly identifies marriage within forbidden degrees of kinship as *zenut* (CD 4:20; 5:7-11), a word translated as *porneia* in the Septuagint ("unchastity" in English).

If this word does refer to what a Jew would consider to be a forbidden union, then Matthew is in agreement with Mark, Luke, and Paul that Jesus forbade divorce without any exception. It has been argued[30] that Matthew added this exception because the infusion of Gentile converts within the Christian community posed a practical dilemma. The predicament was this: if a Gentile Christian was married, and in the eyes of Jewish Christians the relationship was incestuous (see Paul's vehement reaction in 1 Cor. 5:1!), what was to be done? The answer: divorce was required. This is because God could not possibly have joined together two who were forbidden to one another. God could never have recognized this as a marriage. Therefore, Matthew's church, in a mission setting quite different from that of Jesus, adapted Jesus' repudiation of all divorce to make clear that this did not apply to a situation which they believed required divorce. Jesus' prohibition of divorce only applied to valid marriages.[31] The exception clause applies only in quite exceptional cases—marriage within forbidden degrees of kinship—and does not provide an escape hatch for those husbands whose wives have committed adultery.[32]

The Question for Paul

Paul also had to adapt the word of the Lord on divorce in his mission context. When Jesus spoke, he spoke to an audience of Jews who would be married to Jews. When Paul wrote, he wrote to mixed congregations composed of Jews and converted Gentiles, some of whom were formerly God-fearers and some pagans. Many times a Gentile spouse remained unconverted; what then? In keeping with the teaching of Christ, Paul forbade Christians from divorcing their Christian spouse for whatever reason (1 Cor. 7:10-11).[33]

Paul relaxed the prohibition of divorce, however, when he dealt with the question of a Christian married to an unbeliever. This had become a matter of concern at Corinth (see 2 Cor. 6:14-7:1). Would marriage to an infidel defile the Christian in some way? Paul's answer is not that of Malachi or Ezra (Ezra 10:10,11). Paul believed that God honored the marriage of a Christian and an unbeliever. In fact, the Christian in some way "sanctified" the unbelieving spouse. The Christian spouse need not worry about being defiled by marital relations with a non-Christian. Consequently, in keeping with the teaching of Jesus, the Christian spouse is forbidden by Paul from initiating divorce, particularly for religious reasons. But Paul recognized that an unbelieving spouse might wish to end a marriage to a Christian. In that case, the Christian need not feel obligated to cling stubbornly to the marriage relationship. On the one hand, a Christian should never initiate a divorce; but, on the other hand, the Christian is not "bound" to a marriage that an unbelieving partner wants to dissolve.

Divorce and Remarriage

In Luke 16:18a, Jesus states, "Every man who divorces his wife and marries another commits adultery" (Luke 16:18a). In Mark 10:11, the phrase "against her" is added; and it also includes the statement that any wife who divorces and marries another commits adultery. In Matthew 19:9, the exception clause appears. In Matthew 5:32, Jesus does not specifically accuse the husband who divorces his wife of adultery but states that he makes his wife an adulteress and that anyone who should marry her is an adulterer. It is clear

426

from this that Jesus identifies divorce and remarriage as adultery. Adultery by definition is the violation of the marriage bond. If one is guilty of adultery when one remarries after divorcing or having been divorced, this means that for Jesus the marriage relationship continues to exist. Regardless of what legal action a spouse might take to end a marriage, in Jesus' view, the one-flesh relationship cannot be severed.

This attitude toward remarriage would seem to compound the woes of the wife who had been put away. If she married again, she would be guilty of adultery. How was she to survive? But Jesus was not concerned here with the fate of the divorced woman. He was concerned with expressing the will of God concerning marriage and divorce.[34] These statements underline in broad strokes the permanence and sanctity of marriage. No action a man might take and no court decision can ever truly sunder the marriage relationship in the eyes of God. This would have met with an even greater shocked response in Jesus' day than in ours. The essential words of a bill of divorce were: "behold thou art permitted to any man" (*m. Giṭ.* 9:3). The whole point of the procedure was to avoid the charge of adultery on anyone's part should they ever remarry. Jesus' audience must have been as startled as we would be if he said to us, "anyone who sells his car and buys another is guilty of theft."[35]

In Sirach 25:26 one can find the advice that if your wife does not go as you would have her go, you should cut her off from your flesh. Jesus claims that one can never disentangle the one-flesh unity created by marriage, and the spouse can never be considered a disposable appendage. The marriage relationship can be dissolved only by death.[36]

Conclusions

In our book, *Beyond Companionship: Christians in a Marriage,* my wife and I treated sociological trends and issues in light of the biblical revelation; and I would refer the reader to this for a fuller discussion of marriage and divorce.[37] But we can conclude from the analysis above that divorce is clearly a breach of God's will for marriage. It is a sin which springs from a hardness of heart. Consequently, the church needs to take a stand against the rising tide of easy divorce in our society. Many enter marriage today without any sense of it being a lifelong commitment; "to have and to hold as long as we both shall live" has been changed to "as long as my spouse meets my needs and I am fulfilled." But Christians are not to be conformed to this world, and this includes its indifference toward the marriage vow. Marriage is not a temporary, romantic alliance that can be terminated whenever one or both wish. God hates divorce because, like all sin, it destroys. Divorce in particular is like an atomic bomb that leaves deep emotional craters and strikes all kinds of innocent bystanders with the fallout. This is why God hates divorce and why the divorced person usually hates divorce—it is another contribution to chaos in the world. While God hates divorce, the church must always be mindful that God does not hate the divorced

427

person. Therefore, the church must balance on a tightrope by proclaiming the sanctity of marriage while proclaiming God's forgiveness to sinners who violate that sanctity.

Given the divorce statistics in our country, the issue of divorce is constantly before us. We are faced with new dilemmas. Partners have been yoked together, but what should one do when the marriage becomes a yoke of bondage? What should one do when the marriage becomes a legal shell devoid of any personal commitment? Should the quality of the marriage relationship figure into the decision? Can one even expect to have a fulfilling marriage relationship as a right? What should the church do with its members who divorce? Should they be allowed to serve in any capacity? Should they be allowed to attend seminary? Should they be ordained? How is one to be faithful to Scripture as well as being gracious and not legalistic?

The church is called upon to give its counsel in these matters, and some principles can be discerned from our study that may help to guide its counsel. Jesus refused to get mired in the debate about defining proper procedures, terms, and valid grounds for divorce and other legalities. Consequently, we must be careful not to calcify Jesus' teaching into a rigid legalistic system. Legalists inevitably find themselves adrift in a sea of casuistry that has no shore. For example, the way some interpret Jesus' teaching on divorce ensnares the Christian in an incredible Catch 22. It allows divorce on demand with the technical proviso that adultery had to be committed by one of the parties (although the text refers only to the wife). But divorce is not allowed for those who believe that their marriage relationship is irretrievably broken yet have not committed adultery and any attempt by them to divorce would then be labeled adultery.[38] We should avoid casuistry that tries to legitimate divorce, but we should also take note that Jesus made his comments about divorce to opponents who were trying to entrap him and to those who felt that they were doing all that God required if they put away their wives according to the correct procedures. Jesus was not speaking to those who were experiencing the brokenness of a marriage failure. What he might have said to them we can only surmise from what he said to the woman caught in adultery (John 7:53-8:11) and to the Samaritan who had five husbands and was now living with a man who was not her husband (John 4:4-29).

Jesus made radical demands of his disciples and believed that God was working in the world in such a way that they would be able to live up to those demands. It is one thing to stress God's intention for marriage, but what do we do after a couple has failed in that intention? Can they have a second chance by divorcing and beginning again as individuals? Does Jesus' insistence that marriage is indissoluble mean that once a person is divorced that one should never remarry? For some, the answer is yes. W. A. Heth and G. J. Wenham argue that a second marriage rejects the authority of Christ and cite G. L. Archer with approval: "God had not called us to be happy, but He called us to

428

follow Him, with all integrity and devotion. . . . Surely this applies to living with the dismal disappointment and frustration of an unhappy marriage."[39] This is one option that many will consider as the best. It is my conviction, however:

> The church has too often applied the teaching of Jesus on the subject of divorce and remarriage with a legalistic rigor that it suspends when it comes to his other sayings. The principle that should govern our opinion should be the principle of salvage and redemption that governed Jesus' ministry to people. If it is the case that marriage was made for the blessing of humankind, and not humankind for marriage, then it would seem that one who has failed in marriage might have another opportunity to remarry. Any moral superiority that the undivorced might feel toward the divorced who remarry is undermined by Jesus' claim that everyone who lusts after another is guilty of adultery (Matt. 5:28). One may not pass judgments on others. The elder brothers and prodigal brothers are on the same footing when they come before the father who loves them both and wishes them both to be happy.[40]

This does not mean that the slate is wiped clean, particularly when children are involved. Therefore, the failure of the past cannot be dismissed, but it need not rule over us and prevent a new beginning in the grace of God.

---

[1] *Pesikta* 11b.

[2] D. Atkinson, *To Have and to Hold: The Marriage Covenant and the Discipline of Divorce* (London: Collins, 1979), pp. 102-103. See further, D. Daube, *"Repudium* in Deuteronomy," in *Neotestamentica et Semitica,* ed. by E. E. Ellis and M. Wilcox (Edinburgh: T. & T. Clark, 1969), pp. 236-239; and R. Yaron, "The Restoration of Marriage [Deut. 24:4]," *Journal of Jewish Studies,* 17 (1966), 1-11.

[3] W. Rudolf, *Haggai — Sacharja 1-8 — Sacharja 9-14- Maleachi,* KZAW XII/4 (Gütersloh: Gerd Mohn, 1976), p. 271.

[4] Compare 1 Pet. 3:7.

[5] T. V. Moore, *Haggai, Zechariah, and Malachi: A New Translation with Notes* (New York: Robt. Carter & Bros., 1856), pp. 362-363; but Rudolf, *Maleachi,* p. 274, n. 9, thinks that this is overly sentimental and contends that the phrase, "wife of your youth," simply reflects the fact that men generally marry in their youth. The phrase occurs in Prov. 5:18 and Isa. 54:6 (a wife of youth cast off).

[6] D. R. Jones, *Haggai, Zechariah and Malachi,* Torch (London: SCM, 1962), p. 197.

[7] W. C. Kaiser, Jr., *Malachi: God's Unchanging Love* (Grand Rapids: Baker, 1984), pp. 73-74.

[8] Rudolf, *Maleachi,* p. 275.

[9] The great crux of Malachi is 2:15. R. C. Denton, "The Book of Malachi," *The Interpreter's Bible,* vol. 6 (Nashville: Abingdon, 1956), p. 1136, writes: "In the Hebrew this is one of the most obscure verses in the entire Old Testament." F. Horst, "Maleachi," in *Die Zwölf Kleinen Propheten,* HZAW 14 (Tübingen: J. C. B. Mohr/ Paul Siebeck, 1964), p. 270, says that almost every word has its questions. The interpretation that seems to make the best sense assumes that the argument is based on the establishment of marriage in the creation story. God made one man and one woman. God could have made many with the residue of spirit. It was not for lack of a supply of spirit that God did not make more wives for Adam, instead God intended for the marriage to produce godly offspring. Multiple wives would have undermined that purpose as well as the oneness of marriage (so Rudolph, *Maleachi,* p. 274, and Kaiser, *Malachi,* p. 71). If this is the correct context, one could point out that

God created the woman because God did not think it good for man to be alone. Yet now the man does not think twice about abandoning his wife for another and leaving her to be alone.

Another option considers Abraham to be the background. An objector counters, "Has no one done this who has a remnant of the spirit in him? referring to Abraham's relationship with Hagar. The conduct of Abraham is then explained. Abraham took Hagar because he wanted to have a godly seed that would inherit God's promises. Abraham's motives were quite different from those of Malachi's contemporaries. Their consciences are by no means as clear since their motives are entirely different.

Another view sees the oneness of the Jewish people, separated from the rest of the nations, as the context. The reason Israel was separate was because God wanted to make Israel a repository of God's covenant and the stock of the Messiah. By marrying idolaters and polytheists, Israel was destroying its unity, corrupting itself, and rejecting the covenant.

[10] *b. Git.* 90b; *b. Sanh.* 22a.

[11] See H. Anderson, *The Gospel of Mark,* NCB (London: Marshall, Morgan & Scott, 1976), p. 240; D. E. Nineham, *Saint Mark,* Pelican (Philadelphia: Westminster Press, 1978), p. 264.

[12] See Philo, *Spec. Leg.* III:30; and Josephus, *Ant.* 4:253.

[13] Josephus, in his *Life,* 426-427, says that he had been married three times and that he sent away the second wife because he was "displeased with her behavior."

[14] It was considered obscene and absurd to remain with a wife who had been defiled by another man. See Deut. 22:20-22; *m. Yebam.* 2:8; *m. Sot.* 5:1; *m. Ned.* 11:12; and *Num. Rab.* 9:12; and A. Isaksson, *Marriage and Ministry in the New Temple,* trans. N. Tomkinson and J. Grey (Lund: C. W. K. Gleerup, 1965), p. 23. See also Matt. 1:18-25.

[15] According to *m. 'Arak.* 5:6, "The man that divorces is not like the woman that is divorced; for a woman is put away with her consent or without it, but a husband can put away his wife only with his consent" (see also *m. Yebam.* 14:1).

The prerogative of divorce, however, was restricted in certain cases: if the wife were insane and unable to care for herself, if she were in captivity (*m. Ketub.* 4:9), too young to understand (*m. Git.* 6:2), or if the husband had brought false charges of premarital fornication (Deut. 22:13-19) or had seduced her and was required to marry her (Deut. 22:28-29).

[16] *b. 'Erub.* 4lb. Wives did not have the power to divorce their husbands in Israel. Josephus reports that two ruling class women divorced their husbands, but one may not infer from this that the average wife could do this. He reports these incidents as flagrant violations of the law and states unequivocally that wives did not have the right to divorce their husbands and that a wife who was divorced could not marry without her husband's consent (*Ant.* 15:259). They could sue for divorce in a court, however, if their husbands were afflicted with some morbid disease or growth, were engaged in an occupation that caused them to smell, or they were impotent.

[17] Anderson, *Mark,* pp. 241-242.

[18] See D. Daube, "Concession to Sinfulness in Jewish Law," *Journal of Jewish Studies,* 10 (1959), 1-13.

[19] This cuts the legs out from under the notion that divorce was a special privilege granted by God to Israel. See H. Greeven, "Ehe nach dem Neuen Testament," *New Testament Studies,* 15 (1969), 377.

[20] G. Friedrich, *Sexualität und Ehe: Rückfragen an das Neue Testament* (Stuttgart: KBW, 1977), p. 128.

[21] E. Schweizer, *The Good News According to Matthew,* trans. D. E. Green (Atlanta: John Knox, 1975), p. 126.

[22] R. H. Charles, *The Teaching of the New Testament on Divorce* (London: Williams & Norgate, 1921), pp. 18-24. Matthew does display a tendency to add explanations; see H. J. Richards, "Christ and Divorce," *Scripture,* 11 (1959), 22-23.

[23] J. S. Kilgallen, "To What Are the Matthean Exception Texts (5, 32 and 19, 9) an Exception?" *Biblica,* 61 (1980), 102-105; and G. J. Wenham, "Matthew and Divorce: An Old Crux Revisited," *Journal for the Study of the New Testament,* 22 (1984), 95-107.

[24] So U. Luz, *Das Evangelium nach Matthaeus (Mt 1-7)*, EKK 1/1 (Zurich: Benziger/ Neukirchener, 1985), pp. 274-275, who believes that the practice of the Matthean community stood close to that of the Shammaites.

See above, n. 14, for the Jewish abhorrence of living with a wife who was defiled, and Hermas *Mandate* 4.1.4-10, which deals with the question of whether or not it is sinful to live with a wife who has committed adultery. The answer is that the husband is not guilty as long as he does not know about it, but he must put her away if he is aware of it and she does not repent of her sin. The husband is then to remain single and be prepared to take her back if she repents.

[25] *Against Neara* 115.

[26] P. Corbett, *The Roman Law of Marriage* (Oxford: Clarendon, 1930), pp. 133-146. The Early Church Fathers all considered separation to be obligatory when a spouse—not just the wife—was guilty of some sexual sin. See W. A. Heth and G. J. Wenham, *Jesus and Divorce: The Problem with the Evangelical Consensus* (Nashville: Thomas Nelson, 1984), p. 34, for a summary of the views of the early church; and for a more thorough study see H. Crouzel, *L'église primitive face au divorce du premier au cinquième siècle* (Paris: Beauchesne, 1971).

[27] Wenham, "Matthew and Divorce," p. 97.

[28] T. V. Fleming, "Christ on Divorce," *Theological Studies*, 24 (1963), 106-120.

[29] Isaksson, *Marriage and Ministry*, pp. 127-142; E. G. Selwyn, "Christ's Teaching on Marriage and Divorce: A Reply to Dr. Charles," *Theology*, 15 (1927), 88-101; C. D. Stoll, *Ehe und Ehescheidung: Die Weisungen Jesu* (Giessen: Brunnen, 1983).

[30] H. Baltensweiler, *Die Ehe im Neuen Testament: Exegetische Untersuchung über Ehe, Ehelosigukeit und Ehescheidung*, ATANT 52 (Zurich: Zwingli, 1967), pp. 95-101. B. Witherington, "Matthew 5:32 and 19.9—Exception or Exceptional Situation," *New Testament Studies*, 31 (1985), 571-576, makes a case for the exception clause stemming from Jesus.

[31] This should not be taken to imply that the text misrepresents the teaching of Jesus. One should remember that the Evangelist did not have access to the conventions of modern printing such as italics, footnotes, brackets, or parentheses to identify his explanations or comments.

[32] Those who have adopted this view include J. Bonsirven, *Le Divorce dans le Nouveau Testament* (Paris: Desclee & Cie, 1948), p. 46; H. Baltensweiler, "Ehebruchs Klause," *Theologische Zeitschrift*, 15 (1959), 340-356; *Die Ehe*, pp. 87-102; M. Zerwick, "De Matrimonio et divortio in Evangelio," *Verbum Domini*, 38 (1960), 193-212; P. Bonnard, *L' Évangile selon Saint Matthieu*, Commentaire du Noveau Testament, 2nd ed. (Neuchatel: Delachaux & Niestle, 1970), pp. 69-70, 283; J. A. Fitzmyer, "Matthean Divorce Texts," *Theological Studies*, 37 (1976), 197-226; J. P. Meier, *Law and History in Matthew's Gospel*, Analecta Biblica 76 (Rome: Pontifical Biblical Institute, 1976), pp. 140-150; J. Jensen, "Does *Porneia* Mean Fornication?" *Novum Testamentum*, 20 (1978), 161-184; A. Stock, "Matthean Divorce Texts," *Biblical Theology Bulletin*, 8 (1978), 24-33; F. J. Moloney, "Matthew 19, 3-12 and Celibacy: A Redactional and Form Critical Study," *Journal for the Study of the New Testament*, 2 (1979), 44; J. R. Mueller, "The Temple Scroll and the Gospel Divorce Texts," *Revue de Qumran*, (1980), 247-258; R. A. Guelich, *The Sermon on the Mount* (Waco: Word, 1982), pp. 204-210; Witherington, "Matthew 5.32 and 19.9," pp. 571-576.

This interpretation is not without its weaknesses. The two most recent commentaries on Matthew reject it out of hand. Luz, *Matthaeus*, p. 274, calls it a *"Kunststück"* that stems entirely from the conflict this passage has caused in the Catholic church concerning its church law. J. Gnilka, *Das Matthäusevangelium I. Teil*, Herders Theologische Kommentar zum Neuen Testament I/1 (Freiburg/Basel/Vienna: Herder, 1986), p. 168, contends that it belongs in an exegetical curiosity cabinet.

First, it is argued that this interpretation requires an unusually restricted sense for *porneia*, which does not appear in the Greek translation of Lev. 18. The phrase, *logos porneias*, does correspond well to the phrase in Deut. 24:1, *'erwat dabar*, and would translate the transposition of the phrase made by the House of Shammai, *debar 'erwah*. Second, it is contended that incestuous marriages were null and void and would not require divorce, or that a proselyte becomes a new creation on conversion and old relations are no longer valid. Third, it is questioned whether such cases were so frequent that they required adding an explicit exception to the text. Fourth, the reason *porneia* is used instead of *moicheia* is to vary the expression since it included adultery (see Sir. 23:23, Hos. 2:4). Finally, no church father reflects this interpretation of the text.

[33] D. E. Garland, "The Christian's Posture Towards Marriage and Celibacy: 1 Corinthians 7," *Review and Expositor*, 80 (1983), 351-362.

[34] Luz, *Matthäus*, pp. 271-272.

[35] See B. J. Malina, *The New Testament World* (Atlanta: John Knox, 1981), p. 120. The word used in the Greek text for the bill of divorce, *apostasion*, is a technical term for relinquishing property. The rights to the wife are relinquished in the certificate of divorce, and one would be surprised at being found guilty simply for relinquishing property.

[36] Some social scientists have recently drawn the same conclusion, for example, C. A. Whitaker and D. V. Keith, "Counseling the Divorcing Marriage," in *Klemer's Counseling in Marital and Sexual Problems*, ed. R. F. Stahman and W. J. Hiebert, 2nd ed. (Baltimore: Williams and Wilkins, 1977), p. 71.

[37] D. S. R. Garland and D. E. Garland, *Beyond Companionship: Christians in Marriage* (Philadelphia: The Westminster Press, 1986), pp. 151-172.

[38] J. P. Meier, *The Vision of Matthew* (New York: Paulist Press, 1979), p. 253.

[39] W. A. Heth and G. J. Wenham, *Jesus and Divorce*, p. 96.

[40] Garland and Garland, *Beyond Companionship*, p. 166.

A Biblical Approach to Stewardship

W. Clyde Tilley

Every biblical passage is set within contexts and helps to provide the context for all other biblical passages. This interconnectedness of texts and contexts comprises the strong texture within which both the unity and the diversity of Scripture are found.

Among the contexts for any Scripture text are the environing passage, the biblical book, and the whole of Scripture. In addition to these are the varied socio-historical settings which can be partly reconstructed upon the basis of internal and external evidences.

The single passage from Malachi which requires the present article is 3:6-12. The context which most concerns us here is that provided by the whole of Scripture, especially since other passages are being adequately treated elsewhere in this journal. It is unfortunate when this passage is treated in detachment from the total biblical message on stewardship. At the same time, it is a mistake to ignore this passage in deference to more lofty "spiritual" ones, for Malachi 3:6-12 too is a part of the total biblical message on stewardship. Without it we would be much the poorer.

In dealing synoptically with biblical stewardship we begin with the theme in the New Testament, where it attains its fruition. An attempt shall then be made to relate Christian stewardship to the concept of man's dominion over the created order in the Old Testament. We will then need to pay some attention to how the responsibilities of Christian stewardship relate to the total sweep of the Christian life. Following this, the concept of tithing shall be viewed in relation to total stewardship. In conclusion, avenues for further 'Christianizing' the tithe shall be explored.

New Testament Stewardship: An Overview

The New Testament word for stewardship is *oikonomia*, derived from *oikos* (house) and *nemō* (to administer or manage). It refers to the office or role of the *oikonomos* (the steward) who exercises some function of house management.

The socioeconomic background for the word is thus the practice of wealthy landowners who owned or employed *oikonomoi* to manage their affairs of land, house, or business. A steward may be a chief slave, a trusted employee, or even a son. Responsibilities for these persons were as diverse as estate manager, accountant, inspector of goods, housekeeper, or chief cook, as one may be over the entire estate or over some branch of the household.[1] In one biblical passage steward is used interchangeably with servant *(doulos)* (Luke 12:42,43).

The early church usage of *steward* in reference to the Christian's responsibility toward God comes from Jesus' frequent parables of the kingdom relating to stewards, as well as both Pauline and Petrine appropriations of this terminology. The focus of the stewardship metaphor for Jesus (Luke 16:2ff.), Paul (1 Cor. 4:1, 2), and Peter (1 Pet. 4:10-11) is upon the faithfulness with which the steward discharges his duties.

In the New Testament, *oikonomia* is used not only as a metaphor for the believer's position of responsibility to God and its faithful discharge, but also as a way of referring to the plan or administration of salvation itself as it relates to God (Eph. 1:10; 3:9).[2] Thus it denotes God's *stewardship* or *economy* for the ages. The full richness of the theology of our *oikonomia* is not realized until it can be seen against the backdrop of God's *oikonomia* and our participation in it. Thus we are "stewards of the mysteries of God" (1 Cor. 4:1), and stewardship becomes "partnership with Christ, through the Holy Spirit, in fulfilling the purpose of God in the world."[3]

It can now be seen how stewardship in the biblical sense is inclusive of much more than responsibility for material and financial resources, as indeed it was in the socioeconomic heritage that gave us this metaphor, in the parables of Jesus (Luke 12:42), and in its apostolic development (e.g., Eph. 3:2). In fact, it includes our time, talents, and self as well as possessions[4] and so embraces the Christian's responsibility to God for one's total existence.

This is not to minimize or even to remove the focus from our stewardship of material resources, but to set it within a more holistic framework. It is an unfortunate impoverishment of our understanding of stewardship which changes its more life-embracing sweep to a narrower focus upon financial matters, or even to an equation with tithing. This language development is almost the reverse of our usage of the word *talent,* a monetary unit which has come to refer to something more integral to personhood.

Although a look at other related New Testament themes would be required for a total development of Christian stewardship, we must settle here for a concentrated overview. Suffice it to conclude our overview with Paul Stagg's comprehensive definition:

> From the biblical point of view stewardship is grateful and obedient response to God for His undeserved gifts, acknowledging Him as the ultimate owner and sovereign Lord of life, which is held as a trust issuing in the voluntary and responsible use of one's total self and possessions to the glory of God and in loving service to one's neighbor.[5]

434

Human Dominion and Christian Stewardship

Up to now stewardship has been treated as a distinctively New Testament doctrine. Yet, if our understanding of stewardship is (1) to be biblical and (2) to enlighten and be enlightened by our passage in Malachi 3:6-12, attention must be given to whatever antecedent there is for stewardship in Old Testament literature.

I propose to do this by relating Christian stewardship to the Old Testament concept of human dominion over the created order (Gen. 1:26). Although there is little to commend this association philologically,[6] there is much to commend it conceptually.[7] There is, in fact, a very striking theological affinity between human dominion and Christian stewardship:

1. Both dominion and stewardship underscore the imperative of faithfulness in their responsible discharge.
2. In both cases, it is none other than God himself to whom we are responsible—in his role as creator in the first case and as redeemer in the second.
3. In both cases, this responsibility is to be exercised under the aegis of God's sovereignty expressed in the second instance through the Lordship of Jesus Christ.
4. The range of our responsibility is all inclusive in both instances, the scope of the created order defining human dominion comprehensively in much the same way as the sweep of Christian stewardship is defined in the foregoing overview.

Although dominion and stewardship are counterpoised with each other by the two Testaments, they are not equivalent. The same symmetrical relationship is present as appears in the relationship between the Testaments themselves, viz., that of fall and redemption, promise and fulfillment. Thus, in a real sense, stewardship is the heir apparent and true successor of dominion as the old creation gives way to the new.

Just as human beings are in the image of God, human dominion is in the image of God's sovereignty. Human dominion must be exercised under this sovereignty, and the two must never be confused, i.e., dominion must never become domination. But our desire to be our own god and our misuse and abuse of freedom in response to the tempter's promise to that effect (Gen. 3:5) had far-reaching implications for our exercise of dominion.

To confuse the divine image in us with God is to confuse our dominion with God's sovereignty. The attempt to usurp God's sovereign rule is to exercise our dominion in an exploitative manner[8] for our own self-advantage and short-range goals rather than in the sense of responsible trusteeship, a caretaker role that recognizes God's sovereignty. This exploitation has brought our planet closer and closer to ecological chaos, environmental bankruptcy, and nuclear Armageddon. These are only the more drastic of a myriad of more subtle ways by which we confirm the biblical witness to a fallen world order. Not only are we fallen and in need of God's redemptive activity but so is our world, which is no less the object of God's redemptive will and work.[9]

Our dominion over the earth is thus rooted in our creatureliness. Furthermore, it is distorted by our will to fallenness as we exploitatively exercise that dominion as misplaced sovereignty. That dominion, reflective of God's *image* in us, becomes a pseudo-sovereignty as it is mirrored in our *imagination.* Stewardship, by contrast, is rooted in redemption. It belongs to us, not as creatures of the original order but as faith-participants in God's new creation, the redeemed order. The call of stewardship is the call to faithfulness, that faithful responsiveness to God which was thwarted in our rebel exercise of dominion. Stewardship thus belongs to the redeemed order in the same way that dominion belonged to the original but fallen order. It is incumbent upon us by virtue of our willing covenant with God rather than of our unwilling creation by God. Yet choice against covenant is but the extension of rebellious and exploitative dominion. The faithfulness that stewardship requires gathers up into it all the faithfulness that dominion required and more—the stewardship of participation with God in his plan for the ages (1 Cor. 4:1; Eph. 3:2).

A Perspectival Interpretation of Stewardship

Given the comprehensiveness of human responsibility before God, idealized in the creaturely call of dominion and restored in the call to Christian stewardship, we will do well to seek an adequate model for clarifying this stewardship role in relation to the totality of the Christian life. How, for instance, is Christian stewardship related to Christian ethics, Christian discipleship, Christian missions, and Christian evangelism? Perhaps the implicit, popular model for the relationship of these aspects of the Christian life is that of the divided circle. Each wedge-shaped sector of the pie-shaped circle can be variously labeled as stewardship, ethics, missions, etc. The problem with this model is that it does not adequately represent the comprehensiveness of stewardship and of the other aspects of the Christian life, nor do its isolated wedges project the dynamic interaction with the other aspects.

I suggest a perspectival model which represents both the mutual comprehensiveness of these aspects of the Christian life and the dynamic interaction among them. The circle is retained but not divided. From outside the circle, arrows converge in all directions upon the circumference. The shafts of the arrows variously bear the label of stewardship, missions, evangelism, discipleship, worship, and ethics. Each of these aspects of the Christian life is comprehensive in its own function.

This model is called perspectival because each of the aspects represents a different perspective upon the whole. Our life is lived by a variety of action modes—doing, having, growing, telling, going, etc. The circle itself represents the Christian life (being). When viewed from the perspective of having, the Christian life is stewardship; from that of doing, it is ethics; of growing, discipleship; of telling, evangelism; of going, missions. The pattern of perspectivality that characterizes the circle of the Christian life in its entirety may also be used as a model for viewing each single act which may simultaneously be an act of Christian stewardship, of ethics, of evangelism, etc.

The most generic theological concept for speaking of the multiperspective circle of Christian existence is "the Lordship of Jesus Christ." The Christian life owes its undivided existence to Christ's Lordship which is the specifically Christian way that the sovereignty of God is administered over our lives. This Lordship is variously attested in the early Christian confession (1 Cor. 12:3), the risen Christ's claim of comprehensive authority (Matt. 28:18), and Paul's affirmation of the preeminence of Christ (Col. 1:17-18).

The Lordship of Jesus Christ gives not only unity to the Christian life and integrality to all its perspectives. It affirms yet another dimension of its comprehensiveness. The Christian life is all-inclusive, life-embracing. It is not only unified but unifying. No part of life is to be lived outside this Lordship. No other circle can be authentically posited outside the circle of the Christian life.

What is being rejected here is the practice of compartmentalizing life into sacred and secular domains. Attempts at unifying life have proceeded along the lines of attempting to transcend this distinction by secularizing the sacred on the one hand or by sanctifying the secular on the other. The former approach may seek either to implement a nontheistic agenda[10] or a Christian/theistic attempt to shake the sacred free of its associations with irrelevant other worldiness.[11]

A holistic view of life as sacred, lived in a sacramental world, seems most adequate for expressing life lived under the Lordship of Jesus Christ. The otherworldly irrelevance of faith, often institutionalized into relgous life, comes not from an attempt to sanctify the secular but precisely from the failure to do so.[12] This failure is most flagrant when a sacred domain is preserved at the cost of a compartmentalized life. In all fairness, even a compassionate humanism, though secular, is often more "Christian" than the orthodox compartmentalized variety of life so prevalent in our religious culture and in our acculturated religion.

What is the contribution of this discussion to a biblical approach to stewardship? Christian stewardship is the whole of the Christian life (which in turn, is the whole of life) when viewed from the perspective of the action mode of having. Although human *having* in its contrast to human *being* has sometimes been analyzed as inauthentic existence,[13] this is only true when the integrality of having with authentic being is ignored or negated. Authentic Christian existence is only attained when the stewardship of what we have, including life itself, is viewed in full comprehensiveness with life. The example of the Macedonian saints giving themselves to God before they gave their offerings (2 Cor. 8:3-5), Paul's appeal to the Romans to give themselves as living sacrifices to God (Rom. 12:1), and his claim that we no longer belong to ourselves (1 Cor. 6:19-20) best exemplify the mergence of authentic being and responsible having, Christian life and Christian stewardship.

Christian Stewardship and Tithing

Concern for the place of Malachi's oracle on tithing (3:6-12) in the life of the Christian church has prompted our quest for a theological context of Christian stewardship. It may be safe now to look at the place of tithing in relation to the whole of Christian stewardship.

Of all the issues that may be raised about our focal passage in this context, two of them are pressing enough to warrant a place in such a precursory article: (1) Tithing as a requirement, the violation of which involves one in the robbery of God. (2) The place of rewards as a motivation for faithful stewardship (Mal. 3:9-12).

Regarding the first question, it will be helpful if we attempt to delineate both some positive and negative features of tithing as a Christian practice. Several considerations commend tithing to the Christian: (1) It is a regular and systematic way of giving which provides the church with a somewhat predictable income level. (2) It is a disciplined way of giving. A practice like tithing as opposed to a more helter-skelter approach introduces a modicum of discipline into the Christian life, a discipline that is far in advance of where many church members are. *Discipline* is essential to *discipleship*. (3) It is a proportionate way of giving. Although tithing itself is never fully consecrated in the New Testament as a Christian practice,[14] the principle of proportionate giving is (1 Cor. 16:2; 2 Cor. 8:12; Mark 12:41-44).

Conversely, several undesirable features of tithing may caution us against its unqualified approval as *the* Christian approach.

1. It often tends to legalism. The proof-texting method which is used to support it and the judgmental rigidness with which it is often insisted upon knows little of the freedom of divine grace.
2 It is often accompanied by a compartmentalized view of the stewardship of possessions. Whereas Christian stewardship insists upon the divine ownership of all things, the practice of tithing seldom projects the same sense of responsibility for the other nine-tenths as it does the "consecrated" tenth.
3 Tithing is frequently promoted with a bargaining mentality. The same interpretive approach that sees tithing as a biblical mandate tends also to take at face value the seemingly crass promises of materialistic rewards that sometimes accompany this mandate.
4. The proportionality of tithing is a rather rough-hewn proximate one

rather than a perfect one. Even slight sensitivity uncovers the discrepancy between the discipline the tithe imposes upon the retiree with a fixed income and upon the thriving entrepeneur at the peak of his or her earning powers.

5. Tithing can lead to an unwarranted sense of complacency about one's stewardship. If tithing is seen as *the* Christian approach and represents the zenith of stewardship faithfulness, the ongoing life of discipleship can be robbed of much of its adventure and such shortsighted vistas can lead to a self-congratulatory attitude toward oneself and a judgmental perspective upon others.

In all fairness, most of these criticisms of tithing are accompanied by such words as *often, frequently, tends to* or *may lead to.* Except in the case of imperfect proportionality, these cannot then be absolute criticisms since the weaknesses do not express themselves in every instance of tithing. It seems then safe to affirm only that tithing cannot be taken as *the* Christian approach to stewardship, and when it is taken as *a* Christian approach it must be with a spirit of nonjudgmental graciousness and a caution against these excesses. With this spirit there are churches for which a challenge on tithing would represent a welcome advance on the frontier of Christian stewardship and for which this passage from Malachi could warrant a Christianized interpretation.

Concerning rewards for faithful stewardship/tithing, there is undeniably present the promise of reward (Mal. 3:9-12). Many faithful stewards have found these promises to be far from empty. It is one thing, however, to make descriptive statements concerning what often accompanies the faithful exercise of stewardship and quite another to parade these as the exclusive or even primary motivation for faithful stewardship. "A law of spiritual realities" seems justified which represents godly maturity as being decreasingly apprehensive about the certainty of rewards. Moses and Paul are both cases in point (Exod. 32:32; Rom. 9:3).

T. A. Kantonen in a chapter on "The Steward's Reward," notes that "the gospel gives the concept of reward a new meaning quite different from its ordinary connotation of compensation or remuneration for services rendered."[15] It does so with a twofold emphasis upon the sovereignty of grace and the perspective of eternity.

The second emphasis teaches us "both to place stewardship in the perspective of eternity and to place eternity in the perspective of stewardship."[16] Concerning the former emphasis, Kantonen observes "a good steward does his duty because it is his duty, not for the sake of the reward."[17] Illustrating this principle from the story of the laborers in the vineyard (Matt. 20:1-16), he quotes an anonymous poem:

Lord of the vineyard, whose dear word declares,
Our one hour's labor as the day's shall be;

What coin divine can make our wages as theirs
Who had the morning joy of work for thee?[18]

The Concept of the Graduated Tithe

For many of us the problem with the tithe from a Christian perspective is not that it is too stringent but that it is not stringent enough. After all, Jesus' requirement for the rich young man (Mark 10:17-22) and a more general call to discipleship (Luke 12:32-34) was the call to divest oneself of all one's possessions. Zaccheus voluntarily agreed to give away half of his wealth as well as to make a generous settlement of all unjust debts. Even though we may be able to feel good about not taking these commands literally, we should not be too comfortable with our failure to take them seriously as communicating something very important about Christian stewardship in the context of God's present and all-embracing kingdom.

Richard Foster says,

> The tithe simply is not a sufficiently radical concept to embody the carefree unconcern for possessions that marks life in the kingdom of God. Jesus Christ is the Lord of all our goods, not just ten percent. It is quite possible to obey the law without ever dealing with our mammon lust. . . . Perhaps the tithe can be a beginning way to acknowledge God as the owner of all things, but it is only a beginning and not an ending.[19]

To Christianize the tithe further is, among other possible things, to radicalize it further. Ronald J. Sider has experimented with and written about what he calls the graduated tithe. This concept, presented alongside what he calls "other less modest proposals," works something like this: A modest amount of one's income is determined that is required for one's family to live a relatively simple life-style in a world of need. A simple tithe is given on that amount. For each one thousand dollars earned beyond that basic amount the tithe shall be graduated by five additional percentage points. For example, one would give fifteen percent of the first additional $1000, twenty percent on the second additional $1000, and so on. Thus one can, with a more equitable sense of proportion, generously support his or her church as well as other compassionate ministries of relief and development through or beyond one's church.

Implicit in this will to share one's economic resources increasingly in a hurting world is what some have called "voluntary simplicity."[21] This practical growth in the concrete life of Christian stewardship will be responsive both to one's spiritual growth and to one's financial growth. As we grow in the life of stewardship, we may be surprised at how our perspective upon material things will change. We may observe ourselves moving beyond the question, "How much can I afford to give?" toward "How little can I/we afford to live on?" We move beyond that level where material things are important to us to that level

440

where they are not. But do not be surprised if someday in this exciting adventure it may no longer simply be not important for us to have, but important for us not to have certain things.

One other word of caution is necessary if the road to voluntary simplicity is to serve Christian stewardship. The rationale behind this adventure is not that material things are not important. They are so important, in fact, that no one, absolutely no one, should be without a basic amount of them! The will to simplify is the will toward a more equitable distribution of God's resources. We must live simply that others may simply live!

---

[1] O. Michel, *"Oikonomos," Theological Dictionary of the New Testament*, vol. 5, ed. Gerhard Kittel and trans. G. W. Bromiley (Grand Rapids: Wm. B. Eerdmans, 1967), pp. 149-150.

[2] Ibid., p. 151.

[3] A. C. Conrad, *The Divine Economy: A Study in Stewardship* (Grand Rapids: Wm. B. Eerdmans, 1954), p. 27.

[4] C. U. Wolf, "Steward, Stewardship," *The Interpreter's Dictionary of the Bible*, vol. 4 (Nashville: Abingdon, 1962), p. 443.

[5] Paul Leonard Stagg, "An Interpretation of Christian Stewardship," in *What is The Church?* ed. Duke K. McCall (Nashville: Broadman Press), p. 148.

[6] The Hebrew word translated *dominion* in Gen. 1:26ff. is *radah*, to rule, to tread down. This word is translated by the Greek *archetōsan* in the LXX rather than by *oikonomeō*.

[7] J. Morris Ashcraft has rightly observed that "a correct interpretation of Christian stewardship requires a correct understanding of God's creation" and proceeds to develop helpful insights in exploring this relationship ("A Theological Rationale for Christian Stewardship," in *Resource Unlimited*, ed. William L. Hendricks [Nashville: The Stewardship Commission of the Southern Baptist Convention, 1972], pp. 17ff.). In the same anthology James Leo Garrett makes *dominion* an Old Testament point of contact for New Testament stewardship ("A Christian View of Material Things," p. 85).

[8] Ray Summers, among others, has treated the fallen exercise of dominion as exploitation ("Christian Stewardship in the Light of Redemption," in *Resources Unlimited*, pp. 24-26).

[9] For a brief treatment of both Old and New Testament passages on the created order as a victim of the fall and an object of redemption, see J. Morris Ashcraft, "Theological Rationale," pp. 14-15.

[10] An example of this is Paul Kurtz, ed., *The Humanist Alternative: Some Definitions of Humanism* (London: Perberton Books, 1973).

[11] Harvey Cox, *The Secular City* (New York: Macmillan, 1965); John A. T. Robinson, *Honest to God* (London: SCM Press, 1963); Fred Brown, *Secular Evangelism* (London: SCM Press, 1970) and *Faith Without Religion* (London: SCM Press, 1971).

[12] In speaking of sanctifying the secular, this claim refers to the hitherto "secular" dimension of a person's life rather than to the secular or profane in its social setting.

[13] See Gabriel Marcel, *Being and Having* (New York: Harper Torchbooks, 1965); Erich Fromm, *To Be or To Have?* (New York: Harper and Row, 1976).

[14] The commonly quoted proof text for Jesus' approval upon tithing (Matt. 23:23) must be taken within the Judaistic context of his hearer. Even here the approval of tithing is overshadowed by "the weightier matters of the law, justice and mercy and faith."

[15] T. A. Kantonen, *A Theology for Christian Stewardship* (Philadelphia: Muhlenberg Press, 1965), p. 114.

[16] Ibid., p. 118.

[17] Ibid., p. 116.

[18] Ibid., p. 117.

[19] Richard J. Foster, *Freedom of Simplicity* (San Francisco: Harper and Row, 1981), p. 50.

[20] Ronald J. Sider, *Rich Christians in an Age of Hunger* (Downer's Grove, Illinois: Intervarsity Press, 1974), pp. 175-176.

[21] See Duane Elgin, *Voluntary Simplicity: An Ecological Lifestyle that Promotes Personal and Social Renewal* (Toronto: Bantam Books, 1981).

Messianism in the Book of Malachi

Gerald L. Keown

The message of Malachi contains no direct references to the coming of the Messiah, the "anointed one." Nevertheless, at least three elements within Malachi's message must be addressed in any attempt to explore or understand the possible influence of Malachi upon messianic thought. At several points in the development of messianic ideas, these elements of Malachi's message may be seen as a backdrop for key elements in the Messiah traditions.

The three elements, or "ideas," are the following: (1) the reference in Malachi 3:1 to the messenger who comes to prepare the way of the LORD; (2) the reference to Elijah's coming in 4:5a; and (3) the reference to the Day of the LORD in 4:5b. I will attempt in this article to explore how and why these three ideas from Malachi became a part of Hebrew messianic thought.

The Development of Messianic Understanding in Israel

Christian readers of the Old Testament often assume that the expectation of a coming Messiah was present from the earliest days of Israel's existence. Such was not the case. This most significant hope for both Jewish and Christian traditions emerged fairly late in the life of the people of Israel, and there were at least three discernible stages in its development.

With the emergence of the monarchy in Israel, the king obviously occupied a central role in the life of the people. David was the model of the ideal king. In spite of his flaws, which are clearly chronicled in the Old Testament, he remained the epitome of what Israel felt a king should be. The earliest hope for a "messiah," or "anointed one," likely connected the divine promise of a king from David's line who would rule over Israel forever (2 Sam. 22:48-52; Ps. 18:42-52) with the ceremonial "anointing" of Israel's king. *Messiah*, in the way the term is normally used of a coming redeemer, represents an adaptation of a more mundane use of the word to refer to priests (Lev. 4:3, 5, 16) and prophets (1 Kgs. 19:16) as well as any king of Israel (1 Sam. 2:10; 9:16).

By connecting the description *messiah* with the Davidic promise, messianic hope as it is usually understood was born in Israel. Still, what was anticipated in the earliest stage of messianic thinking was no more than the emergence of a Davidic king whom God had blessed and who would lead God's people in ways which would insure the fulfillment of the promise. The connection of specific Israelite kings with overt messianic references demonstrates this pattern of thinking. Hezekiah and Josiah were examples of kings to whom a kind of messianic fervor was attached.

As the monarchy again and again demonstrated its inability to provide the fulfillment of God's promise, messianic understanding underwent some revisions. The Messiah was still seen as God's anointed deliverer, but the process was perceived in other than ordinary terms. For such a deliverer to appear, God had to intervene in the lives of his people. The Messiah would still be the legitimate Davidic king, but he would be far more than the routine successor in the kingly line. The hopes attached to Zerubbabel may be seen as an example of this second stage of messianic thought.

The final stage in the shift of messianic ideas, as they are normally understood in Christian circles,[1] came with the tragedy of the Exile and the recognition that the monarchy was at an end. It had proven to be morally corrupt as well as politically inept. Further, it was clear that there would never again be a "king" for Israel in the usual sense. Therefore, God's Messiah would have to emerge outside of the normal avenues to take his place as deliverer and savior. It was this perspective which was most visible in the first century A.D.

It is impossible to identify the message of Malachi directly with any of these three stages of development. No specific references to the Messiah occur in the book. Evidence from the text suggests the likelihood that the prophet would have at least identified closely with the dominant thinking represented by the second stage described above. The setting of Malachi, as my colleague Marvin Tate has suggested, should probably be seen as the "colonial" period of Israel's history, when attempts were made to rebuild and reestablish life in Palestine. This historical period is consistent with the patterns of what I have termed the second stage of messianism.

The Three "Messianic" Texts in Malachi

Clearly, none of the three passages alluded to (3:1; 4:5a; or 4:5b) is directly related to the "Messiah." They do have impact upon the development of later messianic ideas.

The Messenger (3:1)

The messenger described in Malachi 3:1 is not connected with a coming messiah in this context. The focus is upon one who will prepare, not for the coming of the Messiah, but for the coming of the LORD himself. The task of the messenger is to purify the priests (sons of Levi) and serve as refiner, perhaps to refine all of the people of Israel in preparation for God's coming judgment. The "day of his coming" is probably to be understood as the expected Day of the LORD (see the further discussion on the Day of the LORD below).

In the context of Malachi's message, the prophet is addressing in an uncompromising way those apathetic and faithless Israelites who are his hearers. God's judgment is not in the past, though the trauma of the Exile had brought great hardship to Israel. The ongoing disregard for God's purposes would culminate in that "great and terrible day" of God's judgment. Only by means of the coming messenger could Israel be properly prepared for the LORD's coming to his temple.

Note that within Malachi itself no explicit connection is made between the messenger and Elijah (4:5a). The features of fire and the task of purification, however, both commonly understood as characteristic of Elijah, are allusions which may well explain other references in the Jewish and Christian traditions which do explicitly connect the two.

Elijah (4:5a)

Malachi 4:5a describes the sending of Elijah the prophet before the Day of the LORD. Most Old Testament scholars perceive Malachi 4:4-5 to be additions to the prophetic message proper. These two verses were likely appended to Malachi for very specific reasons. Though it is impossible to determine with any certainty what those reasons might have been, Malachi does mark the close of the Hebrew "Book of the Twelve," the unit of scripture traditionally referred to as the Minor Prophets. In addition, Malachi closes the whole prophetic corpus of the Hebrew Bible. Malachi 4:4-5 (especially 4:4) provides connection between the prophetic material and the Book of the Law. Malachi 4:5 closes the prophetic canon with a reference to the particular prophet Elijah and his role before the "great and terrible day of the LORD." These verses may well have been seen as an appropriate means of closure for the second of the three major divisions of Hebrew scripture as well as a connection of that division of scripture with the first such division, the Torah, or books of the law. Whether it was part of the primary intention or not, these verses tend to identify the messenger of 3:1 with Elijah.

Why should Elijah be the particular prophet mentioned at the close of the prophetic canon? Why is he singled out instead of one of the so-called writing prophets such as Isaiah or Jeremiah? It is impossible to answer these questions conclusively. The best approach is probably to reexamine what is known about Elijah and the role he played in the prophetic tradition.

Elijah is presented as a powerful defender of Yahwistic faith. Against the threat of Baalism in its strongest form, as represented by the evangelistic fervor of Jezebel, Elijah stood firm (more or less) and proved to be a courageous spokesperson for the purity of Yahwistic faith in Israel. The Elijah stories in 1-2 Kings portray Elijah as one associated with the purifying qualities of fire. Not only is that image present at the famous tour de force of Mt. Carmel, but it is also present at the dramatic occasion of Elijah's ascent into the heavens. Characteristics of Elijah, the powerful representative of Yahweh, have applied

445

to numerous enlarged roles for Elijah in the broader expanse of both Jewish and Christian literature.[2] In addition to the obvious role as Yahweh's champion, there is also Elijah's rather unusual departure from the prophetic scene. That image may also be significant in examining the reasons behind Elijah's employment as the particular prophet to close out the prophetic tradition.

Even though no conclusive explanations for the mention of Elijah at this juncture in Malachi may be forthcoming, the passages in Malachi unquestionably provide a foundation for an ever-expanding Elijah tradition in later Jewish and Christian literature. As that tradition grew, it did so in direct relationship to some of the more popular messianic ideas.

The Day of the LORD (4:5b)

The final critical focus in Malachi which has relevance for messianic thought is the focus upon the Day of the LORD. The Day of the LORD was a consistent prophetic emphasis. Popular belief in Israel, as it is set forth by the prophets, anticipated the coming of the Day of the LORD as a time when God would intervene to judge the enemies of Israel. It would be a day of joy for Israel and grief for her traditional enemies. It was seen as a glorious time when the enemies of God's people would get what was coming to them.

The prophets interpreted the Day of the LORD in a radically different way. They, too, saw it as a time of judgment and reward. It was to be a time when God would reward the faithful, who would participate in the joys of his kingdom. For the prophets, the Day of the LORD also included judgment for those enemies of Israel who were deserving of judgment. The radical departure from typical popular thinking, however, lay in the way the prophets turned the judgment inherent in the Day of the LORD until it pointed squarely at Israel herself. Israel had rejected Yahweh and therefore would not escape the judgment she brought upon herself. The ungodly heathen would not escape God's judgment, but neither would faithless Israel.

The concept of the Day of the LORD and ideas which developed in Israel about God's Messiah had no direct connection. That which joins the two images is the common feature of eschatology. As messianic thought was fleshed out, the coming of the Messiah was associated with many of the eschatological images which had been a part of Israelite tradition for a much longer period of time. Ideas which were related to the Day of the LORD rather naturally became associated with the Messiah's coming. Therefore, ideas like those present in Malachi, which may have no direct connection with one another or with specific messianic patterns, became somewhat fused in the ever-expanding eschatological themes of Judaism and Christianity. Perhaps the best way to approach the messianic importance of the Malachi passages is to look more closely at those later eschatological patterns which involve the prophet Elijah, first as they appear in Jewish literature, and finally as they are found in the New Testament.

Jewish Literature

Elijah is clearly present in the eschatological patterns of Jewish literature. References to the prophet can be found in the Apocrypha, the Pseudepigrapha, the Qumran materials, and within the mainstream of rabbinic writings. A sampling of these references follows.[3]

It is readily apparent that only with the development of Jewish Talmudic literature did Elijah begin to appear in a direct relationship to the coming Messiah in Judaism. Elijah references in the Apocrypha, the Pseudepigrapha, Qumran literature, and even in early rabbinic sources are not used in ways that are radically different from the Malachi passages. It could be argued that some transitional ideas develop, but there is certainly no direct contact with explicit Messiah traditions until the Talmudic writings. In the following paragraphs, I will attempt to demonstrate the eschatological patterns which were associated with Elijah in the various streams of Jewish tradition.

The Apocrypha

Ben Sira in Sirach 48:10 draws directly upon Malachi 4:5-6 in his praise portrait of Elijah. He describes the role of Elijah at the "appointed time" as "calming the wrath of God before it breaks out in fury," turning "the heart of the father to the son," and restoring "the tribes of Jacob." A number of Old Testament scholars in the older tradition interpreted this passage in Sirach as indication of Elijah's role as forerunner of the Messiah.[4] A careful reading of Sirach, however, finds no trace whatever of the Messiah, and interpreting Elijah as forerunner of the Messiah from this text is problematic at best.[5] What appears evident in Sirach 48:10 is that Elijah, if a forerunner, is a forerunner of Yahweh, not of the Messiah. This, of course, is the force of the messenger passage in Malachi 3:1. Sirach is concerned with the larger establishment of Yahweh's kingdom and Elijah's role in preparing Israel for that kingdom. Though no messianic connection is visible here, there does appear to be a closer connection between Malachi 3:1 and 4:5-6.

Several references in 2 Esdras are also generally associated with the prophet Elijah. As with the passage in Sirach, there is no connection at all with the Messiah, but a clearly implied association of the prophet with the Day of the LORD.[6]

Apocryphal treatment of Elijah, like that in the canonical Old Testament, connects Elijah with eschatological fulfillment, but not with the Messiah. It may be said, however, that some transition occurs from the portrait of Elijah in Malachi to the portrait of Elijah in apocryphal references.

The Pseudepigrapha

Two works of the Pseudepigrapha provide worthwhile information concerning the role of Elijah as that role was understood within Jewish tradition. Though neither 1 Enoch nor the Testaments of the Twelve Patriarchs provide definitive information about Elijah, references to Elijah in these sources are more pronounced than is true of the remainder of the Pseudepigrapha.

1 Enoch. No explicit references to Elijah are found in 1 Enoch. Traditionally, 1 Enoch 89:52; and 90:31 have been associated with Elijah.[7] The principal figure in these verses is a ram who has a significant eschatological role in the unfolding drama related by the visionary Enoch. Even if the traditional association of the ram with Elijah is accepted, the figure portrayed in 90:31 is eschatological; but there is no direct connection with the Messiah, as forerunner or otherwise.

Testaments of the Twelve Patriarchs. The main contribution which the Testaments makes to the Elijah tradition is the introduction of two messianic figures, the Messiah of Aaron and the Messiah of Israel. A similar concept is also present in the Qumran writings.[8] Some have equated the Messiah of Aaron with an eschatological Elijah figure, a high priest type who comes either as a precursor or partner of the Messiah of Israel.[9] It is he who is often seen to anoint the Messiah of Israel for his task in the messianic age.

Testament of Dan 5:11b is the closest link between the Messiah of Aaron and Elijah. It is possible to make at least a distant connection between this passage and Malachi 4:6 in that the "Lord's salvation" in the Testament of Dan is said to "turn the hearts of the disobedient ones to the Lord." Nevertheless, the reference to Elijah is not clear, and it is not directly connected to the idea of a messianic forerunner.

The Talmud and Post-Talmudic Literature. References to Elijah in the Talmud reflect a growing number of legends and stories about the prophet. Those Elijah references in the Talmud which have a clear eschatological focus are related to the redemption of Israel and Elijah's preparatory role in that redemption.

There is linkage in the *Midrash Rabbah* between Elijah and the coming of the Messiah. Elijah is portrayed both as precursor to the Messiah and as his partner in messianic mission.[10]

The Talmudic and post-Talmudic materials provide the first solid connection of Elijah with the Messiah in Jewish literature. It is significant to note the absence of any such connection elsewhere in Jewish literature.

The New Testament

The New Testament references to Elijah have explicit connections with messianic thought. One issue which must be addressed when the Elijah references in the New Testament are considered is that of the varied ways in which Elijah is treated. Mark 9:11, Matthew 17:10, etc. are traditionally assumed to portray Elijah as forerunner of the Messiah.[11] That understanding must be *assumed*, though, since the texts themselves never directly confirm or deny the scribes' beliefs. Some references seem to identify Elijah *as* the Messiah, and others are fairly consistent with the Malachi portrayal of Elijah as one who prepares the way of the LORD, with no overt messianic connections. The following are samples of the Elijah texts in the New Testament.

Several passages in the Gospels have been traditionally related to an expectation of Elijah's coming prior to the end of time. Mark 9:11, Matthew 17:10, and Luke 1:17 seem to reveal an expectation of Elijah's coming in preparation for the end. Though the texts in Mark and Matthew are usually understood in connection with the Messiah, the Gospels do not make the connection explicit. Instead, the pattern is similar to that which is found in Malachi and could as easily refer to the coming of the LORD himself at the end of time.

The confusion expressed by some of Jesus' followers is a related issue. Some had evidently identified Jesus as Elijah, perhaps, as Jeremias suggested,[12] because of the miracles he performed.

John the Baptist is explicitly linked to Elijah traditions in the Gospels, but in Luke especially there is ambiguity in the pattern. Early on, Luke makes a strong connection between Elijah and John the Baptist. As the Gospel unfolds, however, there appears to be something of a shift in which Elijah patterns are more nearly associated with Jesus.[13]

Traditionally, the New Testament has been understood to profile John the Baptist as an Elijah figure who fulfills a common expectation that Elijah would come to prepare the way for the Messiah. There is at least the possibility of a connection with the task of the messenger in Malachi 3:1. It is necessary, however, to call attention to the inconsistency with which the Elijah traditions are treated.

Conclusions

Elijah plays a significant role in both the Christian and Jewish traditions which are concerned with the end of time. It is equally clear that a number of once disparate traditions associated with the end of time and with Elijah have experienced some fusion across the centuries. The three "ideas" noted from Malachi illustrate this fusion. Not only are the concepts of 3:1 and 4:4-5 joined to each other in the unfolding tradition, they are also connected with other traditions which are concerned with eschatological events. That such fusions would also lead to associations with messianic themes and with the Messiah himself should not be surprising. The striking fact from a careful overview of the biblical and extra-biblical materials is the absence of any overwhelming evidence which would connect Elijah, as noted in Malachi or elsewhere, with the Messiah in any direct way.

What has occurred is the emergence of a *catena,* or a kind of tent, which brings all of the above mentioned ideas under one "roof" of tradition. Even though the connections of Elijah traditions with the Messiah are not direct connections, it is impossible to ignore the very important role those combined traditions have played in the life of the Christian community.

Brevard Childs, noted Old Testament scholar, has argued that the biblical interpreter must address the existing canon of scripture which belongs to the faith community and not spend all the energy of interpretation along the path of its development. Much the same point could be made about this catena of tradition. It is important to pay attention to the long and complex history of the varied traditions which compose the larger biblical tradition, but it is also vital that the impact of the combined traditions not be ignored.

It is therefore crucial to treat both the impact of the portions of Malachi which have later messianic significance within the context of later Christian understanding and their function as a part of the original prophetic message. Ideally, insights from the primary application of the prophet's message will enhance the understanding of its later uses.

The concerns which are addressed to the community of faith in the larger message of Malachi are not isolated from the task of the messenger in 3:1ff. The announcement of the messenger's coming is directly related to the concerns which Malachi identifies within the colonial community of Israel. It is vital that the message be heard, that response be given to the message, and that there be a return to a purity of life which is essential for the people of God.

Any messianic focus which fails to take seriously these most crucial issues is an inappropriate focus. Malachi reflects the consistent emphases of the prophetic tradition, emphases which will not rubber stamp popular thinking as if it were the word of the LORD. Whether it is a denunciation of the apathy of despair, as in Malachi, or the apathy of prosperity, as in much of the pre-exilic prophecy, there is a consistency in the message of the prophets which will not accept a half-hearted way of faith.

I am convinced that the developed messianic traditions which were so crucial for early Christianity retained their identity with the prophetic tradition. The Messiah comes, not to replace the powerful and difficult word of God's prophets, but to fulfill it.

---

[1] Jewish messianism developed a focus upon the nation/state itself which utilized ideas about messiah in a corporate way. Zionism is a modern example of this development.

[2] Some of these are examined below.

[3] For an excellent survey on a more complete scale, see Darrell Reid James, "The Elijah/Elisha Motif in Luke" (Ph.D. dissertation, The Southern Baptist Theological Seminary, 1984), pp. 34-66.

[4] Sigmund Mowinckel, *He that Cometh*, trans. G. W. Anderson (New York: Abingdon Press, 1954), p. 299; J. Klausner, *The Messianic Idea in Israel*, trans. W. F. Stinespring (London: George Allen and Unwin, 1956), pp. 257-258.

[5] For a careful and thorough discussion of the difficulties posed by this interpretation, see M.

Faierstein, "Why Do the Scribes Say that Elijah Must Come First," *Journal of Biblical Literature,* 100 (March 1981), 75-86.

[6] James, "The Elijah/Elisha Motif," p. 47. The passages from 2 Esdras are: 6:26; 7:28; 8:13,19; 12:42; 13:52; 14:9.

[7] See R. H. Charles, ed., *The Apocrypha and the Pseudepigrapha of the Old Testament* (Oxford: Clarendon Press, 1913), 2:263.

[8] The Damascus Document is the primary source for this idea at Qumran. See CD 12:23-13:1; 19:10-11; and 20:1.

[9] See Joachim Jeremias, *"heleias,"* *Theological Dictionary of the New Testament,* ed. Gerhard Kittel and trans. G. W. Bromiley (Grand Rapids: Wm. B. Eerdmans, 1964), 2:932.

[10] See Genesis Rabbah 71:9; Leviticus Rabbah 34:8; Numbers Rabbah 14:1; Ruth Rabbah 5:6; Song of Songs Rabbah 2:13.

[11] *TDNT,* 2:936.

[12] Ibid.

[13] James, "The Elijah/Elisha Motif," pp. 105-110.

Southern Seminary
proudly announces
1987-88 Center Events

November 19-21 "Strengthening the Small Church"
Lecturer: Douglas Walrath, Church Development
    Consultant, Author
Dehoney Center for the Study of the Local Church

March 7-11 National Conference on Biblical Preaching
Mullins Lectures: Calvin Miller, Pastor/Author,
    Omaha, Nebraska
National Center for Christian Preaching

March 21-23 Sixth Annual Congress on Evangelism
Preacher: Ed Young, Second Baptist Church,
    Houston, Texas
Billy Graham Center for World Evangelism

April 14-16 "Lifestyle and Wellness: A Christian Imperative"
Lecturers:
Dr. Steve Wheeler, M.D., Louisville
Phyliss Skonicki, Wellness Promoter,
    State of Kentucky
Dr. Mahan and Janice Siler, Pastor and Specialist
Gheens Center for Christian Family Ministry

April 26-27 "Christian Response to the Biomedical Revolution"
Lecturer: Dr. James B. Nelson, United Theological
    Seminary, Maryland
Clarence Jordan Center for Christian
    Ethical Concerns

July 11-15 First Annual Pastors School
Bible Study, Preaching, Workshops
Sponsored by all centers

For more information, contact the Director of Continuing
Education, The Southern Baptist Theological Seminary, 2825
Lexington Road, Louisville, KY 40280.

Preaching from Malachi
W. Hulitt Gloer

Preaching from Malachi will prove to be an exciting and challenging experience for anyone committed to serious biblical preaching. The faithful proclamation of Malachi's message demands that "the insight of the Word expressed in the passage in that (biblical) day becomes insight and Word for us in our day."[1] Too often, however, the biblical text becomes little more than pretext, a springboard for the preacher's own ideas. The *use* of the text quickly turns into *abuse*. When this happens we are not likely to hear the prophet's penetrating analysis of lifeless religion, an analysis which "strikes at the heart of nominal, easy-going Christianity as it did at the heart of Judaism."[2]

Nowhere is the tendency to *abuse* the biblical text more apparent than in preaching from the Old Testament. To some degree at least this results from the special set of problems which the preacher encounters. While an integral part of the Christian canon, the Old Testament was not written by Christians nor originally for Christians. To many it seems "a foreign land. . . . no Christ, no church, worship by sacrificing animals, strange people with strange customs."[3] How is the preacher to relate Malachi's emphasis on Temple, sacrifices, priestly cult, or purity laws, to Christians at the end of the twentieth century without resorting to fanciful allegory or spiritualization? While the modern methods of biblical criticism learned in seminary are invaluable tools for discerning what the text *meant*, still "the preacher easily becomes frustrated in determining what the text *means* for the audience he must address."[4] How then do we preach from Malachi?[5]

Preaching from Malachi: Some Hermeneutical Considerations

Our commitment to the authority of the Old Testament reminds us that the Old Testament *is* the word of God for the Christian church. We must preserve its integrity by giving attention to this word of God in its original historical setting. We need not rush ahead to link the Old Testament text with some New Testament text or foist a New Testament meaning upon it, thus wrenching it from its historical moorings. We must preach the Old Testament text itself for in its pages we are brought "face to face with the Father of our Lord Jesus Christ and in the encounter God speaks. . . calling, exhorting, warning, judging, condemning, confronting and sanctifying."[6] In and of itself the Old Testament is a valuable witness to what it means to believe in this God.

At the same time we cannot help but read the Old Testament from an A. D. perspective and must ask what the New Testament has done with the facts of Israel's faith in light of Christ. Thus, we must read the Old Testament in two directions: "forward with history in its plain historical meaning and backward in the light of the New Testament affirmations about it."[7] In reading "forward" we must reckon with the difficulties created by the fact that we are far removed from the religious, historical, and cultural life encountered in the biblical text.[8] We cannot assume a simplistic, one-to-one correspondence between the situation reflected in the text and the contemporary setting. Translation from *then* to *now* will be necessary.[9] Some texts will require very little translation because of the commonalities of human experience. Others will demand significant translation in order for there to be a merging of the experience of the people in the text with the experience of the congregation into a single story—an "elision of worlds."[10] Nevertheless, if we affirm the canonical authority of the Old Testament and the significance of history, we must seek to understand how God's word spoken in Israel's history is God's word for us today.

We must be sensitive to the nature and significance of biblical prophecy. This is especially true in a culture which is often preoccupied with the predictive dimension of the prophetic ministry, as though prediction were the prophet's primary concern.[11] Prophetic concern for the future issued from a concern that the people respond to Yahweh in the *present*. Thus the greatest significance of the prophets lies in the fact that they speak of those times in history when God intervened ". . . and because of their explanations of what was happening we can see what is most important to God in the behavior of his people and we can be assured of his intention and the direction of his acts of judgment and redemption."[12]

An awareness of the *two basic hermeneutical modes* reflected in the preaching of the prophets is also important.[13] In times when the believing community needed to hear the comforting word of God's grace and faithfulness to his promises they employed a *constitutive* hermeneutic. In times when it was essential that the same community hear the challenging word of God's freedom to critique and judge, they employed a hermeneutic of *prophetic critique*. We must beware of betraying the intention of the prophetic text by applying a text intended to challenge the oppressed (by affirming God's grace) to the oppressor or a text intended to challenge the oppressor (by affirming God's judgment) to the oppressed. Authentic biblical preaching "should challenge those dynamically equivalent to those challenged by the biblical text."[14]

This axiom means that the preacher must seek to understand the religious, political, and sociological position of those addressed in the text—both the "good guys" (those we tend to identify with) and those who appear to us to be the "bad guys." Are they in a position of power and authority and, therefore, likely to be receptive to materials which confirm and conserve their place and to

454

interpret the traditions in a way that makes life as comfortable as possible? Or do they represent a minority position which stands "over-against" the dominant culture and tends to challenge the values and life-style of that culture? An awareness of these factors can greatly assist the preacher in the attempt to determine dynamic analogies between the situation represented in the biblical text and the contemporary context. Of course this process requires that the preacher ask the same kind of questions about those who will hear the sermon: "The preacher must identify what today's hearers share with the author's original readers so that the text confronts them both."[15] Addressing a contemporary community in a social situation other than that to which the text was written can lead to serious distortion of the biblical message.[16]

What are the implications of these insights for our reading of and preaching from Malachi? While we must read the text from the point of view of the prophet, we must also read it from the point of view of the condemned priests (1:6; 2:1) and of those who question the love and justice of God (1:2; 3:14), with whom we may have more in common than we would like to think! James Sanders suggests a good rule of thumb at this point: "Whenever our reading of the biblical passage makes us feel self-righteous, we can be confident we have misread it."[17]

Finally, the book of Malachi clearly illustrates one of the most noteworthy changes in the study of Israelite prophecy in recent decades. There has been a reversal of the widespread stereotype which portrayed the prophet and priest ranged against one another in sharp antagonism. Both the priest and prophet, however, shared the work of oracular direction, and the prophets were deeply concerned about the cult and its practices. The severe indictment of the cult that often characterizes their preaching is not a rejection of the cult *per se* but a condemnation of the abuse and corruption of the cult which so often occurred.[18]

Preparing to Preach from Malachi: Some Practical Suggestions

1. *Begin your study several months in advance and spend some time each day with the biblical text.* There is no substitute for long-term exposure to the biblical text itself. Shallow sermons and sermons that miss the point are usually the result of limited acquaintance with the text. Powerful preaching results from prolonged exposure.

2. *Get acquainted with the book as a whole.* Read through the book several times at one sitting to get a feel for the flow of the text. If you are not able to work from the Hebrew text, use several different translations. The variations of style and wordings which they offer may stimulate new insights into the meaning of the text. Do not turn to the commentaries and other study tools yet. These initial readings should be "spontaneous, even naive" engagements with the text in which "all faculties of mind and heart are open, with no concern for what one ought to think, much less what one will say later in the sermon. This is

the time to listen, think, feel, imagine and ask."[19] All responses to the text—impressions, questions, and specific texts that arrest your attention—should be noted. These will provide a catalog of sermon starters.

3. *Employ a variety of approaches to engage the text.* We have already discussed the significance of reading the text from more than one point of view. Read Malachi from the perspective of the prophet but also read it from the standpoint of the community to whom the word is addressed. In other words, read the text as if you were one of the priests (1:6; 2:1), or one of those who questions the love and justice of God (1:2; 3:14). An *oral reading* of the text can provide exciting new insights. Read the text aloud several times with feeling and inflection, attentive to volume and timing, and employ a different emphasis and stress each time as you try to imagine how the text may have been spoken and heard. This exercise may set in motion intuitive sympathy with the text "and call to consciousness some of its feelings that would have been evoked by the text in its original setting."[20] It does not take very long to recognize that inflection and tone can make a significant difference in the way a text is interpreted.

4. *Exegete the text.* Once one has become familiar with the text as a whole, move to the stage of careful exegetical study in order to place the text in its proper historical, political, social, and religious context. Turn to the tools and resources provided by biblical scholarship, summarizing your findings as briefly as possible as you compare and contrast the various points of view that surface.

5. *Pose the following questions to the text.*[21] (1) What is the form of the text? It is clear that form and function are inextricably related. The form of the text or sermon will tend to orient our consciousness in relation to it and, therefore, has the effect of predetermining our expectation(s) and response(s). The form of the text may provide the basic form that the sermon needs to take. Most significant, however, is the *how* and *why* of the form. (2) What is the structure, plot, or movement of the text? Does the text reveal patterns, significant repetitions, or the use of certain literary devices that are significant for understanding its message? (3) What points of view are reflected? Many texts will reflect more than one and may shift from one point of view to another. In Malachi, for example, how are the points of view of God, the priests, the doubters, and the righteous reflected? Failure to recognize such point of view shift may result in serious misunderstandings of the text. (4) What is the "addressed world" of the text? Since human consciousness is historical and we do not live in Malachi's world, our tendency is to respond to the text in ways that are more reflective of our world than that of the text. The preacher must understand the addressed world and enable the listeners to understand (and if possible experience) that world. In the case of Malachi this means the world of disappointment, disillusionment, and despair of the post-exilic period and the worlds of the priests and the doubters. (5) What is the text's "field of concern"? John Bright reminds us

that "all biblical texts are expressive of some aspect of the . . . faith of Israel" and thus we must seek to lay bare the theological and ethical concerns that "animate it, that caused it to be said, and said as it was."[22] (6) What is the text trying to do? What is it seeking to accomplish in the lives of those to whom it was addressed? Surely our sermon should share this intention. This question "may well mark the beginning of homiletical obedience."[23]

6. *Determine a strategy for preaching the text.* Early on the preacher must make the listeners aware of the historical context which gives rise to the prophet's message. Contrasting the expectations which had characterized the preaching of the exilic and post-exilic prophets (for example, Ezek. 34:26-30; Isa. 54:1-3; 49:19-23; Jer.23:56; Zech. 8:1-3; Haggai 2:9) with the historical realities will enable listeners to understand the disappointment, disillusionment, and decay which is reflected throughout Malachi (for example, read 2:8, 9; 1:7, 8, 13, 14; 3:8-10; 2:10; 3:5; 2:17; 3:13-15; 2:11, 14-16). It was "the winter of Israel's discontent. . . the summer was over, the harvest was ended and they were not saved."[24]

The form and structure of Malachi are very suggestive for the preacher. The message of Malachi is preserved in the rather unique form of a disputation between God and his people in which the traditional prophetic oracle with its direct statement of sin and judgment is replaced by a *didactic-dialectic* pattern which characterizes later Jewish literature. Elizabeth Achtemeier has made the interesting suggestion that the book has been cast in the form of a court case.[25] As the trial begins, Yahweh is the defendant as the people bring charges against him. Israel is quickly put on the defensive, however, by God's countercharges, and the roles of defendant and plaintiff are reversed. Thus there is a significant element of somewhat shocking reversal in the text that should be captured in one's preaching. The "courtroom" scenario offers interesting possibilities for the preacher. Imagine, for example, a series of sermons based on the notion of "God in the Dock" in which the complaints and questions of the text are rephrased in contemporary terms and argued.

Other ideas for a sermon series from Malachi might focus on "Searching Questions" (for example, "Where is the Love of God?" "Where is the Justice of God?" "Why Serve God?" or "How Do We Despise God's Name?" "When Do We Give God Less than Our Best?" or "How Have We Misrepresented God?" or "The Complaints of God."[26] One might also build a series around the affirmations which introduce each of the oracles: "The Nature of God's Love" (1:2a), "What Does It Mean to Call God Father and Master?" (1:6), "If God is Father . . . " (2:10), "When Words Aren't Enough" (2:17), "God's Unchanging Nature" (3:6), "Bearing False Witness" (3:13-15).

Basically Malachi contains six oracles (1:2-5; 1:6-2:9; 2:10-16; 2:17-3:5; 3:6-12; 3:13-4:3) consisting of (1) an affirmation about Yahweh (for example, 1:2a), (2) an objection in the form of a question placed in the mouths of the people (1:2b), and (3) a response or refutation (1:2c). The book closes with two appendixes in 4:5-6.[27] Sermons based on the oracles of Malachi might adopt a structure similar to that of the oracles themselves, consisting of three basic moves: (1) a statement of the basic affirmation of the oracle translated into contemporary idiom, (2) a consideration of common objections to the affirmation as those might be forming in the minds of your listeners, and (3) a response to these objections emphasizing the content and message of the biblical text. The dialectic form of the text would lend itself well to the use of the dialogue sermon involving other persons or even the whole congregation in the interaction reflected in the text.[28]

A series of sermons on the six oracles of Malachi might be approached in a number of ways. One might present an exposition of each oracle. The appendixes (4:4-6) could be treated in a separate sermon or with an earlier text. For example, 4:4 could be treated with 2:10-16, which emphasizes covenant faithfulness, while 4:5-6 could be treated with 2:17-3:5 since it appears to be something of an explication of this earlier text.

A sermon on the first oracle (1:2-5) would focus on *the love of God*. While some in Israel have come to question that love as a result of recent experiences, the prophet reminds the people that the fact of their election and the history of God's dealings with them is a continuing testimony to the reality of that love. The love of God is the central affirmation of Malachi's message. The book begins and ends with a declaration of that love (4:5-6), thereby framing the entire collection of oracles. For Malachi "each word and deed and movement of God towards men is of infinite love."[29] It is in the context of this unconditional and unrelenting love, a love often unappreciated and unappropriated, that the message of the prophet must be heard!

This "divine love is holy love," however, "and it is precisely the divine love and majesty that have been forgotten by the people" so that there is "a spiritual famine in the land."[30] Thus in the second oracle (1:6-2:9) the prophet turns to focus on "Divine Love Dishonored." He calls the people to recognize that they have despised God's name by allowing their worship to degenerate into "the slavery of selfish interest."[31] While they offer less than their best, the Gentiles offer "a pure offering" to the Lord (1:11-12). Their profession of faith and love for Yahweh are little more than empty words and hollow hymns (1:6): "There is no profanity which is so awful as that of orthodox expression and heterodox heart."[32] The prophet calls the people to genuine and vital worship, recognizing that the nature of our worship is a clear reflection of the state of our relationship with God. Malachi understood the necessity of worship so that while earlier prophets could say 'mercy and not sacrifice,' he "had courage and insight to say 'mercy and sacrifice' was a proper response of God's people."[33] Note that Malachi includes ethical demands in his emphasis on faithfulness in relationships and especially in 3:5! Such an emphasis on worship is sorely needed in our culture!

The third oracle (2:10-16) focuses on divine love dishonored by unfaithfulness to the covenant. For Malachi the love of God is most clearly manifested in *the covenant of God.*

> Fundamental to Malachi's teaching is the concept of the covenant. It is implicit in the opening theme, the Lord's love for Israel (1:2-5) and the book ends with a call to fulfill the obligations of the covenant as expressed in the law.[34]

The priests have profaned the covenant of Levi by their unfaithfulness to Temple service and people. The people have profaned the covenant of the fathers (2:10) by their faithlessness to one another (2:10), a fact clearly revealed in violation of the marriage covenant (2:13-16). Furthermore, they have married "the daughter of a foreign god" (as did their ancestor Judah) and whether this is understood literally or figuratively, it is still a clear violation of the Sinai covenant.[35] For Malachi righteousness is covenant faithfulness, which means faithfulness in *relationships*—to God and to one another. If people are not faithful to these relationships, though they may "cover the Lord's altar with tears" as a sign of repentance and devotion, their behavior belies their profession. They are a people who are "holding the form of religion but denying the power of it" (2 Tim. 3:4).

The fourth oracle (2:17-3:5) raises the age-old issue of theodicy. How does one reconcile *the ways of God* with the character of God? Traditional theological answers are being questioned. The wicked prosper, the righteous suffer, and the promises remain unfulfilled. Such despair leads to a kind of "functional atheism" which does not deny God's existence but doubts his ability to intervene effectively in human affairs or keep his promises. Malachi's response to such despair and doubt is a call to *faith*. While current events may seem to present evidence to the contrary, Yahweh is the Lord of all the earth, and he is very much in charge of history. He will appear to purify his people (3:2c-4), to execute judgment against the unfaithful (3:5; 4:1), and to save the righteous (3:16-18; 4:2-3). Until then, the people must wait in faith (cf. Heb. 11-12):

> Faith according to the Bible consists in waiting for God to act—waiting with the expectation that he will act; acting with the assurance that he will keep his words, trusting that the future will indeed bring that which he has promised. . . . so Israel was to trust and obey.[36]

There is a sense, however, in which present events bear prophetic witness to this great eschatological judgment, for according to the prophet the unhappy circumstances in which the people languish are a result of their own faithlessness. It is God's judgment on their disobedience (3:7a). Malachi knows that "a just God does not tolerate shoddy worship or lives lived contradictory to his holiness,"[37] and while God's grace abounds it is not "cheap grace." Thus his judgment comes, but it is a judgment borne out of his love: "All this talk about

God being such a God of love that he passes lightly over sin is the misunderstanding of what love is. . . the instant God begins to excuse sin. . . He proves He does not love us."[38] The judgment of God comes upon his people to purify them (3:2c-4), and he calls them to return to a relationship in which his faithfulness can be experienced: "Return to me, and I will return to you, says the Lord of hosts" (3:7b). He yearns for the return of the prodigal, and he stands ready to "open the windows of heaven" and "pour down. . . an overflowing blessing" (3:10). But we must be prepared for his coming! "Can I say, 'Come' to Christ's announcement that He is coming?. . . There is no test concerning holiness of life and character equal to that."[39]

The fifth oracle (3:6-12) focuses on *the faithfulness of God*. He has not consumed his people despite their turning from his statutes. His desire continues to be the same: "We have to do with an unchanging love and with a faithfulness that never departs from its word and with a purpose of blessing that will not be turned aside."[40] This undying love is mocked by the people, however, as their unwillingness to bring the tithe demonstrates. For Malachi this failure represents a far deeper problem. It bespeaks a lack of confidence in God's providential care: "Small giving and small faith go hand in hand and indeed the former may be a symptom of the latter."[41] At this point we must be quick to recognize that Malachi's allusion to failure to pay the tithe is but one example of the way we may rob God: "This God of the Bible is Lord, King, Father, Judge, Savior, Redeemer over our lives and world. If in the conduct of our daily existence we try to make him less than that we most assuredly rob him."[42] On the other hand, God is faithful and "when men can say, 'Here we are, our interests, ourselves, our business, everything,' then the windows of heaven are never shut—never."[43]

The final oracle (3:13-4:3) speaks of the dangers of misrepresenting God: "The worst form of blasphemy is the misrepresentation of God by people who profess to love him."[44] Those who say, "It is vain to serve the Lord. What is to be gained from it?" betray the fact that theirs is little better than "mercenary" service! The righteous in Israel, however, "fear the Lord" (3:16; cf. 1:6), "think on his name" (3:16; cf. Prov. 23:7: "As a man thinketh. . . "), and "speak with one another," that is , encourage one another in faithfulness. They are God's "special possession" (3:18; cf. Deut. 7:6-14-2; 1 Pet. 2:9) and for these "the sun of righteousness shall rise with healing in his wings" (Mal. 4:2).

The message of the book concludes with a final affirmation and challenge in 4:4-6. Faithfulness is manifested in obedience to the law of Moses (4:4) and anticipation of God's eschatological action of salvation and judgment (4:5-6). Thus memory and hope are the two poles between which faithfulness is fleshed out. For the Jew, of course, remembering always involves action! The implication is clear: "Do the law. . . until I come!"[45] Then there is a final appeal:

The Old Testament does not end with a curse pronounced but

with a curse threatened, not with a declaring that hope is forever past and that there can be no redemption and no deliverance, no further word, but with a statement intended to teach that God has not yet pronounced this curse and that he does not desire to do so. . . [it] is the last appeal of love.[46]

Besides the themes alluded to above one might preach on "Marriage: A Sacred Covenant" (2:13-16) in which God is a partner because he is "witness to the covenant." Here Malachi appeals to the creative purposes of God in marriage (2:10, 14-15; cf. Jesus' discussion of marriage where he takes the same approach) and the significance of the family for sustaining and nurturing faith (2:15).

Malachi emphasizes "God's Electing Love" in 1:2-5.[47] God's election of Israel has a purpose which extends beyond Israel for he is the Lord of the whole earth (1:5). He is the creator God (2:10), worshiped by righteous Gentiles (1:11) while unrighteous Gentiles (like the Edomites[48]) feel his wrath. Israel has been chosen to be the vessel through which God's love would be communicated to all the nations. Thus while God loved the Israelites for themselves he desired to love others through them, but Israel's failure to respond to God's love stymied both purposes.

Malachi warns of God's "Contempt for Casual Faith" as he reminds us that complacency can result from the knowledge of God's gracious love. This state of mind is clearly seen in the people's questions (1:6-7; 2:13, 17; 3:8, 13) and even more clearly in the unrelenting condemnation of the priests (1:6-2:9). Note that they are going through the motions of ministry. They are performing their assigned tasks. In fact they are doing them to the point of tedium (1:13). The problem is the way they are doing them! By offering blemished sacrifices they violate the law by the very acts with which they seem to adhere to it. (Cf. Mark's marvelous *inclusio* of Jesus and the Temple and fig tree in 11:11-20).

Malachi's beautiful description of the role of the priest in 2:5-7 sets before us a significant standard by which to determine "The Measure of Our Ministry." The priest functions as God's messenger (2:7; cf. the use of the same term in 3:1) mediating to the people the knowledge of God which is derived from his own intimate communion with the Lord. In short, the priest is to "walk with" God (2:6; this term is used only here and in Gen. 5:22; 6:9): "Priests should not only have the knowledge but should keep it, that is , walk in it, be obedient to it, be the embodiment of the knowledge he holds."[49] The implications of Malachi's teaching are clear when we remember that in Christ we have become God's "Royal Priesthood" (1 Pet. 2:9).

Malachi 1:5,11-12 presents a powerful challenge to narrow parochialism and challenges us to ask "How Big Is Our God" as the prophet contrasts the "fragrant sacrifice" and "pure offerings" of the nations with those offered in Israel. This text was so surprising to the translators of the King James Version that they translated its present tense as future, making it a reference to a future time. It was difficult in Israel, in England in 1611, and it remains difficult to allow God to be at work in the lives of those outside the prescribed boundaries!

Finally, a sermon on Malachi's "Great Expectations" could focus on the prophet's eschatological significance. He alone presents the idea that God would send a messenger before his final advent (3:1). One might trace the use of Malachi by Jesus and early Christians by referring to specific New Testament texts (Matt. 16:14; 17:10ff.; Mark 6:15; 8:28; 11; Luke 1:17; 9:18). Malachi's eschatological interest is basically an expression of his confidence that Yahweh is in control of history and that his purposes will be accomplished. His primary concern is not forecasting the future but affecting the lives of people in the present!

[1] Ronald Sleeth, *God's Word and Our Words: Basic Homiletics* (Atlanta: John Knox, 1986), p. 53. In his book *The Bible in the Pulpit* (Nashville: Abingdon, 1978), p. 106, Leander Keck gives the following definition: "Preaching is biblical when (a) the Bible governs the content of the sermon and when (b) the function of the sermon is analogous to that of the text."

[2] Joyce Baldwin, *Haggai, Zechariah, Malachi* (Downers Grove: InterVarsity Press, 1972), p. 218.

[3] Donald Gowan, *Reclaiming the Old Testament for the Christian Pulpit* (Atlanta: John Knox, 1980), p. 6.

[4] See the discussion of this problem by Foster McCurley in his book *Proclaiming the Promise* (Philadelphia: Fortress, 1974), pp. 4ff. A most helpful book which attempts to show how contemporary methods of biblical criticism *can* help the preacher determine what the text *means* for today is Ronald Allen's, *Contemporary Biblical Interpretation for Preaching* (Valley Forge: Judson, 1984).

[5] The most helpful discussions of the problem of preaching from the Old Testament are found in: Elizabeth Achtemeier, *The Old Testament and the Proclamation of the Gospel* (Philadelphia: Westminster, 1983); John Bright, *The Authority of the Old Testament* (Nashville: Abingdon, 1987); Donald Gowan, *Reclaiming the Old Testament for the Christian Pulpit* (Atlanta: John Knox, 1980); Foster R. McCurley, *Proclaiming the Promise* (Philadelphia: Fortress, 1974).

[6] Terence Fretheim, "The Old Testament in Christian Proclamation," *Word and World,* 3 (1983), 223.

[7] Bright, *The Authority of the Old Testament* p. 162.

[8] A succinct treatment of the fundamental differences in situation, culture, and worldview is presented by William Thompson in "Text and Sermon," *Interpretation,* 35 (1981), 32-45.

[9] For a significant and helpful discussion of the variety of approaches to this task, see Ernest Best, *From Text to Sermon* (Atlanta: John Knox, 1978), pp. 54-96; Fred Craddock, *Preaching* (Nashville: Abingdon, 1987), pp. 125-150.

[10] For further discussion of this matter, see Fretheim, "The Old Testament," pp. 228ff.; Gowan, *Reclaiming the Old Testament*, pp. 4ff.; and Lawrence Toombs, "The Problematic of Preaching from the Old Testament," *Interpretation,* 23 (1969), 302-314.

[11] For a survey of basic approaches to understanding the prophets, see Gowan, *Reclaiming the Old Testament,* pp. 119ff. A practical treatment of this problem is found in Gordon Fee and Douglas Stuart, *How to Read the Bible for All Its Worth* (Grand Rapids: Zondervan, 1982), pp. 150ff.

[12] Gowan, *Reclaiming the Old Testament,* p. 126.

[13] A stimulating discussion of these two hermeneutical modes and their significance for the preacher is given by James A. Sanders in his book, *God Has a Story Too: Sermons in Context* (Philadelphia: Fortress, 1979). A briefer version of this discussion is found in his article, "Hermeneutics," in the *Interpreter's Dictionary of the Bible,* Supplementary Volume, ed. Keith Crim (Nashville:

Abingdon, 1976), pp. 402-407.

[14] Sanders, "Hermeneutics,"p. 406. The use of the term *dynamic equivalent* rather than *parallel* is deliberate and significant. The search for parallels often leads to a quest for one-to-one correspondences which may actually result in moving one away from the intention of the text!

[15] Keck, *The Bible in the Pulpit*, pp. 11ff. Thompson, "Text and Sermon," p. 33, reminds us that "Every preacher faces two dangers in preparing a sermon from a biblical text: Failing to take seriously the text's agenda and failing to take seriously the congregation's agenda."

[16] A most helpful discussion of this process can be found in Allen, *Contemporary Biblical Interpretation*.

[17] Sanders, "Hermeneutics," p. 407.

[18] See, for example, James Muilenburg, "Old Testament Prophecy," *Peakes Commentary on the Bible*, ed. Matthew Black and H. H. Rowley (Middlesex: Thomas Nelson and Sons, 1962), pp. 475-483.

[19] Craddock, *Preaching*, p. 105.

[20] Allen, *Contemporary Biblical Interpretation*, p. 25. For a basic word on oral interpretation, see Charlotte Lee, *Oral Reading of the Scripture* (Boston: Houghton Mifflin, 1961).

[21] The following questions are basically derived from David Buttrick, "Interpretation and Preaching," *Interpretation*, 35 (1981), 50-57. A more traditional approach is reflected in Dwight Stevenson, *In the Biblical Preacher's Workshop* (Nashville: Abingdon, 1967), pp. 69-70.

[22] John Bright, "An Exercise in Hermeneutics," *Interpretation*, 20 (1966), 190. Buttrick, "Interpretation," p. 57, suggests that this is the "theo-logic" of the text.

[23] Buttrick, "Interpretation and Preaching," p. 58.

[24] James Hastings, ed., *The Speaker's Bible: The Minor Prophets* (Aberdeen: The Speakers Bible Office), p. 211.

[25] Elizabeth Achtemeier, *Nahum-Malachi* (Waco: Word, 1986), p. 172.

[26] See, for example, the interesting treatment of God's complaints by G. Campbell Morgan, *Wherein Have We Robbed God? Malachi's Message to the Men of Today* (New York: Fleming Revell, 1898). Morgan's treatment is still quite stimulating for the preacher.

[27] See the helpful treatment by James Fischer, "Notes on the Literary Form and Message of Malachi," *Catholic Biblical Quarterly*, 34 (1972), 315-320.

[28] Morgan, *Wherein*, p. 69.

[29] Ibid.

[30] John Paterson, *The Goodly Fellowship of the Prophets* (New York: Charles Scribner's Sons (1948), p. 248.

[31] Morgan, *Wherein*, p. 51.

[32] Ibid., pp. 46-47.

[33] Rex Mason,"The Prophets of the Restoration," *Israel's Prophetic Tradition: Essays in Honor of Peter Ackroyd*, ed. Richard Coggins, Anthony Phillips, and Michael Knibb (Cambridge: Cambridge University Press, 1982), p. 140.

[34] Baldwin, *Haggai, Zechariah, Malachi*, p. 216.

[35] See the treatment of this text in major commentaries, and the interesting treatment by A. S. van der Woude, "Malachi's Struggle for a Pure Community: Reflections on Malachi 2:10-16," in *Tradition and Reinterpretation in Jewish and Early Christian Literature* (Leiden: E. J. Brill, 1986), pp. 65-71.

[36] Achtemeier, *Nahum-Malachi*, pp. 174-175.

[37] Ralph Klein, "A Valentine for Those Who Fear Yahweh: The Book of Malachi," *Currents in Theology and Mission*, 13 (1986), 152.

[38] Morgan, *Wherein*, p. 130.

[39] Ibid.

[40] Alexander MacLaren, *Exposition of Holy Scriptures*, vol. 4 (Grand Rapids: Wm. B. Eerdmans, 1959), p. 353.

[41] Peter Craigie, *Twelve Prophets* (Philadelphia: Westminster, 1985), p. 243.

[42] Achtemeier, *Nahum-Malachi*, p. 191.

[43] Morgan, *Wherein*, p. 78.

[44] Ibid., p. 61.

[45] It is interesting at this point to note the striking parallels with Jesus' instruction to his disciples in the upper room ("Do this . . . Until I come"). See, for example, 1 Cor. 11:23-26; Mark 11:22-25 par.

[46] Morgan, *Wherein*, p. 113.

[47] Note Paul's use of Mal. 1:2-3 in Rom. 9:13, 18 in a discussion of God's freedom to choose or to reject whomever he will.

[48] In Israelite prophecy Edom was understood as a type of all those who oppose God, and the downfall of Edom was seen as an indispensable part of the Messianic Age (Isa. 34:5-6; 63:1-6; Jer. 49:13, 17, 18).

[49] Morgan, *Wherein*, p. 32.

"You Say": Confrontational Dialogue in Malachi
John D. Hendrix

I am learning the meaning of a new word. The word is *recursiveness*, a concept used in the design of teaching and training programs which illustrates the importance of congruency. For teaching to be congruent, the approach used to present the material (the *process*) should reflect the material being covered (the *content*). Reflection is a process of holding up mirrors. If we held a mirror behind the process and another mirror behind the content the images reflected would be consistent and harmonious, or congruent.

Recursiveness is an issue in congruency. A recursive statement is a statement which refers to itself. For example, the sentence, "Let's examine all sentences which contain eight words," is recursive because it has eight words and therefore refers to itself.

The idea of recursiveness in teaching and learning was brought to light by the Pulitzer Prize winning book *Godel, Escher, Bach: An Eternal Golden Braid* by Douglas R. Hofstadter, who adapted the mathematical concept of recursion to a wide range of issues. According to Hofstadter, any situation where there is more than one level of meaning has the potential to be recursive:

> The concept is very general. (Stories inside stories, movies inside movies, paintings inside paintings, Russian dolls inside Russian dolls (even parenthetical comments inside parenthetical comments!)—these are just a few of the charms of recursion.)[1]

Examples of recursion are often seen as we watch the daily news on television. The commentator will switch to some foreign correspondent who then has a tape of some local reporter interviewing someone. We now have news interpretation within news interpretation within news interpretation—three levels down. We keep track of it very easily in our subconscious minds and are scarcely aware of the movement.

The art of teaching constantly calls our attention to recursiveness and congruency. When the process of education reflects the subject matter being taught we have a recursive design. The word might be new but the teaching concept will be familiar to those who have studied the methods of Jesus. When Jesus washed the disciples' feet to get across the idea of servanthood he was being recursive. Jesus wisely chose or utilized his environment and designed activities to fit the concept he wanted to teach. Over and over again he let the message direct the medium.

Recursive teaching takes the content seriously for it suggests that content *drives* or directs the process in a particular way. A teacher who uses the same methodology regardless of the content is not being recursive. A teacher of methodology is aware that the issues of recursion and congruence are always present in the climate of a classroom. What is worse than a boring unimaginative lecture on lecturing? What is going on when a teacher lectures on small group interaction? (A student reminded me one day that I had used copious notes in a lecture on memory.) The repertoire of the teacher calls for a flexible methodology that allows the content to direct process.

Teaching Prophetic Literature Recursively

Recursiveness means that teaching prophetic literature is different from teaching other types of biblical material. Walter Brueggemann suggests canonical criticism as a way that Old Testament studies interface with teaching methodologies. Canon criticism gives attention to how the biblical material reached its present form and the shape of its presentation. The shaping process is a clue to communicating the message. Therefore Brueggemann suggests that "canon is a clue to education, both as substance and process."[2] The educational process can be faithfully carried out only by those who give close attention to the canonical process.

The prophetic literature has a different function, proceeds with a different epistemology, and evokes a different response. Brueggemann is calling for recursiveness, the shape and process of the content drives the methodology: "Shape and process, how and what, substance and method are bound together."[3] Teachers are not permitted to focus exclusively on the substance of knowledge or on the process of knowing but must attend to the interaction between the two.

Would we teach Malachi the same way we would teach Exodus or Deuteronomy? The answer is no. In the law we have what is narrative, known, given. We teach through the accurate communication of principles and concepts. There is a general consensus around the content that is known and settled.

In contrast the word of the prophet is immediate, intrusive, and spontaneous. It is improvisational, "winging it," "shooting from the hip." I have been reflecting on this process during the football season. The teacher is not the quarterback who stays in the pocket, buffeted and protected by numerous defenses and committed and programmed for predesigned routes and patterns. The teacher of prophetic literature is the scrambler, breaking loose from protection, and making up plays on the spot:

> The word of the prophet is something immediate, intrusive, and surprising. It is not normative. It is not known in advance. It is a way of knowledge that is not known until it is uttered.[4]

466

The teacher is amazed at himself or herself: "I can't believe I really said that. Where did that come from? That wasn't a part of my notes."

The prophetic task in Malachi is to bring to the surface those fears and unexpressed emotions that have been ignored and suppressed. The numb and denying posture of the people is simply verbalized. The prophet speaks evocatively in the indirect language of questions so that the expression can be heard in different ways by many different people. The prophet articulates what the people feel but ignore or deny. He brings to light the self-deception and asks people to face up to what is real. You can almost see the injured look on their faces: "I don't want to hear it. Who—me? I don't know what you are talking about. What do you mean?"

Since Malachi's method is consistently different from that of any other prophet, recursiveness calls for a unique and different teaching method. Nothing energizes and stretches the teacher more than expanding the teaching repertoire. Malachi gives us that opportunity. He uses the question and answer method with interesting variations. A declarative truth is followed by the people's objection to this truth. Malachi responds by a forceful restatement of his original proposition. In the same way, the teacher intentionally creates the tension and scaffolds the argument.

Perception and Reaction

Malachi offers us in contemporary educational terminology a study of perception and reaction. Malachi perceives what is happening in Israel differently from anyone else. The meanings come from within. As a teacher you are trying to help people discover and clarify many meanings. As you teach you must be aware that learners bring different perceptual maps.

But there is another part of the process of perception that is quite important to teaching/learning—one that creates a contextual problem for the teacher. The perception of the learners is selective. That is, they see only what they want to see. Selective perception is amazing. For example, you can watch a television program so intently that suddenly you notice that someone has been talking to you for several minutes and you have not heard a word of it.

The teacher, like the prophet, is doing something very difficult—helping people see things they do not want to see and pay attention to things that they would just as soon not pay for. Teachers do that by putting into words what *they think* is going on in the listeners' heads. In other words, teachers are so close to their audience that they ask themselves the questions the listeners would rather ignore.

This brings us to the second part of the process. The teacher carries on a running internal dialogue. How will they react if I explain it this way or that way? Will it have meaning if I give this concrete example? How can I make this meaning so vivid that they will act on it? How can I predict how they will react?

How do I know if I have gotten through? (Sometimes I say, "When their eyes get big and they start blinking at you, you know you have gotten through.")

If this is what Malachi is doing (predicting the response of others and responding), he is doing something very natural to human communication. We make predictions all the time about how people will react to things we say and do. When we ask a salesman the price of a new pair of shoes, ask the usher to give us a seat on the aisle in church, request a double dip chocolate mint ice cream cone, we assume that people will act in a predictable way. We predict almost by intuition. And, in most situations, that works well enough.

But we must be careful to remember that we will never be skillful enough to predict perfectly how others react to our messages. What teachers do in confrontational dialogue is to bring to light their predictions (intuitions and hunches) concerning the learner's response. They do that by asking questions of themselves. How would I react to that message in that situation? What does the inner voice say when I own the indictment, "You are robbing God." That is to say we look inside ourselves, reflecting and looking for the mirror that shows us something of ourselves. Would others respond the same way?

Robert D. Young in *Religious Imagination* shows the crucial weakness in teaching and preaching when the biblical story is not joined to personal creative power and energy. It is not that teachers shun the hard work of interpretation and exegesis: "However, though they are highly trained in using their minds, they are not highly trained in listening to their inner voices. Again the result is copying rather than proclaiming."[5] There is a certain ignorance in all of this, an ignorance of our own best personal insights as they are prodded and stimulated by the interaction of Scripture with experience. Only in giving attention to the inner voice and visions do we produce, in Robert Louis Stevenson's words, "Your own stuff."

The price to be paid in being deaf to "your own stuff" is teaching that is dull and safe:

> Messages that do not spring from the viscera are apt to be dull. They take popular ideas and repeat them. Whether of heaven or hell, the messages do not break new ground. They are "safe" even if they deal with Armageddon. The audience loves to hear that old story. They will judge the orthodoxy by the familiar sounds. That is the danger of neglecting your inner vision. Visions break new ground.[6]

Method in Malachi

What is the medium that carries the message in Malachi? The style is rare if not unique. There are strands of interrogative methodology in Old Testament literature (Amos 3:3-7; Jer. 13:12-14; Ezek. 18:1-24), but none as sharply developed as in Malachi. Malachi has been called the "Hebrew Socrates" and calls our attention to the Socratic method of teaching.

Socrates taught everywhere—the streets, the marketplace, and the gymnasium. He taught by questioning his listeners and showing them the inadequacies of their answers. Inevitably, he made enemies. He was brought to trial, charged with corrupting the young and showing disrespect.

Socrates believed that the correct method of discovering truth was by inductive means—reasoning from particular facts to general ideas. This process took the form of dialectic conversation which became known as the Socratic method. Two people would begin a discussion with common assumptions about key ideas. The conversation first showed that assumptions were different and inadequate. Through the conversation more adequate definitions were developed and broader meanings were made applicable.

Scholars do not agree on the type of question and answer methodology used. Ralph L. Smith in the Word Biblical Commentary describes these confrontations as disputes:

> The style of the book of Malachi is that of disputation. Some have called it "discussions." Others call it "Socratic" or "catechetical," or question and answer style.[7]

Smith does not see this style as new or unique to Malachi, although the form of the discourse is more standardized than in previous passages.

Elizabeth Achtemeier sees the book made up largely of disputations in the form of questions and answers between the prophet and his contemporary Israelites.[8] She sees the setting as a court of law where charges and defenses are made. In each dispute the people ask, "Wherein have we done, or not done, what is charged?" In spite of the overwhelming evidence of the people's guilt, Malachi has a pastoral concern for the people filled with love, comfort, and assurance.

T. Miles Bennett in the Broadman Commentary on Malachi describes this process as a "new method" that Malachi refines to such a degree that it is used consistently among later Jewish rabbis.

> This new method is easily understood and was employed by the prophet with telling effect. First a charge or accusation was made against the people. Then with the words "But you say," the prophet proposed an objection on the part of his hearers. This objection was next refuted in some detail, and in so doing the truth of his original charge or affirmation was driven home in true prophetic fashion. Seven distinct examples of this unique method of prophetic instruction are found in this short book of only 55 verses.[10]

Socrates, Kierkegaard, and Malachi

Whether Malachi's method be Socratic (the streets), catechetical (the schools), or disputational (the courts), communication still remains the primary issue. Malachi stands in the tradition of Socrates and Kierkegaard in proposing an indirect method of teaching. The cultural situations in Greece, Palestine, and Denmark are similar—a people up to their ears in information, their senses dulled by too much hearing, and their spirits swamped with a rationalism requiring a logical and reasoned argument.

No one has described this process better than Fred Craddock's treatment of Socrates and Kierkegaard in *Overhearing the Gospel.* Craddock centers his study of indirect methodology on Kierkegaard's judgment of his own times: "There is no lack of information in a Christian land; something else is lacking, and this is something which the one man cannot directly communicate to the other."[10] The nuances that tie the three together in an indirect teaching style are the prophetic feeling for the unfamiliar and an indirect way of communication.

How do we communicate the inner vision of Scripture to another? How does the immediacy of one person's experience become immediate to another?

> The ideal requirement of Christian speech consists of this:. . . it must not only talk about the listener's situation between the twin possibilities of offense and faith, but must place him in that situation—and in order to do this must first create that situation.[11]

I have found no better statement of Malachi's methodology in the seven charges he makes against the people.

Seven Confrontations

Do the people actually get into verbal discourse? Or, is the prophet verbalizing feelings and attitudes that the people cannot verbalize for themselves? "You say" may carry the meaning "you think" or "you say to yourself." The people's response comes closer to being unconscious conclusions that filter and distract everything the prophet says. Instead of ignoring these "feeling" responses of the people, the prophet pays close attention to them and makes their perceived unconscious attitudes a part of the communication process.

The Interpreter's Bible commentary on Malachi 2:7 gives insight into the "you say" passages.

> The RSV renders more idiomatically "thinking." "Say" in Hebrew not unfrequently has the sense "say to oneself." In the present case one is not to suppose that they had come to the deliberate and reasoned conclusion that the worship of God was unimportant. The prophet means merely that their attitude shows that *unconsciously* they really *feel* the performance of the ritual to be a secondary matter which requires no particular care on their part.[12] (author's italics).

In the seven confrontations I have attempted to model a teaching methodology through a short lecturette. First, there is the charge, in the explanation of the meaning of the text. Second, is the anticipated response of the people in listening to my "inner voice." The lecturette is part of the structured experience, "I Say. . . I Hear You Say."

470

The First Confrontation: You Say, How Has God Loved Us? (1:2)

Malachi begins with a charge that the people have been blessed by God but have lost their awareness that all good things come from him. Malachi puts into words what many people "think" but are afraid to say. When the prophet says "God loves you," the people think, "Does God really love us? Look at all the bad things that happen to us. If God really loved us, these things would not happen." The people want more proofs. Listen closely and you will find that need in people. "Surround us with evidences, engulf us with proofs, assure us with concrete testimonies, show us with spectacular results, and perhaps we will believe." This constant insatiable need for proofs is a form of denial. Nothing is more damaging to interpersonal relationships than the incessant need for others to prove their care and affection. To ask God for proofs constantly is to say that he is capricious, unreliable, and faithless. What the people expect is a recitation of the mighty acts of God in the past. But they say, "Don't start telling us the stories of the past again. We want to know what God is doing for us now."

The Second Confrontation: You Say, How Have We Despised God's Name? (1:6)

Malachi gives new meaning to the third commandment of the Decalogue. The prophet accuses the priests of despising the name of God. The people dishonor the name of God by giving indifferent service. Hearts had turned so far away from the tenderness of God that they were unable to recognize their own attitudes. Again, the priests do not consciously despise God's name. But the prophet follows good rules of confrontation feedback. The prophet does not talk about intent but actual behavior that perhaps expresses itself in unconscious ways. The prophet attacks attitudes in worship. They say, "Worship is important, but not that important. Most worship is knowing the right times to stand and sit. Since we're just going through the motions one way is just as good as the other." That kind of worship is polluted or blemished or flawed. Malachi is confronting the indifferent professionalism of the priests. "We have been here many times before. We can do this with our eyes closed." Going through the motions simply means that the body and mind know what to do, and that can be done regardless of the inner attitude.

Nothing deflates the worship of God more than mechanical routine and tiresome duty. This attitude spreads quickly from worship leaders to congregation. No one is touched, no tears are shed, no lives are changed. "What happened at church today?" one asks. "Nothing," is the perceived response. When nothing happens, God is despised.

The Third Confrontation: You Say, How Have We
Polluted God's Altar? (1:7)

The third confrontation Malachi brings before the people is a charge of polluted offerings. The people come to God's house with a flippant attitude, half-hearted, talkative, saucy, and impertinent. Their gifts on God's altar are blemished—coins that are residues of weekend spending, discarded clothes for the poor, remnants of their time, and halfhearted gifts of their talents. What the people offer to God they would not dare offer to civil authorities (1:8). It would be better to close the doors of God's house and forget the whole thing than to continue this flippant attitude of worship (1:10).

Malachi anticipates or predicts the response of the people. "What a weariness this is, you say, and you sniff at me," says the Lord of hosts (1:13). The people think, "Accept what we give and be thankful for what we are doing. At least, we are doing something, and that's more than can be said for most." With a deep sigh, throwing the head back and turning up the nose, they sniff. "How weary this is making us. We get so tired of hearing about all the things we should be doing, this is such a bother. Everyone knows we are doing the best we can."

The Fourth Confrontation: You Say, How Have We
Wearied God? (2:17)

The people have wearied God by their worship. Now, they weary God with their words. The charge is the cynical spirit that reasons God's influence in behalf of the wicked rather than the righteous. The people constantly badger God with complaints about the wicked who seem to get so much out of life in contrast to the righteous who seem to get so little.

You would think from their response that they are living obedient, faithful lives. But they are not, and it doesn't matter anyway! The issue is self-centeredness that shows itself in disbelief. Self-centeredness is a vicious cycle that draws a circle and leaves God out. When they ask, "Where is the God of justice?" (2:17) they are expressing doubt that he is anywhere, and frankly, they do not care. What they are concerned about is the neighbor down the street.

We can predict the response. "It is simply not right. I can't help thinking of Fred who lives down the street. Some people get away with everything. Everyone knows he is a gangster. Every penny he has made comes from cheating and lying. And he hasn't set foot in a church for twenty years."

The Fifth Confrontation: But You Say, How Shall
We Return? (3:7)

Malachi's words suggest an intentional false turn even when the true way is clearly marked. The people have chosen to go down the wrong road and beyond the boundaries of faithful obedience. Returning is not simply a change of direction but a retracing one's steps, finding the road again after wandering. Repentance calls for a change in attitude, but it also calls for action. Retracing steps calls for cleaning up the clutter along the way.

If they return to God, he will meet them on the way. The people are lovingly invited to the way clearly marked by God and to walk with God in that way. Again, they pretend ignorance. Can't you hear their reply? "What do you mean return? What's all this talk about revival and renewal? How can we return since we're already here? How can we come back when we haven't been anywhere? I don't see anything wrong with things just the way they are."

The Sixth Confrontation: You Say, How Are We Robbing God? (3:8)

The prophet moves from a general charge of unfaithfulness to the specific one of robbing God. The audience in the prophet's mind presses for an interpretation of the charges. He replies that they are ignoring the giving of the tithe and other offerings for the support of the temple. To rob God is an attempt to hide ourselves and our substance from him. Like thieves, we rob God by appearing to be less visible. We hide from God by ignoring his commands, by failing to pray and worship, by keeping silent about our witness, and by a paralysis of action in compassion and love. Robbing God is a way of dropping into the shadows and becoming anonymous. That is why people become so sensitive to the attention focused on them in times of stewardship emphasis. No doubt the people claimed that times were hard and there were many causes demanding their attention.

Can we predict the response during budget planning and promotion? Perhaps it would go something like this: "Well, it's that time of year again. This is the only time the pastor writes a column in the newsletter. This is the only time a lay person's testimony is heard from the pulpit. This is the only time we ever get a letter from the church. We get tired of all these appeals for money. We aren't robbing God. We're just trying to keep life and limb together. We have a lot of calls for money, and we've always given what we could. We've heard the old saying. 'The more you give, the more you have,' but that's not been true for us."

The Seventh Confrontation: You Say, How Have We Spoken Against God? (3:13)

The people are skeptical because they feel that God has treated them badly. It is doubtful that the people would actually speak "stout" words against God. They are not so bold as to scoff openly at God. But Malachi is not talking about their speech. He is openly verbalizing the doubts that surface in people's minds and the cynical attitude that develops as a result. Perhaps Malachi is saying, "Although you would not dare say it, you 'think' harsh things about God. How can he bless you if you are not responsive to him?"

The people's response may go something like this. "How do you know we think harshly of God? I know I shouldn't think bad things about him. But God does not pay attention even when I do all the right things. God has said, 'Put me to the test' (3:10). But the test has been carried out every day, and only those who are disobedient receive the good things of life. It's not fair, and it's certainly not worth all the trouble of trying to live the way you want us to."

Recursive Teaching Design

The seven confrontational dialogues provide an example of the charges and the "inner dialogue" that takes place in the "thinking" of the teacher in predicting and anticipating responses. How can these processes be developed into a full teaching design for the book of Malachi? The diagram suggests a process of increasing experiential meaning for the learner. This is followed by a *structured experience*, an inductive methodology which gives each learner opportunity to experience and practice confrontational dialogue.

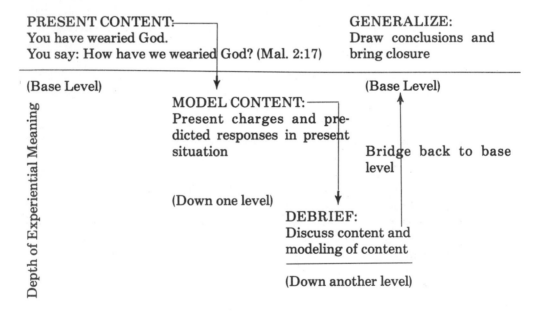

PRESENT CONTENT:
You have wearied God.
You say: How have we wearied God? (Mal. 2:17)

GENERALIZE:
Draw conclusions and bring closure

Depth of Experiential Meaning

(Base Level)

(Base Level)

MODEL CONTENT:
Present charges and predicted responses in present situation

Bridge back to base level

(Down one level)

DEBRIEF:
Discuss content and modeling of content

(Down another level)

The teacher models a recursive design by presenting Malachi's charges and the anticipatory responses of the people (base level). These charges are applied to the immediate situation by predicting and verbalizing how listeners are responding to charges. The teacher says, "Here's what I think you are thinking when I make the charge that you are wearying God." Down one level: Speaker and listeners debrief the interaction. What happens in interaction between speaker and listeners? What feelings are generated? What understandings and misunderstandings result? Down another level: Speaker and listener draw

474

conclusions and make applications about content of Malachi and question-answer process. (Return to base level.)

This recursive teaching design can be developed into a one-hour teaching plan for each of the seven disputes. This design is a "structured experience" using an inductive method and drawing from each person's experience and insight.

Title: "I Say . . . I Hear You Say." Confrontational Dialogue in Malachi

A. Goals:
　　1. To establish a climate conducive for confrontational dialogue.
　　2. To practice question and answer process as suggested in the seven Malachi disputes.
　　3. To draw meanings from dialogues that will give insight into the nature of the seven Malachi disputes.

B. Setting, Time, Materials
　　1. The same process can be used for any or all of the seven disputes. Group may include any number of dyads (pairs). Participants will need blank paper and pencils. The room needs to be large enough to accommodate pairings where each pair can work relatively undisturbed.
　　2. Each of the seven disputes can be designed in one-hour sessions.

C. The Process
　　1. The leader introduces the goals of the exercise. The nature of the question-answer process is described in detail.
　　　　a. A declaration of truth.
　　　　b. The people's objection to truth (as perceived by the speaker).
　　　　c. A forceful restatement of original declaration.
　　2. The text is introduced through a short lecturette that explains the charge and predicts the response of the listeners.
　　　　The facilitator then divides the total group into dyads (pairs) and states that both partners will have a chance to play roles of accuser (the prophet) and defender (the people).
　　3. The facilitator writes one of the seven disputes on chalkboard or newsprint and asks partners to build a case for both accusations and defense or denials.

Example from Malachi 3:8

　　　　a. Will man rob God? Yet, you are robbing me. (Write down evidences that people are robbing God.)
　　　　b. But you say, How are we robbing God? (Write down perceived responses that would defend against or deny the charges.)
　　4. Partners are divided into accusers and defenders. The dyads are given time for confrontational dialogues. The accusers make charges and verbalize perceived responses. The defenders make reasoned responses or

denials. The roles are reversed between accuser and defender, and the process is repeated.

5. After several minutes the exchange is completed and partners take notes on responses. Participants then select new partners and repeat the process. This process may be continued until responses are exchanged with 3-4 group members.
6. Participants are instructed to review privately both the meaning of the Malachi dispute (content) and the interaction that takes place in accuser and defender roles (process).
7. Participants are then asked to contribute their findings to the total group. Responses are noted on chalkboard or newsprint.
   a. What meanings have been generated concerning Malachi's confrontation with the people?
   b. What application of meanings can be applied to contemporary church life?
   c. How accurate are the accuser's perceptions and defender's reactions?
   d. What feelings are generated between accusers and defenders?
   e. What has been the intensity and involvement level during the entire experience?
   f. What have group members learned from the experience that will be useful in daily living?

D. Variations
   1. The teacher/facilitator may take the role of accuser who makes charges and verbalizes perceived responses. The audience acts as defenders with responses and denials. Both content and process are debriefed.
   2. A small group of accusers and defenders may role play the dispute in a "fishbowl" (role play group in the center with audience encircling them as observers). The debriefing process is initiated by the observers.

Conclusion

Since I am convinced that recursiveness is the route to good teaching, how do I make this essay recursive? I see you reading this essay, and several questions come into your mind. "How useful are these concepts? Is he really saying anything worth hearing?" In confrontational dialogue I say, "You fail yourself and the people you teach by not expanding your teaching repertoire. The content of biblical literature leads us toward different teaching methodologies. The style of Malachi calls for a teaching style that I have called confrontational dialogue."

Then, I predict or anticipate your response by listening to my own inner voice and vision. You look at me with raised eyebrows and surprise. You throw your head back with the appearance of great weariness and "sniff" (Malachi 1:13). You say, "Who does he think he is, anyway? I have been teaching the Bible for twenty-five years, and some educator comes along and says I have to

476

teach each book differently? Why isn't he out there teaching it rather than telling us. George Bernard Shaw was right—those who can, do; those who can't, teach." That is not the end of the conversation, but only the beginning.

[1] Douglas R. Hofstadter, *Godel, Escher, Bach: An Eternal Golden Braid* (New York: Vintage, 1979), p. 127.

[2] Walter Brueggemann, *The Creative Word* (Philadelphia: Fortress, 1982), p. 3.

[3] Ibid., p. 10.

[4] Ibid., p. 33.

[5] Robert D. Young, *Religious Imagination* (Philadelphia: Westminster, 1979), p. 113.

[6] Ibid., p. 124.

[7] Ralph L. Smith, *Micah-Malachi*, Word Biblical Commentary, vol. 32 (Waco: Word, 1984), p. 300.

[8] Elizabeth Achtemeier, *Nahum-Malachi*, Interpretation (Atlanta: John Knox, 1986), p. 171.

[9] T. Miles Bennett, "Malachi," *The Broadman Bible Commentary*, vol. 7 (Nashville: Broadman, 1972), p. 369.

[10] Fred B. Craddock, *Overhearing the Gospel* (Nashville: Abingdon, 1978), p. 9.

[11] H. Diem, "Kierkegaard's Bequest to Theology," *A Kierkegaard Critique*, ed. Howard Johnson and Niels Thulstruip (New York: Harper, 1962), p. 260.

[12] Robert C. Denton, "The Book of Malachi," *The Interpreter's Bible*, vol. 6 (Nashville: Abingdon, 1956), p. 1126.

The frightened, unwed teenager who thinks abortion is the only answer . . .

The distraught five-year-old who doesn't know why Daddy hits Mommy and makes her cry . . .

The aloneness of single adults amidst the togetherness of the "prescribed" Christian family . . .

The confused bulimic coed who doesn't think *anyone* will understand . . .

Concerned Christians face these cries for help—and so many others—every day. And it is difficult to always be prepared. Many crises of today were not those of yesterday, last week, even last year, and seldom do you have the luxury of time to research every issue. Word Publishing has responded to the need for up-to-date, at-your-fingertips information with . . .

RESOURCES FOR CHRISTIAN COUNSELING

Practical, understandable, biblically sound approaches to contemporary counseling situations in a new series under the professional guidance of Dr. Gary Collins. Written by counseling experts, these volumes will serve as an invaluable reference for ministers, laypersons and church libraries.

NOW AVAILABLE . . .

Counseling Those with Eating Disorders/
Raymond E. Vath, M.D.

Counseling the Depressed/
Archibald D. Hart, Ph.D.

Counseling for Family Violence and Abuse/
Grant L. Martin, Ph.D.

Counseling and Guilt/*Earl Wilson, Ph.D.*

Innovative Approaches to Counseling/*Gary R. Collins, Ph.D.*

Self-talk, Imagery, and Prayer in Counseling/*H. Norman Wright, M.A.*

Counseling Christian Workers/*Louis McBurney, M.D.*

Counseling in Times of Crisis/
Judson Swihart, Ph.D., and Gerald Richardson, D. Min.

WORD BOOKS
Waco, Texas 76796

AND MANY MORE COMING SOON

Available in Christian bookstores everywhere

Gary R. Collins, Ph.D. is professor of psychology at Trinity Evangelical Divinity School in Deerfield, IL. He is a licensed clinical psychologist and a widely published author and editor. His vision for this series has been rewarded by the acclaim the first volumes have already received.

Worship Resources for Malachi
Paul A. Richardson

The study of Malachi can have more meaning if materials used in worship reinforce the concepts contained in the scripture. This article is designed to assist those who plan worship. Included are suggested scripture readings, prayers, hymns, anthems, and solos. Though there are few direct quotations from the book in the literature for worship, there are some allusions and many topical parallels.

The principal sources for scripture readings, prayers, and hymns are three hymnals widely used among Baptists in North America: *Baptist Hymnal* (1956),[1] *Hymnbook for Christian Worship*,[2] and *Baptist Hymnal* (1975).[3] Hereafter these hymnals are abbreviated BH56, HCW, and BH75. Two limitations have been made because of the constraints of space: many texts of general praise, though related to the subject matter of Malachi, have been omitted; and texts which might be listed under several topics are cited only under a single heading.

Scripture Readings and Prayers

Quotations from Malachi
    Mal. 3:10   BH56: 99   BH75: 629

Related Texts, Arranged Topically
   Acceptable Worship
BH56: 26, 27, 102
HCW: 455, 456, 457, 458, 466, 582, 583, 588, 601, 604
BH75: 522, 524, 529, 576, 639

   Confession and Forgiveness
BH56: 11, 54, 61, 69, 91
HCW: 474, 489, 566, 573, 601, 611, 612, 613, 616, 626
BH75: 534, 568, 569, 570, 573

Divine Faithfulness
BH56: 1, 7, 8, 24, 25, 37, 39
HCW: 572, 580, 584, 587, 595
BH75: 515, 521, 527, 564, 574, 578, 626, 636

Divine Love
BH56: 15, 43, 44, 80
HCW: 472, 477, 479, 508, 509, 557, 561, 563, 565, 570, 579, 591, 593, 596, 597, 598
BH75: 536, 575

Judgment
BH56: 55, 57, 58, 87
HCW: 517, 620
BH75: 532, 597, 622

Marriage Covenant
BH75: 611, 618

Righteousness and Stewardship of Life
BH56: 21, 29, 40, 41, 60, 66
HCW: 486, 538, 544, 545, 548, 554, 562, 567, 607
BH75: 528, 541, 572, 609, 621

Tithes and Offerings
BH56: 50, 99
HCW: 650, 651, 652, 653, 654, 655, 656, 657, 658, 659, 660, 661, 662
BH75: 525, 581, 590, 600, 608, 623, 624, 629, 632

Unity of Worship and Service
BH56: 13, 96
HCW: 457, 481, 510, 569, 605, 619

Hymns

Quotations from and Allusions to Malachi

Verse	Hymn	BH56	HCW	BH75
3:1	Angels from the realms of glory (st. 4)	76	124	87
	Love divine, all loves excelling (st. 3)	2	297	58

Verse	Hymn	BH56	HCW	BH75
3:2	Day of judgment! Day of won- ders! (cf. 3:5; 4:2)			502
3:3	Judge eternal, throned in splen- dor[4] (cf. 4:2)			
3:10	Bring ye all the tithes into the storehouse	404		
4:2	Christ, whose glory fills the skies	22	285	
	Hark! the herald angels sing (st. 3)	81	123	83
	O come, O come, Emmanuel (st. 2)		108,109	78
	O very God of very God[5]			
	Sometimes a light surprises			221
	Sun of Righteousness[6]			
	The heavens declare thy glory, Lord (st. 3)[7]	187		

Related Texts, Arranged Topically
Divine Faithfulness

	BH56	HCW	BH75
All my hope on God is founded		20	
Begin, my tongue, some heavenly theme	49		
Cast thy burden upon the Lord	254		
Children of the heavenly Father		30	207
Father, long before creation		211	
God almighty, God eternal		203	
God hath spoken by his prophets		34	
God of our life		28	
Great is thy faithfulness	47	14	216
How firm a foundation	262,263	35	383
Immortal, invisible, God only wise	43	75	32
Let us with a gladsome mind		3	27
O God, our help in ages past	286	23	223
O worship the King	20	67	30
Praise, my soul, the King of heaven	18	73	8
Serve the Lord with gladness	434		411
The God of Abraham praise		81	25
Unto the hills		21	

Divine Love

	BH56	HCW	BH75
God is love; his mercy brightens	50		36
I sought the Lord		11	

	BH56	HCW	BH75
O love of God, how strong and true		16	
O love of God most full	52		482
O love that wilt not let me go	290	17	368
The cattle on a thousand hills			152
The King of love my Shepherd is	280	49	215
The Lord is my Shepherd	57		
The Lord's my Shepherd		40, 41	341
There's a wideness in God's mercy	48	13	171

Human Commitment

	BH56	HCW	BH75
A charge to keep I have	358		407
Christian hearts, in love united			253
He who would valiant be		252	384
Lord, dismiss us with thy blessing	31		
Make room within my heart, O God			321
O God of earth and altar		373	
O God of our fathers, we praise	500		507
O God, whose love compels us		18	
O Jesus, I have promised	386	213	365
O Master, let me walk with thee	426	218	369
So let our lips and lives express	323		456

Judgment

	BH56	HCW	BH75
Come, ye thankful people, come[8]	490		233
O day of God, draw nigh		266	
The God who sent the prophets[9]			
The Lord will come	126		128
Thou Judge by whom each empire fell		372	

Marriage Covenant

Most of these texts were written for use in the marriage service. Their use in a general worship setting will require a clear explanation of relevance.

	BH56	HCW	BH75
As we before thine altar bow		380	
Before thee, Lord, we join our hearts		375	
O Father, all creating		381	
O God in heaven, whose loving plan			396
O God, who to a loyal home		277	398
O Love divine and golden		376	
O perfect Love	501	378, 379	395
O thou whose favor hallows		377	
Our Father, by whose name		275	

482

	BH56	HCW	BH75
Social Responsibility and Service			
Hope of the world	282	236	364
Jesus, friend of thronging pilgrims		144	100
Let there be light	444	331	
Lord, speak to me	340	344	276
Mid blackness of the city's night		336	
O God of every time and place			320
O Lord, who came to earth to show			309
Renew thy church, her ministries		335	
Stir thy church, O God our Father			269
The light of God is falling	442		
The voice of God is calling		271	
We are called to be God's people			405
We lift our hearts			416
Where cross the crowded ways of life	464	268	311
Where restless crowds are thronging		272	
Stewardship of Life and Posses-sions			
All things are thine	403	262	
As men of old their first fruits		98	
Awake, awake to love and work			413
Because I have been given much			414
Come, all Christians, be committed			362
Give to the Lord, as he has blessed			415
Glorious is thy name, most Holy			419
Hear ye the Master's call	437		
Master, no offering	401		
Praise to God, immortal praise	14	95	
Savior, thy dying love	400	260	418
Take my life, and let it be	356, 357	94	373, 374
The wise may bring their learning	513	263	
We give thee but thine own	402	261	
Unity of Worship and Service			
Lord, whose love through humble serv-ice		145	
O gracious Lord, accept our praise			19
Thou whose purpose is to kindle			313
When the church of Jesus			319

Anthems

Quotations from or Allusions to Malachi

Verse	Composer	Title	Publisher	Voicing
1:11	Ouseley	From the rising of the sun	Oxford	SATB
	Powell	From the rising of the sun	Abingdon	SATB
	West	In every place incense shall be offered up	Novello	SATB
2:2	Sateren	Return unto me	Schmitt	SATB
2:10	Beck	Song of Exaltation	G. Schirmer	SATB
3:3	Handel	And he shall purify (*Messiah*)	various	SATB
4:2	Angell	Christ, whose glory fills the skies	Pro Art	SATB
	Burroughs	Christ, whose glory	New Music	SATB
	Candlyn	Christ, whose glory	C. Fischer	SATB
	Darke	Christ, whose glory	Royal Sch.	SATB
	Graves	Christ, whose glory	Oxford	2-part
	Knight	Christ, whose glory	Royal Sch.	Unison
	Werner	Christ, whose glory	Augsburg	2-part
	Willan	Christ, whose glory	Concordia	SATB
	Wolff	Christ, whose glory	Concordia	SAB

Related Texts

Berger	Psalm 57	Flammer	SATB
Blakley	Draw nigh to God	Schmitt, Hall & McCreary	SATB
Blakley	If with all your heart	Hinshaw	SATB
Brahms	Create in me a clean heart	G. Schirmer	SATBB
Carter	Seek the Lord	Hope	SATB
Dietterich	Wilt thou not turn again	Abingdon	SATB
Farrant	Lord, for thy tender mercies' sake	E. C. Schirmer	SATB
Gibbs	O God of earth and altar	G. Schirmer	SATB
Glarum	Be merciful unto me, O God	Abingdon	SAB
Graf	Great Lord of all	Hall & McCreary	SATB
Lovelace	What shall I render to my God	E. C. Kirby	SATB

Marchant	Judge eternal	Novello	SATB
Marshall	Blessed is the man	Abingdon	SATB
Marshall	We would offer thee this day	Sacred Music	SATB
Martin	Anthem of Dedication	Presser	SATB
Mueller	Create in me a clean heart	G. Schirmer	SATB
Pelz	Show me thy ways	Augsburg	SATB
Pelz	Who shall abide	Augsburg	SAB
Pote	Create in me a clean heart	Hinshaw	SATB
Powell	Lord, Sanctify me wholly	Augsburg	SATB
Price	Do not I love thee, O my Lord	Hope	SATB
Purcell	Lord, how long wilt thou be angry	Mercury	SSATB
Purcell	Thou knowest, Lord, the secrets of our hearts	E. C. Schirmer	SATB
Roberts	Seek ye the Lord	G. Schirmer	SATB
Routley	The Second Song of Isaiah	Hinshaw	SATB
Schmutz	Be merciful unto me	Abingdon	SATB
Schütz	Lord, create in me a clean heart	Capella	2-part
Schwoebel	Psalm 1	Broadman	SATB
Smith	Do not I love thee	Triune	SATB
Wesley	Lead me, Lord	various	SATB
Wesley	Wash me throughly	Novello	SATB
Willan	Create in me a clean heart	Concordia	Unison
Wyton	Seek the Lord	Hinshaw	Unison

Solos

Quotations from or Allusions to Malachi

Verse	Composer	Title	Publisher	Voicing
1:11	Greene	The Lord's name is praised	Bosworth	high/low
3:1	Handel	Thus saith the Lord (*Messiah*)	various	medium
3:2	Handel	But who may abide (Messiah)	various	medium
3:2, 3	MacDermid	The Spirit of the Lord God	Forster	high/low

485

3:10	MacDermid	Bring ye all the tithes into the storehouse	Forster	high/low
4:1, 2	Scott	I know in whom I have believed	Presser	high/low

Related Texts

Butler	The Lord reigns	Sacred Music	medium
Caldwell	O love that wilt not let me go	Triune	medium
Ellsasser	O love that wilt not let me go	Word	high/low
Evans	Create in me a clean heart	Abingdon	high
Greene	O that my ways	Bosworth	high/low
Mendelssohn	Be thou faithful unto death (*St. Paul*)	various	high
Mendelssohn	If with all your hearts (*Elijah*)	various	high
Mendelssohn	O God, have mercy (*St. Paul*)	various	medium
Powell	I will sing of the mercies of the Lord	Sacred Music	medium
Powers	Create in me	Abingdon	high
Roberts	Seek ye the Lord	G. Schirmer	high/low
Starer	Have mercy on me, O God	Southern	medium

---

[1] Walter Hines Sims, ed., *Baptist Hymnal* (Nashville: Convention Press, 1956).

[2] Charles Huddleston Heaton, ed., *Hymnbook for Christian Worship* (Valley Forge: The Judson Press, 1970).

[3] William J. Reynolds, gen. ed., *Baptist Hymnal* (Nashville: Convention Press, 1975).

[4] *The Hymnal 1982* (New York: The Church Hymnal Corporation, 1985), no. 596; this text is in the public domain.

[5] Ibid., no. 672; this text is in the public domain.

[6] *The Hymns and Ballads of Fred Pratt Green* (Carol Stream, Ill.: Hope Publishing Co., 1982), no. 179; permission to use this text must be obtained from the publisher.

[7] The version of this text at no. 325 in HCW does not contain the pertinent stanza.

[8] The version of this text at no. 101 in HCW is a revision which suits the hymn for harvest, rather than judgment, emphasis.

[9] Pratt Green, no. 88; permission to use this text must be obtained from the publisher.

Early Chautauqua Institution as a Model Lifelong Learning Enterprise

R. Michael Harton

Lifelong learning has been described as "a conceptual framework for conceiving, planning, implementing, and coordinating activities designed to facilitate learning by all Americans throughout their lifetimes."[1] Although lifelong learning is now a popular idiom in education, Kellogg Foundation President Russell Mawby said in his 1985 Foundation report, "Most Americans have not fully grasped the concept of lifelong learning. Conditioned by the educational system they have experienced, they think of education as an institutional ladder constructed for children and youth."[2]

The 1976 "Lifelong Learning Act" (or Mondale Act) was a kind of manifesto on the need to focus on lifelong learning. Nineteen different types of programs were included in the scope of lifelong learning under the Act, from literary to personal development.

Strange as it may seem, the roots of this contemporary idea of lifelong learning may be found in the history of a 112 year old institution in the southwest corner of New York State. Its two founders shared a religious conviction that education was the right and duty of all, and that all persons should have equal access to knowledge. The founders were years ahead of their time in their assertion that the mind is at its best for reading, reflection, and production in adulthood. In their view the school disciplined the mind of the child; the activities of everyday life disciplined the mind of the adult. "Between the ages of twenty and eighty lie a person's best intellectual and educational opportunities."[3]

My purpose is to trace briefly the history of this unique institution, its founders, and some of the outstanding personages who both touched and were touched by it. My goal is to show the contribution of Chautauqua Institution to the concept of lifelong learning.

Historical Context

There were precious few educational opportunities for adults in nineteenth-century America. Therefore, one of the prime resources an adolescent nation needed to cope with the problems of urbanization, industrialization, and immigration was sorely lacking. In the latter third of the century a number of diverse issues plagued the socially conscious and the religious minded in the growing nation. Susan B. Anthony was a popular if not fully respected speaker on the subject of women's suffrage, and temperance drew its share of vocal advocates. Slaves had been freed, and the nation was trying to find a place for them off the plantations.

The need for a general education for the young was also an issue, but few thought of the need for educating adults. Gradually, however, homemakers, farmers, and factory laborers were finding new labor saving devices which had the effect of producing more leisure. Along with scattered pleas for organized general education many who realized their own deficiencies in education were forming mechanics institutes, library associations, and book clubs. Newspapers were gaining more power as an adolescent nation thirsted for information about its world. Papers often carried excerpts of books, poetry, and Sunday School lessons.

Early Antecedents

A number of early educational experiments focused on bringing enrichment and enlightenment to the masses in a day when formal education was largely reserved for the wealthy. The Workingmen's Institutes, for example, sought to provide a means for the common laborer to learn about the world, not so much with the idea of helping him advance in job or society but simply to enrich his life and broaden his horizons whatever his circumstances.

The Lyceum became something of an institution itself prior to the Civil War as hundreds of local groups were formed, attracting itinerant orators to provide both entertainment and enrichment. Josiah Holbrook was a self-made scientist who lectured throughout Connecticut and Massachusetts on geology, mineralogy, and other natural sciences, while encouraging local groups to form for discussion and exploration of topics of interest to members. Across the stage of Lyceum moved such august figures as Daniel Webster, Edward Everett, William Jennings Bryan, Horace Mann, and Ralph Waldo Emerson. Emerson called Lyceum his "free pulpit" and saw it as an "active focus of the intellectual and spiritual life of the village."[4] The National Lyceum established by Holbrook lasted only eight years, but John S. Noffsinger claims it was one of the most powerful influences in the establishment of public schools.[5]

Chautauqua Institution outlived all its predecessors and peers, however, and it is on that institution that I wish to focus.

Chautauqua Offspring

To many the word *Chautauqua* describes the early traveling troupes which moved into a town with much fanfare, put up circus-sized tents and conducted a show that would rival the wild west medicine shows. Peyton Thurman told me he remembers a traveling Chautauqua held in Louisville in the late 1920s; the tent was staked out on the grounds of the waterworks on Frankfort and Stiltz Avenues.

The traveling Chautauquas were an attempt to imitate the Institution in cities and towns through the midwest and east. These were all independent, and neither the traveling Chautauquas nor the local imitators matched the vision and inspiration of the original. They were in many respects more related to the pre-Civil War Lyceum.

What Was Unique about Chautauqua?

Where did this strange sounding name come from--SHA-TOC-KWA? Some have thought it to mean a special meeting or even a special approach to education. Today people often think of it as a conference for older adults. Actually the name came from the lake on which the original assembly was held. No one really knows the origin of the name, but most believe it to be an Indian name meaning "bag tied in the middle," which would describe the shape of the lake, and there is nothing more exotic than that to the name!

The uniqueness of Chautauqua lies in the ideology on which it was based, the extraordinary character and vision of its founders, and its innovations and history.

The founders provided creative avenues for the aforementioned increased leisure being experienced by many sectors of the populace. They brought together in one place and way many popular community activities: the platform of the Lyceum, reading circles, coeducation, and new zeal for religion following the war.

The Founders: Separate Dreams, Common Concerns

Chautauqua was born from the dreams of two very different men from very diverse backgrounds who nonetheless shared in common a deep faith and burning concern for a prominent institution of the day, the Sunday School.

John Vincent was the grandson of a French Huguenot who fled to America to escape religious persecution. Born in Tuscaloosa, Alabama, John's family joined the Methodist church before moving north. Religion became a strong influence in their home. John often mimicked the preachers, preaching to the slave children and literally "sharing the gospel" with them by tearing out and distributing pages from his red Testament.[6]

Vincent grew up with an unquenchable thirst for learning, and wanted desperately to attend college. Coming from a family which was at once deeply religious and with relatively little formal education, Vincent was convinced by the considerable pressure from his father to forego wasting his time on learning (his father told him it would be selfish) when there was such a crying need for young, energetic ministers. Thus Vincent became an itinerant Methodist minister at age 17, and at age 21 was appointed to his first church. Methodist policy at the time allowed a minister to stay with one church only two years. Where he had opportunity, even during his short tenures, he would enroll in college or seminary to help quench his thirst for knowledge.

Bible instruction was an important ministry to Vincent, and while pastor in Irvington, New Jersey, he began his first "Palestine Class." A map of Palestine was staked out on the lawn of the church, and his students became very familiar with its layout and geography. Students took examinations and were passed from grade to grade—not conventional grades, but: first Pilgrim, then "Resident" of a given place, then Explorer in Other Regions, Dweller in Jerusalem, and finally "Templar."[7]

From 1866 to 1888 Vincent served the Methodist Episcopal Church as Sunday School agent and Secretary, and in 1888 was made a Bishop. While General Agent of the Sunday School Union Vincent organized the Berean Uniform Lessons, which later became the International Lesson series. In his "Hints and Maxims for Teachers" he admonished that "Every lesson should be historically developed, graphically pictured, spiritually and familiarly interpreted, practically applied, indelibly impressed."[8]

Vincent gave much attention to the Sunday School Institutes held in various places around the country. But these were too brief to offer the intensive guidance and instruction Sunday School teachers needed. He dreamed of something of longer duration, in a setting where a total learning experience of lectures by experts, workshops, and conferences interspersed with relaxation could be realized. His dream included a place for persons from all denominations and all parts of the country.

It was at one of the Sunday School Institutes that Vincent met Lewis Miller, soon to become his partner in a grand educational venture. Miller was a prominent inventor/businessman and member of First Methodist Church, Akron, Ohio. Born in Stark County, Ohio, in 1829, he was reared on a farm and as a young man took up farming with his father. He soon realized, however, that farming would leave little time to pursue the education he so urgently desired, so he became a plasterer. This allowed him to work in the summer and go to school in the winter. But Miller found his "niche" when he became a mechanic working on reaping machines. He had a logical mind which aided him in problem solving and developing better designs for the equipment on which he worked. His undaunting pursuit of a "better way" landed him the job of designer and manager of a firm owned by several of his relatives. At twenty-six he invented what would be his key to prosperity, influence, and leisure: the Buckeye Mower and Reaper.

Miller's interest and involvement in the Sunday School indicate both his ability to transfer his energy, logic, and organizational skills to nonbusiness settings and his concern for a more liberal view of life. His interest and innovative ideas in education did not go unnoticed in wider circles either. In 1867 Miller was made President of Mount Union College Board of trustees and subsequently was appointed by the Governor of Ohio to a state board whose purpose was to develop a land grant plan for a state school of mechanical and agricultural arts.[9]

When Miller became the Superintendent of the Sunday School at First Methodist in Akron, he set about to make it a model place of education for the church. He graded the classes, systematized the curriculum, and held weekly conferences of teachers to study the next lesson. The weekly discussions included not only the Bible passages but history, science, and nature as appropriate. The focus for Miller was not the storing up of religious knowledge but fitting persons for effective service to their God in the community. A lasting influence of Miller, beyond his own Akron church, was a unique architectural design which was widely copied. Eventually called the Akron Plan, the design called for a large room surrounded by individual classrooms that could be separated by folding doors.

It did not take Vincent and Miller long to discover their common zeal for improving the quality of Sunday Schools. The two talked frequently about how this might be accomplished. Vincent shared his dream for a summer school. When the idea was met with enthusiasm from Miller, Vincent suggested that the school might be held at Miller's own church to showcase his new architectural design. Miller, however, had a different idea. He was on the board of directors of the Chautauqua Lake Camp Meeting Association at Fair Point, New York. When Vincent visited the site with Miller, he could see that it was indeed the picturesque setting he had envisioned originally.

First Assembly

The grounds were leased from the Camp Meeting Association for a two-week period in the summer of 1874. At the opening of the first Sunday School Assembly, Vincent and Miller found the response beyond their expectations. Teachers, superintendents, and pastors arrived by rail, horseback, and steamboat from many states and many denominations. Arriving at Fair Point, visitors found that activities were concentrated in an area near the boat landing called Miller Park. Rows of backless benches faced a roofed platform. This open-air meeting place was called the Auditorium and had seating for about 2,000 persons. It was circled by tents brought or rented by the participants and a few cottages already a part of the grounds. Up the hill from the Auditorium was a large tent called the Tabernacle which could accommodate the crowd in case the rains permeated the natural tree-shaded outdoor meeting.

A popular attraction which still exists today beside the lake and near the site of the Auditorium was an extension of Vincent's Palestine classes from his early pastorates. It was a scale relief model of Palestine with the general contour of the Holy Land, complete with model cities of plaster, mountains, valleys, lakes, and seas. Chautauqua Lake represented the Mediterranean Sea, necessitating that the poles be reversed. "Palestine Park" was 120 feet long and 75 feet across and was a regularly used visual aid for teaching Holy Land geography.

Vincent was justly proud of his planning. One writer observed,

> No phase, no aspect, no problem of Sunday School work seems to have evaded attention in the addresses, conferences and sermons which were crowded into the next two weeks. Preachers, Sunday School superintendents, teachers, and students found sessions arranged especially for them. They had opportunity to discuss their problems relating to the church, and the home, indeed to the whole of human life![10]

Twenty-two lectures on the theory and practice of Sunday School work were provided, as well as others on Bible history, geography of Bible lands, and discourses on "Language and Illustration in Teaching" and "Helps of Science in Religious Teaching."[11]

The first assembly ended with an extensive examination in which 200 people gathered to answer fifty questions on the Bible and teaching. Most were women, but it was still a diverse group. According to a reporter from the *Western Christian Advocate*, the group included a lawyer who "took off his hat, coat, collar, and cuffs the better to grapple with his test, and a boy from Iowa who made a table out of a log and heaped dry beech leaves together to keep his kneecaps from rubbing sore while he knelt to his task."[12] Twenty candidates quit, while others worked five hours on the examination. Diplomas were finally awarded to 152 candidates.[13]

Second Assembly

There were apparently no designs for carrying on the Sunday School Assembly past the first experiment. It was such an overwhelming success, however (an estimated 4,000 persons per day participated in the activities of the assembly with a total of 25,000 attending over the two weeks), that the camp meeting board urged the Assembly to return the next year and offered to add its representatives to the Camp Meeting board.

Before the conclusion of the first Assembly, Vincent and Miller were contemplating such a return, but Vincent wanted no identification with the Camp Meeting. Perhaps Vincent shunned the Camp Meeting atmosphere as much on theological grounds as any. Strongly influenced by Horace Bushnell, he believed that a person's nature was a seed to be nurtured, not a mutant plant needing transformation.[14] Instead of the Camp Meeting absorbing the Assembly, somehow (it is not clear how except to speculate that it was due to Miller's influence as a board member and substantial contributor), the Camp Meeting board was actually reorganized as the Assembly Board, and Miller became both president of the board and the Assembly.[15]

Another Assembly confined to a Sunday School Institute was too limiting to contain Vincent's ambitious dream. Vincent realized that concentration on Sunday School pedagogy could reach a limit of usefulness. "Sunday School workers," he granted, "could not content themselves, year after year, with the discussion of the same old practical questions of organization, administration, and method." Enterprising religious workers

> . . . detest ruts. They want radical ideas, and new applications of them to everyday service. But the compass of pedagogical and governmental philosophy as applied to the Sunday Schools is not wide; and thoughtful, earnest souls loathe husks and platitudes and repetitions.[16]

"It is possible to insist upon too many hours of Bible study each day. Even a good thing can be carried to excess," Vincent said.[17] He had already realized that in an expanded Assembly he could begin to implement an idea he had nurtured since his days as a young pastor: the development of a program which would give persons a "college outlook," exposing them to great ideas and great thinkers. It would take him several years to realize his dream, but in the conception of his idea Vincent never questioned the ability of adults to learn. As previously noted, he thought the mind was at its best for reading, reflection, and production in adulthood.

The second Chautauqua was even more successful than the first, word having spread rapidly about the unique and fulfilling experience of the first assembly. This time the study of Hebrew was added to the curriculum. Nightly concerts by the lake and a chorus of 150 voices from Miller's Akron church inspired huge audiences. Vincent felt he needed a celebrity to attract more national attention, and would have invited his friend Henry Ward Beecher, but Beecher had lately been accused of indiscretions with a female parishioner. So Vincent turned to another friend and member of his former church in Gelena, Illinois, Ulysses S. Grant, then President of the United States. Grant attended, with much pomp and circumstance, but apparently did little public speaking on the occasion, having little to contribute to discussions of Sunday School pedagogy or the relation of science and nature. Grant was the first of a succession of United States presidents to visit Chautauqua.

By the end of the 1875 assembly Vincent and Miller knew they had a going concern. Plans were rapidly laid for even further expansion of the program. A Temperance Convention and a huge "Scientific Congress" highlighted the 1876 program. Professor Ogden Doremus brought with him three tons of scientific equipment for demonstrations and lectures. These were interspersed with frequent lectures by other platform personalities on subjects such as "Latest Results of Scientific Investigation and Their Bearing upon the Bible Idea of Heaven" and "Bible Miracles and Modern Science."[18] Chautauqua was addressing such issues thirty-eight years before the Norton Lectures were established

493

at Southern Seminary to address "Science and Philosophy and Their Relation to Religion."

By 1877 Fair Point had changed its name to Chautauqua, and the Chautauqua Lake Camp Meeting Association became the Chautauqua Lake Sunday School Assembly and then simply, Chautauqua Assembly.

It would be several years before Vincent would retrospectively describe the Chautauqua ideal, but it was nonetheless operative from the beginning.

> Now the doctrine which Chautauqua teaches is this, that every man has a right to be all that he can be, to know all that he can know, to do all that he pleases to do—so long as [this] . . . does not keep another man from knowing all that he can know, being all that he can be and doing all that he pleased to do. And the Christian idea of Chautauqua movement sees that the Christian elements enter into it as one of its essential features. It is the duty of every man to help every other man to be all that he can be, know all that he can know and do all that he pleases to do under the limitations already indicated. And position in life has nothing to do with it. A man is a man who has a man's motive, a man's purpose, a man's will, and who bows reverently before God that he may worship Him and gain strength to help his neighbor. That is Chautauqua.[19]

The Chautauqua Literary and Scientific Circle

One of the far-reaching experiments of founder Vincent was a plan, the seeds of which again dated to his early days in the pastorate, for an individual reading plan to make general education the property of all. Vincent said he

> felt the importance and saw the practicality of providing a course of popular reading which should open the college world to the people deprived of college training. The "student's outlook" may be enjoyed by those who have not been subjected to the student's discipline. The discipline is far more valuable than the outlook; but the latter is not to be lightly taken since it is likely to lead to the other.[20]

Vincent wished to provide a well-rounded education for all.

> Business men and mechanics, hard-working women in kitchen, nursery, or shop, may turn to good account the training-power of everyday service, and rejoice in a glorious possession of truth to which they have as much right as professional students, or "favorites of fortune."[21]

In introducing the Chautauqua Scientific and Literary Circle Vincent again revealed his philosophy, almost a theology of education.

> Knowledge promotes power. It gives to a man wide vision, enlarging the world into which he was born, and multiplying worlds to which

494

from time to time he is introduced. It is microscope and telescope to the man who possesses it. In the scheme of redemption, God has connected all grace and spiritual power with knowledge.[22]

Years later Vincent would explain his conceptualization of this new endeavor:

The "CLCS" is a school at home, a school after school, a "college" for one's own house. It is for busy people who left school years ago, and who desire to pursue some systematic course of instruction. It is for high school and college graduates, for people who never entered either high school or college, for merchants, mechanics, apprentices, mothers, busy house-keepers, farmer-boys, shop-girls, and for people of leisure and wealth who do not know what to do with their time.[23]

Vincent was so dynamic and popular that it is said that even his presence in the auditorium to introduce a speaker would draw a crowd. It was crowded August 10, 1978, when Vincent announced his plan for a "directed adult self-education." In his introduction Vincent laid before his hearers his dream, and in so doing revealed what he meant by a "college outlook": the association with other learners, a feeling of oneness with cohorts of a noble institution of learning.

All things that are legitimate are of God. In our studies in the school that is to be, let us keep the thought of our Father in the midst of nature, the thought of our Father in the midst of literature and the thought of our Father in every-day life. So this every-day college, this Chautauqua Literary and Scientific Circle [CLSC], will grow. It must grow. . . . We shall invite people all over the United States to unite with us. . . . Student lamps will be trimmed on many a little table over the land this coming winter. Fellowships will be formed. The thought that we are one, engaged in a common purpose of culture of God's glory, will help us; and we shall return to Chautauqua year after year, members and Alumni of the CLSC proud of our Alma Mater, and determined to exalt and honor her wherever we are. . . . And I say to you, with all your getting, get understanding. Look through microscopes, but find God. Look for him revealed in the throbbing life about you, in the palpitating stars above, in the marvelous records of the earth beneath you, and make of yourselves all that you can. . . . Go on to KNOW and WILL, to DO and BE. . . . [24]

Vincent had said he would be happy if ten people signed up for this new venture. To his amazement, 8,400 persons were enrolled by the following fall. His new plan challenged adults to learn. It made learning convenient, and, most significantly, it brought order to learning. Pastors enrolled their members in CLSC, homemakers propped books on the cabinet while cooking, homebound persons found escape, railroaders waiting in a caboose on a siding read, as did even lumberjacks. One steamboat captain on the Mississippi wrote, "When I stand on the deck on stormy nights I have something to think about; and you know when one has not taken care of his thoughts they will run away with him, and he will think about what he ought not."[25]

The first year ten books were assigned, in English literature, Greek history and literature, astronomy, physiology, biblical history and interpretation. The readings were subsequently organized into a four-year course with an English year, an American year, a Greek, and a Roman year. By 1887 membership numbered 80,000.

The advent of the CLSC gave rise to the CHAUTAUQUAN, a tabloid that served to link the Chautauqua faithful, particularly members of the CLSC. It carried news of the assembly and, more importantly, the reading list for the Circles. It is said that by the middle 1880s 100,000 persons were reading the CHAUTAUQUAN.[26] In the first twenty years 10,000 local CLSC groups were formed, half being in small towns of less than 3,500 population.[27]

By 1884 the program of Chautauqua was very complex. It included: a Missionary Institute, the American Church School of Church Work for laymen and ministers in the efficient management of churches, the Youth League, Boys and Girls Class for religious training, and Temperance Classmates (a series of Sunday lectures), along with the society of Christian Ethics. And there were lectures on the duties of young people between age twelve and twenty-one.

The Look-up Legion held special meetings revolving around the concept of self-help. The Sunday School Normal Department and the Teachers Retreat focused on methods of teaching. A School of Languages was begun in 1879, and a School of Theology in 1881. It was felt that Sunday School teachers should teach hymns so music classes were provided in 1880. Nine years later a School of Music opened.

But the full range of Vincent's educational plan could not be developed without providing for a centralized university-type system. Vincent convinced his board to establish a College of Liberal Arts, and in 1883 Chautauqua University was born, offering bachelors degrees in the classics, humanities, social sciences, mathematics, modern languages, and the natural sciences. The State University of New York also impowered Chautauqua University to offer the M.A. and Ph.D. degrees.

Correspondence courses proliferated under the new system with study available in five areas: history, literature, science, and pedagogy. The School of Theology conducted correspondence courses and granted the B.D. degree.[28]

William Rainey Harper

If the CLSC was one of Vincent's keys to the success and legacy of Chautauqua, his persuasion of William Rainey Harper to become Superintendent of Instruction was the other. New Chautauquas were springing up around the country, and Vincent aided and encouraged as many as he could, often traveling far to make appearances and give advice. There was one Chautauqua that he did not encourage, however. It began just across the lake under the auspices of the Baptists. Vincent realized that it could bring damaging competition to his enterprise and did some investigating on his own to determine to whom the Baptists might turn for leadership. He concluded that it might be Harper, who was teaching at the seminary at Morgan Park (three years before he went to teach at Yale). Vincent persuaded Harper to join him at Chautauqua. Little more is known about the Baptist Chautauqua. Vincent's strategy apparently worked.

Harper was an extraordinary person. Born in New Concord, Ohio, in 1856, he entered college at the age of ten. At seventeen he became a graduate student at Yale, becoming so absorbed in his studies that it is said he could study for seventeen hours a day without tiring. He received his Ph.D. before his nineteenth birthday. Upon graduation he became principal of Masonic College in Macon, Tennessee.

In 1876 Harper went to Denison University to teach. While there, he began attending a student prayer meeting and expressed a desire to become a Christian. Shortly, he became a Baptist, although his parents were Presbyterian. From Denison University Harper went to Morgan Park to teach Hebrew, and while there began his famous American Institute of Hebrew.

One biographer of Harper's opined that Chautauqua was "only a passing incident in his busy life."[29] That writer obviously was not familiar with how engrossed Harper became in his fifteen years with Chautauqua. Harper found at Chautauqua an opportunity to expand some of his own educational interest, for it was here that he added one of his first summer Hebrew schools. Its work began in 1883 as a part of the Department of Theology and continued for five weeks of very intensive study. One of Harper's students at Chautauqua recalled:

> Once at Chautauqua he told his Hebrew class in which I studied, "You are neither to eat, drink, or sleep. You will recite three times a day, six days a week. Study nothing but Hebrew. Go to no side interest. Begin with the rising of the sun Monday and stop with the chimes Saturday night."[30]

In 1885 Harper was made Principal of the Chautauqua College of Liberal Arts. In this role he was responsible for securing fifteen department heads in languages, literature, mathematics, the natural sciences, education, music, art, physical education, and the "practical arts." In addition to securing this staff of one hundred, he edited the catalog; planned courses of study; supervised the promotion of the summer schools; directed the public program of sermons, lectures, readings, and concerts; and generally supervised some three hundred events during the sixty-day session.[31]

The program and enrollment grew every year that Harper was associated with Chautauqua, as he gave himself feverishly to its work. Part of what drove him must have been the almost immediate results evident with each initiative. Harper wrote to his friend Thomas Wakefield Goodspeed in 1889 that,

> We have had a most glorious season at Chautauqua. The increase in every department is over forty percent. We do not know what we are to do with the people who are to come in this week and next. As matters stand today the grounds are crowded. We have enrolled over 550 college students in four weeks as against 330 last year in six weeks. This does not include between 800 and 900 general students in special departments. The pressure has been very great, but I think I am coming through all right.[32]

It should be noted that another contributing factor in Chautauqua's growth was Melvil Dewey's decision to hold his Great Library School there.

No one understood the significant impact the Chautauqua experience was to have on Harper until years later when he was at Chicago. His biographer wrote,

> [Harper] did for [Chautauqua] a highly useful service, but in doing it he received himself a perhaps indispensable training for the great future of which he had no conception when he became the Chautauqua principal of instruction. He was brought into intimate association with Dr. Vincent. He became acquainted with the hundreds of leading educators, lecturers, preachers, and statesmen who served in the Schools of Chautauqua. . . . He came to know the men and methods of the universities and colleges of the country and of other countries. . . . Through every year of his Chautauqua connection he grew in mental stature, in knowledge of the educational world, and in the practical skill of the administrator.[33]

While Chautauqua was a major concern of Harper's, it was not his principal work. He was professor of Hebrew at Yale and spent his summers at Chautauqua, even though much of the planning had to be done around his teaching at Yale. Through his writing and his work at Yale and Chautauqua he had become quite well known. It is not surprising that when American Baptists set about to establish a major university at Chicago, Harper would ultimately be the one to whom they turned for leadership. Actually, the choice of Harper was as much John D. Rockefeller's as anyone's. The success of the endeavor depended upon astute leadership and sound financial backing, for which the denomination looked to Rockefeller. Denominational officer Northup wrote to encourage Harper in his decision, "It is self-evident that you are the only man in the denomination that Mr. R. would think of having at the head of the proposed institution, and in this feeling and judgment all intelligent Baptists would heartily concur."[34] Actually, the latter was an overstatement, since Harper's

498

orthodoxy had been challenged on the grounds of his use of higher criticism in Hebrew studies.

The story of Harper's ultimate acceptance of the Presidency of the University of Chicago is interesting in and of itself but more germane to this topic is the profound evidence of how Chautauqua was in essence transplanted, or at least the idea was transformed into a major university under Harper's guidance. Comparing the outlines of the two institutions as reported in their publications reveals the striking similarity.

In 1885 Vincent proposed the following organization:
I. The Chautauqua Association
   A. The summer meetings
   B. The Sunday School Normal Department
   C. The School of Languages
   D. The Chautauqua Teachers' Retreat
II. The Chautauqua Literary and Scientific Circles
III. The Chautauqua School of Liberal Arts (formally Chautauqua U.)
IV. The Chautauqua School of Theology
V. The Chautauqua Press

In 1891, Harper published in Chicago's OFFICIAL BULLETIN No. I an outline for the University:
I. The University Proper
   A. The Academies of the University
   B. The Colleges of the University
   C. The Graduate Schools of the University
   D. The Divinity Schools of the University
   E. Affiliated Colleges of the University
II. The University Extension Work
   A. Regular courses of lecture
   B. Evening courses in University subjects
   C. Correspondence courses
   D. Special courses in a scientific study of the Bible
   E. Library Extension
III. The University Press

Harper's University Proper had its counterpart in Chautauqua's College of Liberal Arts (formally Chautauqua University), meeting in four quarters (or assemblies) instead of once in the summer. The CLSC became Chicago's University Extension. Gould suggests that "the plan for affiliation of colleges with Chicago may have had its inspiration from the many 'little Chautauquas' that had sprung up all over the country, and which received much help from Vincent and his staff."[35] It is clear that one of the most influential innovations to make the University of Chicago famous under Harper's leadership, education by extension, had its roots in Chautauqua. This writer could find no indication in the literature of anything but support and affirmation from Vincent regarding

Harper's work, which would seem to indicate absence of any ill will toward Harper's instituting a Chautauqua-type plan at Chicago.

For several years Harper resisted appeals from colleagues to give up his work at Chautauqua and devote full attention to the work of the University. He loved Chautauqua and his role in its leadership. He did, however, find it necessary in 1894 to bring his work there to a close in favor of the demands of a burgeoning and increasingly complex university.

George Vincent and Shailer Mathews

Space and time do not permit mention of the numerous other prominent personages who led Chautauqua through the years. George Vincent, son of founder John Heyl Vincent, became president in 1898. It was he who broadened the scope of Chautauqua to include contemporary concerns. He organized the programs into weeks, each with its own theme. The opening week of 1902 was "Social Settlement Week," with lecture and discussion topics like Graft in American Life, Social Unrest, the Juvenile Problems, and Organizations of Discontent.

Shailer Mathews, a colorful and somewhat controversial figure, became Director of Religious Work in 1912 despite criticism from conservative ministers for his "social application of the gospel" as a lecturer at Chautauqua.

Mathews said it was the opportunity to "remake religious opinion among church members" that led him to Chautauqua.

> . . . the opportunity to get in touch with the type of people who compose the churches and women's clubs. . . was really great. Chautauqua Institution is attended by thousands of people each year and has been a great influence in the development of intellectual life of America. . . . The majority of those attending it are undoubtedly conservative economically and theologically, but there is also a considerable number of persons distinctly progressive.[36]

Criticism of Chautauqua

Chautauqua was not without its critics. It has been noted that the dream of an educated populace was not shared by all. Why, workers might become discontent if allowed to learn about their world! Superficiality was perhaps the most frequently heard criticism, however. Of the CLSC one writer was reported to have said, "What can be the result of a year spent upon this set of books but an intensification of the American fault of pretentious superficiality."[37] Vincent responded to the charge:

> . . . superficiality is better than absolute ignorance. It is better for a man to take a general survey, to catch somewhere a point that assists him; for the man who never takes a survey never catches the point in

which dwell the possibilities of power for him. By this superficial view he develops taste and power. When you sow seed, it is not the weight of the seed put into the soil that tells, but it is the weight of the harvest that comes after.[38]

Chautauqua published many of its own textbooks. These were also criticized as being shallow treatments of their subjects. An economics student answered this criticism by asserting, "I do not so much feel that I really know a great deal about political economy as that I am in a position to learn something."[39]

The most cutting criticism, even if not taken seriously by many, came from Rudyard Kipling. He wrote:

> Lectures on the Chautauqua stamp I have heard before. People don't get educated that way. They must dig for it, and cry for it, and sit up o'nights for it; and when they have got it they must call it by another name or their struggle is of no avail.... You can get a degree from this Lawn Tennis Tabernacle of all the arts and sciences.... Mercifully the students are mostly womenfolk, and if they marry the degree is forgotten, and if they become school-teachers they can only instruct young American in the art of mispronouncing his own language. I don't like Chautauqua. There's something wrong with it, and I haven't time to find out where. But it is wrong.[40]

Chautauqua in the Twentieth Century

While Vincent took criticism seriously, it was not criticism which spelled trouble for Chautauqua. The advent of the automobile, radio, and the moving picture brought new forms of entertainment and diversion; and formal, stronger institutions took the initiative in higher education. Dunn observes that the ideals of Vincent faded as America awoke from its moral slumbers, and Chautauqua had to be content to provide a supporting role to other institutions of society. [41] But perhaps Chautauqua provided much of the "wake up call" in that consciousness raising.

Reflecting on the development of Chautauqua, Dunn sees three distinctive phases.[42] Through the 1880s the emphasis was on teaching methods and Bible study, broadening to general secular educational programs with concern for providing educational credentials. In the 1990s a concern began for general learning and information through cultural and entertaining lectures and concerts and few formal educational offerings.

By 1900 all of the formal study programs had been eliminated except for a few (mostly in teacher training and music) held during the summers. Dunn writes:

> This third phase, continuing to the present, is a cultural experience with a variety of leisure activities including recreation, lectures on a

variety of subjects and general classes. It seems to be focused in creative use of leisure instead of changing society, credentially, or on consciousness raising. [43]

Still, a reader of Vincent's autobiography gets the impression that his approach to education was flexible enough to make the necessary adjustments and that he would not be altogether displeased with its present state. Vincent liked to entertain outstanding personalities. In fact, it was Miller's good fortune for his daughter to marry Thomas Edison, a frequent visitor, who personally saw to the installation of electric lights at Chautauqua, making it one of the first communities in the country to have them. Edison often entertained his friends Harvey Firestone and Henry Ford at Chautauqua. Vincent probably would have been pleased with the array of presidents and dignitaries who have continued to visit and lecture at Chautauqua in this century. Roosevelt delivered his famous "I Hate War" speech there, and even today's visitor is treated to contact with a variety of public figures whom one would not ordinarily hear and see, at least in one place. For example, in the summer of 1986 this visitor to Chautauqua heard first black congress woman Shirley Chisholm discuss the future of higher education, dynamic black theologian James Forbes of Union Seminary talk about "Trust as an Antidote to Economic Anxiety," and , among others, he heard former Iranian hostage Morehead Kennedy criticize our government's refusal to deal with terrorism.

Today one can find at Chautauqua a variety of popular educational activities from lectures to discussion groups, a center for the exploration of theological and philosophical ideas, and a festive center for the arts set in the midst of a vacation resort. There is a summer music school sponsored by the State University of New York, which includes voice, instrumental instruction, composition, and conducting. One may study painting, sculpture, or all types of dance. The religion department, while not as important as it once was, still provides daily lectures and discussions and leads daily devotionals and weekly worship. The summer program of eight and a half weeks in the 700 acre compound will see 8,000 to 10,000 participants per week.

Chautauqua struggles with the same problems of its founders: how to keep programming both interesting and challenging (educational vs. entertaining) and how to structure pricing to attract moderate income and younger families, a necessity if Chautauqua is to survive. The balance is still there between spiritual, physical, and academic self-improvement.

Conclusion

UNESCO's International Commission on the Development of Education published a statement a few years ago that asserted, "Every person must be in a position to keep learning throughout life. Education must be carried on at all ages. . . according to each individual's need and convenience."[44] Further, they said,

502

Education should be dispensed and acquired through a multiplicity of means. All kinds of existing institutions, whether designed for teaching or not, and many forms of social and economic activity, must be used for educational purposes. The important thing is not the path an individual has followed, but what he has learned or acquired.[45]

One can see clearly the roots of such an ambitious ideal embodied in the ideals of Chautauqua founders John Heyl Vincent and Lewis Miller:
—a religious conviction that education is the right and duty of all;
—a theory of self-culture;
—a conviction that all persons have a right to equal access to knowledge;
—a belief that adulthood is a unique time for learning;
—that education should continue beyond formal schooling when one has a chance to pursue what one wants and needs to learn;
—a belief that life is a school
—that agencies of society should cooperate in promoting and providing adult learning;
—that adults should come in contact through education with current thought on scientific and social issues.[46]

In 1903, during the twenty-fifth anniversary celebration of the CLSC, Vincent summarized the ideology of Chautauqua: "this then is the Chautauqua thought: self-improvement in all the faculties for all folks, through all time, for all the greatest good of all people."[47]

Historically, Chautauqua Institution made its mark on America:

John Vincent's belief in education as lifelong process and his determination in making it available to everyone regardless of condition vibrated in sympathy with the American idea. Chautauqua jibed perfectly with the grand American passion for self-improvement.[48]

Vincent himself recognized Chautauqua's leadership in the contemporary thought of the time:

The finger of Chautauqua seemed to be placed on the pulse of the age, and to recognize the various signs of life, and to follow promptly every tendency of the great American people toward a higher personal, intellectual, social, industrial, political, ecclesiastical, and spiritual life.[49]

A number of independent Chautauquas still operate and hundreds of imitators can be found, including our own Ridgecrest and Glorieta conference centers. One noteworthy offspring is Glen Echoe, on the shores of the Potomac in Maryland. Once an independent Chautauqua headquarters, now a state park, it truly echoes the ideals of its ancestors. A wide curriculum for all ages aims to foster "human growth and creative potential, serve as a center for the broad and

503

open exchange of resources and skills, and reflect the attitude that each human being has a responsibility to the environment.[50]

More important than organizational survival, the ideal still lives: access to knowledge is not only the right of every person, but the act of acquiring and appropriating that knowledge glorifies the Creator.

A Faculty address, delivered November 5, 1986.

[1] Richard Peterson and Association, *Lifelong Learning in America* (San Francisco: Jossey-Bass Publishers, 1980), p. 5.

[2] Russel Mawby, *Adult and Continuing Education Today*, 16 (July 14, 1986) 108.

[3] John H. Vincent, *The Chautauqua Movement* (Boston: Chautauqua Press, 1886), p. 13.

[4] Emerson quoted in Rebecca Richmond, *Chautauqua: An American Place* (New York: Duell, Sloan and Pearce, 1924), p. 24.

[5] John S.Noffsinger, *Correspondence Schools, Lyceums, Chautauquas* (New York, 1926), p. 103.

[6] Richmond, *Chautauqua*, p. 41.

[7] Ibid., p. 48.

[8] Ibid., p. 50.

[9] David N. Portman, *The Universities and the Public* (Chicago: Nelson-Hall, 1978), p. 39.

[10] Richmond, *Chautauqua*, p. 55.

[11] Theodore Morrison, *Chautauqua: A Center for Education, Religion, and the Arts in America* (Chicago: University of Chicago Press, 1974), p. 36.

[12] Ibid., p. 37.

[13] Ibid.

[14] Harold W. Stubblefield, "The Idea of Lifelong Learning in the Chautauqua Movement." *Adult Education*, 31 (Summer 1981), 201.

[15] Irwin, *Three Taps of the Gravel: The Chautauqua Story* (Westfield, New York, 1970), p. 18.

[16] Vincent, *The Chautauqua Movement*, p. 29.

[17] Ibid., p. 30.

[18] Morrison, *Chautauqua: A Center for Education*, p. 43.

[19] Vincent's Recognition Day Address, 1888, in *Scrapbook* No. II, Westcott, p. 25. VIII. CLSC.

[20] Vincent, *The Chautauqua Movement*, p. 76.

[21] Ibid., pp. 76-77.

[22] Ibid., p. 82.

[23] Ibid., p. 75.

[24] Ibid., pp. 90-91.

[25] CLSC Handbook, 1881.

[26] E. Hale, "The Chautauqua Literary and Scientific Circle," *Century*, 9 (November 1885), 147-150.

[27] Noffsinger, *Correspondence Schools, Lycuems, Chautauquas*, p. 109.

[28] Portman, *The Universities and the Public*, p. 44.

[29] Thomas Wakefield Goodspeed, *A History of the University of Chicago* (Chicago: University of Chicago Press, 1916), p. 103.

[30] Thomas Wakefield Goodspeed, *William Rainey Harper* (Chicago: University of Chicago Press, 1928), p. 69.

[31] Ibid., p. 71.

[32] Ibid., p. 102.

[33] Ibid., p. 73.

[34] Goodspeed, *A History of the University of Chicago* p. 106.

[35] Joseph E. Gould, *The Chautauqua Movement* (New York: State University of New York, 1961), pp. 60-61.

[36] Shailer Mathews, *New Faith for Old: An Autobiography* (New York: Macmillan, 1936), p. 76.

[37] Portman, *The Universities and the Public*, p. 47.

[38] Vincent, *The Chautauqua Movement.* pp. 87-88.

[39] C. A. W., "A Plea for Chautauqua," *Nation*, 490 (October, 1889), 350.

[40] Rudyard Kipling, *Abaft the Funnel* (New York: B. W. Dodge, 1909), pp. 195-203.

[41] Walter S. Dunn, "A Historian Looks at Chautauqua," an unpublished paper, July, 1974 (Smith Memorial Library, Chautauqua Institution), p. 20.

[42] Ibid.

[43] Ibid.

[44] E. Faure, *Learning to Be: The World of Education Today and Tomorrow* (New York: Unipub., 1972), p. 181.

[45] Ibid., p. 185.

[46] Stubblefield, "The Idea of Lifelong Learning," p. 205.

[47] John Vincent, *The Chautauquan*, vol. 37, p. 340.

[48] Walter Erbland, "Chautauqua Institution," *The Conservationalist* (State of New York, Dept. of Environmental Conservation, March-April, 1978), p. 17.

[49] Vincent, *The Chautauquan*, vol. 37, p. 338.

[50] Mark Travaglini, "From the Echoes of Chautauqua," *American Education*, (May, 1977), 18.

Bibliography

Adams, Herbert Baxter. "Summer Schools and University Extension," *Education in the United States*, Vol. 2. Ed. Nicholas Murray Butler. Albany: J. B. Lyon, 1900.

Adult & Continuing Education Today, 16 (July 14, 1986).

Bester, Arthur Eugene. *Chautauqua Publications: An Historical and Bibliographical Guide.* Chautauqua, New York: Chautauqua Press, 1934.

C. A. W. "A Plea for Chautauqua," *Nation*, 49 (October 31, 1889).

Chautauqua Assembly Herald, August 12, 1878, p. 1, col. 6.

Dunn, Walter S. "A Historian Looks at Chautauqua," An unpublished paper, July, 1974. Smith Memorial Library, Chautauqua Institution.

Ellwood, Hendricks. *Lewis Miller: A Biographical Essay.* New York: G. P. Putnam's Sons, 1925.

Erbland, Walter. "Chautauqua Institution," *The Conservationist.* State of New York, Dept. of Environmental Conservation, March-April, 1978. Pp.14-18.

Faure, E. *Learning to Be: The World of Education Today and Tomorrow.* New York: Unipub., 1972.

Goodspeed, Thomas Wakefield. *A History of the University of Chicago.* Chicago: University of Chicago Press, 1916.

Goodspeed, Thomas Wakefield. *William Rainey Harper.* Chicago: University of Chicago Press, 1928.

Gould, Joseph E. *The Chautauqua Movement.* New York: State University of New York, 1961.

Hale, Edward Everett. "The Chautauqua Literary and Scientific Circle," *Century*, 9 (November, 1985).

Harper, William Rainey. "The Founder of the Chautauqua Movement," *Outlook*, 54 (September 26, 1896), 546.

Hurlbut, Jesse L. *The Story of Chautauqua.* New York: G. P. Putnam's Sons, 1921.

Irwin. *Three Taps of the Gravel: The Chautauqua Story.* Westfield, New York, 1970.

Kipling, Rudyard. *Abaft the Funnel.* New York: B. W. Dodge, 1909.

Malcom, John Philip. *An Historical Investigation of, and a Visual Supplement to, the Educational Innovations of the Chautauqua Institution in the Late Nineteenth Century.* Unpublished Ph.D. dissertation. Syracuse University, 1972.

Mathews, Shailer. *New Faith for Old: An Autobiography.* New York: Macmillan, 1936.

Morrison, Theodore. *Chautauqua: A Center for Education, Religion, and the Arts in America.* Chicago: University of Chicago Press, 1974.

Noffsinger, John S. *Correspondence Schools, Lyceums, Chautauqua.* New York, 1926.

Peterson, Richard, and Associates. *Lifelong Learning in America.* San Francisco: Jossey-Bass, 1980.

Portman, David N. *The Universities and the Public.* Chicago: Nelson-Hall, 1978.

Richmond, Rebecca. *Chautauqua: An American Place.* New York: Duell, Sloan and Pearce, 1974.

Stewart, Sonja Marie. *John Heyl Vincent: His Theory and Practice of Protestant Religious Education from 1855-1920.* Unpublished Ph.D dissertation. Notre Dame, Indiana, May 1977.

Storr, Richard J. *Harper's University, the Beginnings.* Chicago: University of Chicago Press, 1966.

Stubblefield, Harold W. "The Idea of Lifelong Learning in the Chautauqua Movement," *Adult Education*, 31 (Summer, 1981), 199-208.

Travaglini, Mark. "From the Echoes of Chautauqua," *American Education*, 13 (May, 1977), 18.

Vincent, John H. *The Chautauqua Movement.* Boston: Chautauqua Press, 1886.

Book Reviews
I. Faculty

The Art of Human Relations, by Ernest O. White. Nashville: Broadman Press, 1985. pp. 194. $6.95.

Persons have been created as relational beings. We live our lives in relationship with God, others, and our selves. We relate to God's creation (nature), to society (world), and to our vocation.

Having delineated these relationships, Dr. White proceeds to offer a most thoughtful and thorough guide in developing and nurturing the art of human relations. The choice of the word "art" is very telling and significant.

Drawing upon his rich and mature background as a pastor and counselor, and reflecting comfortable acquaintance with research and literature in the field of human relations, White moves from examining one's relationship to a discussion of a most common and convenient model of relationships. This rigid ladder model consists of the initiating, developing, and perfecting steps in a relationship. The perfecting stage is followed by a high achievement level. The many problems with this model are explored and the various points of "fall" and "death" are accented.

The heart of the book is an insightful presentation and explanation of a cyclical model of relationships. It is based on the creative research and work of Sherwood and Glidewell of Purdue University. This wheel model starts with the various types of contracts that begin a relationship. Following this initial phase is the critical and important gift of commitment. White contends that this is the most vital of all aspects of a relationship. He studies the barriers against and clues toward this necessary element in a relationship.

The honeymoon phase of the relationship is colored by much productivity, but honeymoons do end and a "pinch" time occurs. Pinch produces disruption, but rather than being viewed as a negative or cause for termination, the disruption can be a constructive tool to reshape the relationship. This reshaping includes some renegotiation and recommitment. White spends time in discussing all aspects of this process.

A very helpful chapter is developed around the care and feeding of a relationship. The reader is reminded that a healthy and thriving relationship does not just happen and maintain. It requires work. This is an important work.

Dr. White concludes the book with a positive and encouraging statement on the potential and power of relationships. He calls the reader to remember that "God did not choose ideas to change the world. He chose relationships to change and transform the world and persons" (pg. 194).

As one who has served as a minister in the local church for some time now, I know how needed White's words are among church staffs, staff members and congregation, church members, and families within the church.

This book could be very useful for a staff retreat, deacon retreat, church council retreat, church training class, and in other creative groupings within and beyond the church. We are indebted to Dr. White for his fine work in this volume. I commend it to you.

William M. Johnson
Minister of Education
Crescent Hill Baptist Church
Louisville,KY

Isaiah 1-33, by John D. W. Watts. Word Biblical Commentary, Vol. 24. Waco, TX: Word Books, 1985. $24.95. 449 pp.

The format of the series of which this book is a part should be familiar by now since more than sixteen volumes have appeared. It is designed to address different audiences in each of its sections. Working on the basis of the original languages, the commentator includes a translation, each unit of which is preceded by a bibliography and followed by notes that deal with relatively technical matters of textual criticism, philol-ogy, and grammar. A section called "Form/Structure/Setting" tends to report the results of critical work on those topics, although Watts often uses this section to present his own literary analysis of individual units. Under "Comment" specific words . phrases or verses are treated sequentially; finally, the meaning of the passage as a whole is summarized under "Explanation." The translation, these final two sections, and the Introduction to the book are for the readers who do not use the original languages and are not interested in the history of critical interpretation.

It is not easy to bring a fresh perspective to the interpretation of a book such as Isaiah, but Watts has managed to do so in several ways. His distinctive approach is spelled out in the Introduction, which addresses the traditional questions of the literary and historical questions concerning the book, but in ways that go against many widely-held views about Isaiah. The decisive step that defines the others is Watts' decision to examine the final form of the Book of Isaiah from a literary perspective, an approach that he considers incompatible with historical exegesis (p. xxiii).

But the strictly literary, nonhistorical exegesis is difficult to sustain. Watts has not rejected historical exegesis, but only some aspects of it. He establishes and takes seriously an historical context for the final form of the book, ca. 435 B.C. (pp. xxix-xxx), and speaks of the anonymous author of Isa. 65:1-16 as "likely the one responsible for collecting, editing, and writing the Vision" (p. xxxii). While he is well aware that older traditions and written materials were used in the creation of the book, and of the history of the investigation of those questions, Watts is not interested in distinguishing among those materials or dating them. A fifth century date is certainly too early for the final form of the book, but since Watts does not argue the case in terms of the dates of the individual parts, it is difficult to evaluate his reasons for this conclusion. Moreover, throughout the discussion of the individual units he repeatedly refers to the historical framework, e.g., of the kings of the eighth century to whom the original prophet addressed himself. Since a prophet such as Isaiah was deeply involved in the concrete historical events of his time, why should one be reluctant to link his words to those events when the evidence for such links presents itself?

Concluding that the title in 1:1 refers to the full sixty-six chapters, Watts identifies the genre of the book as a "Vision," defining the genre--in terms of what he takes its form and contents to be--as a drama. The drama has twelve acts (the title page before the commentary proper incorrectly says ten), five of which are covered in the present volume. "Because the Vision genre has been understood to be like drama, the translation is here presented in that form. The larger sections are called 'acts' while the smaller ones are

'scenes,' which in turn contain 'episodes.' Suggested designations of speakers, found at the left of the translation, serve also to note the limits of the speeches" (p. xxiv). Watts spells out some of the characteristics of drama, argues that the book has many of those features, and hints at the possibility that it may have been presented orally-- presumably in the fifth and subsequent centuries--by a troop of players (pp. xxiv, xlv-lii).

This reading of Isaiah as a drama is a bold attempt to bring a new perspective to the analysis of the book, but it is forced and in the last analysis totally unconvincing. Watts' list of the features of drama does not give sufficent attention to the one that is most fundamental: It is to be performed by characters before an audience, or—as "literary drama"— it is modeled after or written for such a presentation. This is by no means the case in Isaiah, and it has not been shown at all. Sometimes the attempts to identify the shifts of speaker and addressee with the translation are right on target, and very helpful, as in the song of the vineyard (5:1-7). In other cases the shifts have nothing to do with "drama" but are the typical pattern in prophetic speech, distinguishing between the prophet (or herald) and direct quotations from Yahweh. At other times Watts' identifications are simply arbitrary. Why, for example, shift from the prophet as speaker in 3:16-17 to heavens and earth in 3:18-23, then back to the prophet in 3:24? How do we know that the prophet is speaking to heavens and earth in the first place? The basis in this case must be the dubious link to 1:2.

Both in the Introduction and throughout the commentary—especially under "Explanation"—Watts is sensitive to theological issues, particularly as posed from the perspective of Christian faith. His approach has the advantage of attempting to make sense of the theology of the final form of the Book of Isaiah, which concerns God's plan and policies concerning Jerusalem, Judah, Israel, and all the nations. "The book proclaims that Isaiah in the eighth century revealed Yahweh's decisions and strategy concerning Israel, Judah, and the empires. It claims that Yahweh's strategy has not varied through that period and that Isaiah's words continued to be valid in 435 B.C. . . ." (p. xxiv). More specifically, the book advocates that "the people of God be separate from the state, a spiritual gathering of those who would serve God in spirit and in truth. It teaches that God's power can more appropriately be shown in and through such a group than through national power" (p. lvii).

The disadvantage of this approach is a tendency to flatten out the theology, to mute the distinct voices present in traditions that span centuries. For example, Watts does not try to explain the dramatic differences between 4:2-6 and its context, that is, that is announcement of the day of Yahweh as time of salvation when the previous announcements are the reverse. More dramatically, given the anti-nationalistic interpretation of both the final form of the book and of the original Isaiah, what is one to do with such clearly Davidic passages as 9:1-7 and 11:1-ff? For Watts these are the voice of the opposition, the traditionalists whom both Isaiah of Jerusalem and the final author of the Vision oppose!

One does not need to agree with all of Watts' distinctive interpretations to find a great deal that is valuable in this commentary. There is, for example, a particularly good discussion (pp. 102-104) of how Isa. 7:14 in its Greek (LXX) translation served the purposes of Matthew. The issue is addressed both historically and theologically, showing Matthew's basis for taking the text as a prophecy of the virgin birth, the exegetical practices current in his time, those who followed and those who disagreed with him in the church, and why the christological treatment of the matter is more appropriate to a commentary on Matthew than one on Isaiah. Nevertheless, Watts argues here and throughout the commentary for the theological significance of the OT text in and for the Christian faith.

Gene M. Tucker
Candler School of Theology
Emory University
Atlanta, Georgia 30322

II. Biblical

A Critical and Exegetical Commentary on Jeremiah, Vol. I. by William McKane. *The International Critical Commentary*. Edinburgh: T. & T. Clark, Ltd. 1986. 658 pp. No price given.

This volume on Jeremiah is the first OT volume to appear in the ICC in 35 years. It is great to see this series re-established, and this reviewer hopes the editors will complete those volumes which have not appeared, and revise or totally rewrite the older ones on the basis of current scholarship.

It is also quite surprising to find such a spate of major commentaries on Jeremiah in English. The last major works were those of Hyatt (Interpreter's Bible) and Bright (Anchor Bible) in the 1950's and 1960's, and from a more conservative perspective, Thompson's volume in the New International Commentary on the Old Testament (1980). Suddenly in a six month period three significant volumes appear (or in two of the cases, volume one of a two volume commentary), the ICC of this review, Old Testament Library, and Hermeneia.

In a short review, it is impossible to deal adequately with all the features of a commentary, so this review will concentrate on the approach McKane takes. It does seem that McKane has tried to maintain much of the approach of the ICC, especially with his heavy emphasis on the evidence of the ancient versions. Indeed, he stipulates that concern with ancient versions is primary to his work (p. xv).

A chief issue for McKane in this volume is the fact that the Septuagint of Jeremiah is considerably shorter than the Masoretic Text. His conclusion based on his textual study is that behind the Septuagint lay a shorter Hebrew text that was expanded to give our current Masoretic text. To overly simplify his view, McKane argues that a Jeremianic core of material was expanded over a long period of time, into the post-exilic period, by many additions. But these additions were not for the most part made on the basis of an overall plan; instead, most of the additions dealt with only a small unit of text and related only to that unit. Thus McKane accounts for the lack of apparent unity and organization in our present text of Jeremiah.

McKane does give an excellent summary of scholarly positions both in the introduction and in the text. He presents a variety of positions with his own critique. Then he will state whether he holds to one of the positions given, or he will present his own position. McKane is more skeptical than many previous commentators about positing a historical setting for every passage. Of poetic passages in chapters 1-25, he states that attempts to relate them to historical settings "are much more shaky and speculative than has been generally recognized" (p. lxxxix). McKane does not mean to rule our any historical context, but simply to question the primacy of historical concerns above the message of the book.

This reviewer was quite positive toward the book. It is an excellent addition to the ICC. There are only a few shortcomings, and those primarily of format. While not necessarily a fault , the writing style does assume that the reader has a Hebrew old Testament open as one reads. Only a portion of the text is given along with comment, and the English translation given will not explain many of the comments based on the Hebrew. Thus this commentary is intended primarily for one with fairly good skills in Hebrew and Greek. The type face is a bit small and tedious to read: it looks as though it has been reduced in size and that is unfortunate. The bibliography (pp. ciii-cxxii) is excellent, but the format (with no indentations or spaces between entries) makes it almost unreadable. The Hebrew is typeset rather than transliterated; this is excellent (and is to be commended for it is certainly more expensive--in comparison, the Old Testament Library series transliterates). But the typeface is small, unpointed, and certain letters are extremely difficult to differentiate. In this regard, Hermeneia is vastly more readable. Again on the positive side, the proof-reading (English and Hebrew, Greek, etc.) is superb! The binding is unfortunately not very

512

good. For a $40.00 book, one should expect good quality binding. Alas, the back of mine broke almost immediately, not from abuse, but from poor binding. Those few negatives aside, I commend the work heartily. It is an excellent scholarly addition to current Jeremiah study.

Joel F. Drinkard, Jr.

Robert P. Carroll, *Jeremiah, A, Commentary*. Philadelphia: Westminster Press, 1986. 874 pp. $38.95.

Robert P. Carroll's commentary in the Old Testament Library series is a welcome addition to the available resources for the study of Jeremiah, if only because it treats all fifty-two chapters of the book--We are not left waiting for volume two! The printed biblical text is the Revised Standard Version. A list of the units in which Carroll has analyzed Jeremiah appears in the form of an outline (pp. 86-88). Their arrangement follows the Septuagint's order, with chapters 46-51 preceding chapter 26. The selective bibliography is both extensive and up-to-date.

Carroll's approach to Jeremiah has been determined by two facts about the book: the existence of substantial differences of content and order between the Masoretic (Hebrew) and the Septuagint (Greek translation), and the presence of a wide variety of material, much more diverse than the usual categories of poetry, prose sermons, and narratives would indicate. (He describes Jeremiah as "at times a sprawling, untidy and exasperating collection of discrete and disparate units whose order and meaning baffle the exegete" (p. 46)). The "Notes" on each unit document the first phenomenon and compare the meanings of the Hebrew and Greek text traditions, while the "Commentary" section carries forward the literary analysis and considers questions of origin and point of view. Carroll makes no attempt to bring unity to this diversity, either by means of a comprehensive theory of redaction or by a unifying literary principle. Even the figure of the prophet himself only provides evidence of the complexity, not its solution. Carroll's contribution in this commentary is to expose the tensions and contradictions within the book of Jeremiah, and to account for this variety by identifying the products of redaction and inner-biblical exegesis which contributed to its present form. There is no attempt to smooth the book's rough edges or to harmonize its inconsistencies, but he does offer readings of individual units which show how the parts contribute to the meaning of the whole (e.g., chapter 26).

The reader in search of exposition, theological reflection, and homiletical inspiration will find this a difficult book to use, for Carroll's exegesis only brings one to the point where these tasks begin.

Pamela J. Scalise

Jeremiah 1, by William L. Holladay. In the Hermeneia series, edited by Paul D. Hanson. Philadelphia: Fortress Press, 1986. 682 pp.

Every now and then a commentary appears as the outgrowth of a lifetime of research on the part ot its author. Such is the commentary by William L. Holladay on chapters 1-25 of the book of Jeremiah. For over a quarter of a century he has been publishing articles in leading theological journals on various topics related to the book of Jeremiah. Certainly no one in America is better qualified to treat this long-neglected prophet than he.

The format already well known to users of the Hermeneia series is followed in this volume. There is, however, one surprising and somewhat frustrating feature to Holladay's book. In an effort to speed its publication, it was decided to postpone the introduction, the indexes, and the bibliography of general works on Jeremiah until the second volume appears. This certainly limits the volume's usefulness in the classroom.

Holladay does include a brief section on "A Chronology of Jeremiah's Career."Without this, it would be almost impossible to understand what Holladay has written. This is because he structures the entire ministry of Jeremiah around the "septennial reading" of the book of Deuteronomy. Holladay argues with Hyatt that 627 B.C. was the date of Jeremiah's birth and not of his call.

When Deuteronomy was discovered in 622 B.C., it was read then and at subsequent celebrations of the feast of tabernacles at seven year intervals. This would have placed its subsequent readings in the autumn of 615, 608, 601, 594, and 587 B.C.

Holladay strives valiantly to prove that Jeremiah received his call to be a prophet at the recitation of 615, and that his sermons and confessions cluster around the other recitations. It must be said to Holladay's credit that he takes the historicity of the prophet more seriously than either McKane or Carroll.

Still I remain unconvinced by his restructuring of Jeremiah's career around a seven-year cycle. He spends entirely too much time throughout the commentary trying to fit the pieces into his predetermined scheme. It is regrettable that a major work like this should depend so heavily on one's acceptance of a hypothetical chronological framework.

Holladay denies that the prose sermons in Jeremiah are "Deuteronomistic," and argues instead that they are closely related to the poetry of the prophet. He sees the temple sermon in chapter 7 as an accurate reflection of "what Jeremiah said on that occasion, or at least what he himself recalls having said on that occasion" (p. 240). He sees no reason to doubt that Jeremiah himself delivered the sermon "probably in late summer or early autumn of 609" (p. 240). Such confidence would not be shared by other

scholars like Nicholson. Still it has much to commend itself.

I have placed this book on the required list in my course on Jeremiah. It is in my opinion far superior to any other work presently available on this prophet. But one still wonders why it was issued without an introduction.

Page H. Kelley

Ezra, Nehemiah, by H. G. M. Williamson. Word Biblical Commentary, Vol. 16. Waco, Texas: Word Books, 1985. 417 pp. $22.95.

If I could have only one commentary on Ezra and Nehemiah, it would have to be this volume written by H. G. M. Williamson, lecturer in Hebrew and Aramaic at Cambridge University. While the commentary, like others in the same series, is addressed primarily to those who have a working knowledge of the biblical languages, it nevertheless contains a wealth of material easily available to those who do not. Even those who are not theologically trained could come to a fresh understanding of these two biblical books by studying Williamson's commentary.

The author is eminently qualified to write in this area. His commentary on 1 and 2 Chronicles appeared in The New Century Bible Commentary in 1982. He has also published numerous articles on topics related to the period under study. Perhaps even more importantly, he seems to have collected and read almost all the literature related to the field, included foreign language literature. He brings this vast knowledge to the service of his readers as he draws out the meaning of the text in Ezra and Nehemiah.

Some commentators seem to feel that to justify their work they must propound a new theory regarding a book's structure and purpose. Often the theory borders on the bizarre and time is spent defending the theory that could better be spent explaining the biblical book. Williamson avoids this pitfall. His is a straightforward presentation of the text, its background, its problems, and its meaning. He often adopts traditional views presenting convincing evidence that these views are correct. He never avoids a problem because it is difficult nor adopts a solution because it is easy.

A few illustrations will have to suffice. Williamson rejects the view that Ezra and Nehemiah are part of the same work as 1 and 2 Chronicles, thus rejecting a longstanding tradition of their unity. On the other hand, he accepts the traditional view that Ezra probably came to Jerusalem in 458 B.C. He also concludes on the basis of Nehemiah 13:6 that Nehemiah was governor of Jerusalem for twelve years, then was recalled to Babylon, and later returned to Jerusalem to finish out his career.

Of particular interest is Williamson's discussion of the composition of these two books. He identifies three stages in this process: (1) the writing of the various primary sources, all more or less contemporary with the events they relate; (2) the combination of the Ezra Memoirs, the Nehemiah Memoirs, and other sources to form Ezra 7:1-Neh. 11:20; 12:27-13:31 (Williamson sees 11:21-12:26 as added separately); (3) the later addition of Ezra 1-6 as an introduction to the whole work. He would place the completion of the entire work around 300 B.C.

This is in my opinion a commentary that admirably fulfills its purpose. I would especially like to thank the author for his lucid style.

Page H. Kelley

Amos, by A. G. Auld. Old Testament guides. Sheffield, England: JSOT Press, 1986. 89 pages. $3.95.

Where would one find annotated bibliography of studies on Amos between 1800 and 1983 that runs to 177 pages and covers over 1,100 articles and books? What evidence is there to support the view that the five visions in Amos 7, 8, and 9 may be seen as a single composition going back to Amos himself? Was Amos a prophet, and just how is the answer to this question influenced by 3:3-8 and 7:14-15? What can be said about the unity and authenticity of 1:3-2:16? How has the study of Amos been influenced by the recent attention to literary structure in the biblical books? What contributions have the social sciences, especially anthropology and social history, made to the study of Amos? How is the essential message of Amos reflected in the doxologies that are scattered throughout the book?

These are the questions that Auld raises in this provocative little book, which he modestly calls "our scamper through the texts." The book is one in a series of guides to Old Testament books published by JSOT Press for the Society for Old Testament Study. It is not a commentary but a guide to the current state of Amos studies. Auld skillfully outlines the problem areas and past and current attempts to deal with these. He puts the reader on the cutting edge of Amos research, including modern literary approaches to the book. A notable feature of the book is its summary and analysis of recent articles from a wide range of scholarly journals. A section on "Further Reading" comes at the end of each chapter and is arranged by themes and accompanied by brief annotations.

This is not a book for casual readers. Its thoroughgoing scholarship makes it rather a useful tool for serious students of the Hebrew text of Amos. In fact, such students could hardly do without it.

Page H. Kelley

Old Testament Exegesis: A Primer for Students and Pastors, by

Douglas Stuart. Second Edition. Westminster Press,1984. $7.95 142 pp.

Douglas Stuart has revised his already excellent book on Old Testament exegesis and has greatly improved its usefulness. As the subtitle states, this book is meant primarily for students and pastors. The book gives a thorough outline for doing an exegesis (twelve steps for a full exegesis). Not only does Stuart explain each step in an exegesis carefully, but he also gives biblical examples working from the Hebrew text. This exegetical guide is most helpful for students. Indeed, this reviewer has recommended this book to his students in his Old Testament Introduction classes as well as exegesis classes.

Of special interest to the pastor is a chapter entitled "Short Guide for Sermon Exegesis." This abbreviated outline for exegesis combines essential items for sermon preparation. Stuart even suggests the approximate time one should spend on each part of the exegesis.

The final chapter in the book includes additional suggested reading to aid in carrying out each step of exegesis. These books provide excellent bibliography for the student or pastor who wishes to delve deeper into some aspect of exegesis.

In summary, I highly recommend this book for anyone who does exegetical work.

Joel F. Drinkard

Old Testament Faith, by John Drane. San Fransisco: Harper and Row, 1986. 160 pp. $10.95.

This book is one in a series by John Drane that is intended to introduce the Bible to the lay person. And he does the job superbly in this volume. *Old Testament Faith* gives an introduction to the religion of the Old Testament. It gives a non-technical summary of the major aspects of Israel's faith and how this faith is related to that of the New Testament. This text is easy to follow and written in a manner that can be followed easily by the non-specialist. Yet the major technical terms and problems of Old Testament religion are presented and optional interpretations are given.

Drane has chapters dealing with the nature of God; the nature of creation and sin; the nature of humanity in relation to God, other humans, and the world; the worship of God; and the relationship between Old and New Testaments. Ethical issues such as the preaching of the prophets are set in their larger context and are related to the nature of God.

The book has only one major drawback. When longer explanations are given, they are set in a smaller typeface. The typeface chosen is too small to be read comfortably and so an otherwise fine book suffers somewhat. Many black-and-white photographs are included in the book, including numerous examples from modern Near Eastern life. Some of the photographs illustrate pointedly modern social ills.

For the person wanting a non-specialist introduction to the religion of the Old Testament, I cannot think of a better source than this book. I recommend it highly. Even the person with technical expertise will find Drane's insight and organization helpful.

Joel F. Drinkard, Jr.

The Quest for the Kingdom of God, ed. by H. B. Huffmon, F. A. Spina, and A. R. W. Green. Winona Lake, IN: Eisenbrauns, 1983. 316 pp. $20.00.

This volume is composed of 20 essays given in honor of George E. Mendenhall plus an appreciation and bibliography of Mendenhall's works. Mendenhall is known for his studies concerning early Israel, especially covenant and law, and the sociological development of Israel. This volume has sections of essays dealing with these major concerns: Federation and Early Monarchy, Covenant and Law, Archaeology and History. In addition there are sections on Prophecy and Poetry, and Biblical Ideology.

Among the essays with broader interest, Norman Gottwald has written about "Two Models for the Origins of Ancient Israel." In this essay, he critiques a frontier model and supports his model of social revolution. In "The Sack of Israel," John McKenzie raises the issue of the Davidic monarchy as being basically ruled by a foreign, conquering aristocracy. Robert Wilson, in "The Mechanisms of Judicial Authority in Early Israel," posits that beyond the level of the extended family judicial authority was complex, involving at times the elders, or the entire tribal assembly, and even invoked Yahweh in assessing guilt and punishment.

Walter Harrelson discusses an interpretation of Isaiah 8:23-9:6 in his essay "Prophetic Eschatological Visions and the Kingdom of God." David Noel Freedman discusses Micah 3:1-8 and 1:2-16 in "Discourse on Prophetic Discourse." Freedman argues that chapters 3 and 1 may deal with the same situation, chapter 3 in a poetic manner and chapter 1:10-16 in an ecstatic expression.

John Lundquist gives a number of common typological features of ancient Near Eastern temples in his contribution, "What is a Temple? A Preliminary Typology." Among the features he isolates are: temple is the architectural embodiment of the cosmic mountain; temple is associated with the waters of life; temple is built on sacral space; temple is oriented to the 4 cardinal directions; temple plan is revealed by God; communal meals are part of temple ritual; temple is a place of sacrifice; and temple and its ritual are shrouded in secrecy.

In evaluating this work, I would have to say this is not a book for the average lay person. The essays are technical and specialized. But for the pastor or student with a keen inter-est in the Old Testament and Archaeology, the book has many interesting essays near the cutting edge of current scholarship.

Joel F. Drinkard, Jr.

Foes from the Northern Frontier, by Edwin M. Yamauchi. Grand Rapids: Baker Book House, 1982. 148 pp. $6.95.

Professor Yamauchi has provided in this short work a summary of the archaeological and historical evidence for the Scythians and other non-Semitic peoples who lived to the north of Syria-Palestine and Mesopotamia, and who are mentioned in the Bible and other ancient Near Eastern sources. After first rejecting the popular identity of Gog, Magog, Meschech, and Tubal (Exek. 38) with modern Russia, Yamauchi begins a careful analysis of the identity and history of the Urartians, Manneans, Cimmerians, and Scythians. Among his conclusions is a call to reconsider the Scythians as the foe from the north mentioned by Jeremiah.

Yamauchi has included evidence from recent archaeological excavations, including Russian work in the Caucasus mountains and east of the Caspian Sea. He also correlates archaeological data with references from Assyrian, Babylonian, and Persian historical sources. One chapter deals with a reassessment of and vindication of Herodotus' references to the Scythians.

Yamauchi's work is thorough, well-documented, and very readable. For the person interested in learning of the people who lived north of Syria-Palestine and Mesopotamia and their influence on Biblical and ancient Near Eastern history, this book is an excellent resource.

Joel F. Drinkard, Jr.

Egypt and Bible History From Earliest Times to 1000 B.C., by Charles F. Aling. Grand Rapids: Baker Book House. 1981. 145 pp. $5.95.

The purpose of this book is to fit the history of Egypt into the author's view of Biblical history. The author adheres to what he calls the early date for the Exodus, ca. 1446 B.C. Building from this presupposition, he then fits Biblical references to Egypt related to Abraham, Joseph, and Moses with particular pharaohs or time periods of Egypt's history. Abraham's sojourn in Egypt is dated to ca. 2091 B.C. and is associated with Wahkare-Kheti III during the First Intermediate period. Joseph in Egypt is related to the reigns of Amenemhat II, Sesostris II, and Sesostris III (1897-1843 B.C.) The bondage of the Hebrews began during the Hyksos period (after 1675 B.C.) and reached its height during the Eighteenth Dynasty (16th century B.C.). Moses was born about 1526 B.C. and the Exodus occurred during the reign of Amenhotep II about 1446 B.C. This chronology fits precisely the statement of I Kings 6:1 which dates the building of the Solomonic Temple 180 years after the Exodus.

Problems with this dating scheme are explained away. Josephus' statement, taken from Manetho, that Joseph was in Egypt during the Hyksos period is disregarded without reason: "It is best to disregard Josephus unless there is archaeological confirmation of his assertions . . . (pp. 29-30). Likewise the difficulty with the name Potiphar containing elements not found until a later time period is dealt with by positing that Potiphar is not a proper name but an epithet. The use of the word "pharaoh" as a title in Joseph's time (Genesis 37:36, etc.) five centuries before it is found in Egyptian usage is explained by appealing to Mosaic authorship. Since Moses wrote Genesis, he used the term "pharaoh" as it was used in his own day. However, Aling admits that the first attested usage of the term in that manner in Egypt does not appear until after Moses' death.

Even silence from historical evidence is used by Aling to support his reconstruction. The silence of historical records in Egypt to military campaigns by Amenhotep II after his ninth year is related to the Exodus. Amenhotep II is identified as the pharaoh of the Exodus. Because he lost 600 chariots and soldiers at the Red Sea (Exod. 14), his army was so crippled that he could never again mount a major campaign. At best such a reconstruction is a creative possibility; it certainly cannot be proven.

Aling's summary of Egyptian history is helpful. But his reconstruction of Biblical episodes as related to those events is only speculative. The book is quite readable and will be appealing to the lay person. The danger is that many readers may not separate Aling's summary of Egyptian history from his reconstruction of Biblical history.

Joel F. Drinkard, Jr.

Introducing the New Testament, by John Drane. San Francisco: Harper and Row, Publishers, 1986. 479 pp. $19.95.

Not infrequently I am asked to recommend an introduction to the New Testament that reflects modern critical scholarship without going out on a limb, that is not so simple as to insult the reader's intelligence yet not so academic as to overwhelm the lay student. Now I can recommend Drane's new introduction as ideal for meeting this need. This introduction is an expansion and adaptation of three previous books by the author, *Paul, Jesus and the Four Gospels,* and *The Life of the Early Church.*

Although it covers the standard topics that one expects an introduction to treat, this book is different. Unlike the technical introductions to the New Testament by Kuemmel, Guthrie, Koester or even Martin, I

can imagine the interested person getting caught up with the story of the New Testament and wanting to read more. The reason is that this book is produced with the *USA Today* generation in mind. It is chocked full of fascinating pictures, charts, and diagrams that illuminate the text. The pictures are not only from relevant archaeological discoveries but include interesting scenes from contemporary life that suggest the modern relevance of the text--for example, there is a picture of a woman celebrating mass, Sun Myung Moon, an auction of a black slave, and Russian Christians worshiping secretly in the woods. This is a unique approach, but scholarship is not slighted in the interest of relevance. Drane reflects the best of scholarship and his conclusions are eminently sane. All of this is complemented by an engaging style. Anyone who is interested in the Southern Baptist Sunday School board periodical, *Biblical Illustrator,* will certainly find this book an interesting and useful source for knowledge of the New Testament.

David E. Garland

Jesus and Paul: Signs of Contradiction, by Wilfrid Harrington. Wilmington, Del.: Michael Glazier, 1987. 207 pp. $8.95. ISBN 0-89453-591-9

Harrington's major thesis in *Jesus and Paul* is that both men--Jesus and Paul—were signs of contradiction in their own day and that "a singular and tragic achievement of historical Christianity has been the effective domestication of Jesus and Paul" (p. 16). Closely tied to this thesis is another thesis: that no one else has ever understood Jesus as well as Paul has. Rather then seeing Paul as one who distorted the simple religion of Jesus, Harrington perceives Paul to be *the* exegete of Jesus.

For Harrington, Mark's gospel is the main source for recovering the historical Jesus. Already within the N.T. gospels, he sees signs of the church domesticating Jesus. Seven letters of Paul—1 Thessalonians, 1, 2 Corinthians, Galations, Romans, Philemon, and Philippians—are the main source for recovering the historical Paul. Already in the N.T., letters claiming to be by Paul (2 Thessalonians, Colossians, Ephesians, the Pastoral Epistles) have begun the process of domesticating Paul. Indeed, Paul has been so misunderstood, according to Harrington, that "Paul's 'religion' has [not] ever in

Christian history—not even by the Reformers—been given a chance" (p. 182).

This book is divided in to two parts: I. Jesus, and II. Paul. Each part has seven chapters basically parallel. For example, chapter 4- Jesus and women, chapter 11- Paul and woman; chapter 5- Jesus and religion, chapter 12- Paul and religion; chapter 6- The Triumph of Failure, chapter 13- Theology of the Cross; chapter 7- A Respectable Jesus, chapter 14- The Taming of Paul.

Although one may disagree with Harrington at various points, his major thesis is will argued. His evaluation of the Pastoral Epistles as a betrayal of Paul in some regards may well be correct, but unfortunately he does not give guidance to the reader how these writings—also canonical— are to be used along with Paul's writings to guide the life of the church today.

Roger L. Omanson

III. Historical-Theological

The Southern Baptist Holy War by Joe Edward Barnhart. Austin: Texas Monthly Press, 1986. 273 pp. $16.95. ISBN 0-87719-037-2

Joe Barnhart is Professor of Philosophy at North Texas State University in Denton, Texas. He holds degrees from Southern Seminary and Boston university and has writ-

ten earlier studies of the evangelical phenomenon in America. In this book he examines the current political-theological upheaval in the Southern Baptist Convention and numerous issues and personalities involved in the controversy. It is a timely topic. Southern Baptists need some summary of the complex problems and political intrigues which have recently seized the energy and attention of America's largest Protestant body.

Barnhart is sincerely concerned to tell the story, present the issues, and analyze the situation. He has read certain materials on the subject and interviewed numerous protagonists—Fundamentalist, moderate, Liberal, and non-committed individuals. He is particularly sympathetic toward the plight of seminary professors—an approach I naturally appreciate. Likewise, he points out many of the intellectual and theological problems inherent in any effort to promote inerrancy as the only orthodox approach to Holy Scripture. Professor Barnhart makes some good points and provides some telling analyses of the current struggle.

Perhaps his greatest insight is that the controversy over inerrancy will continue because it distracts Southern Baptists, fundamentalists and moderates alike, from the essential failure of their evangelical task. He writes, "If those who reject inerrancy are forced to leave the convention, the Inerrancy Party will lose its scapegoat and have only itself to blame for failing to bring about the great revival and missionary triumph" (p. 174).

In other words, Southern Baptist evangelical impetus and methodology is rapidly losing its ability to reach "the world" for Christ. Liberalism is a convenient scapegoat for a much more complex evangelical conundrum.

Barnhart also reflects on the serious textual problems which inerrantists must confront in order to maintain their position, i.e. the evolution of the New Testament canon, word usage, translation, and other such questions. He writes, "There is even the problem of articulating one's theory of inerrancy of specifying the necessary degree of inerrancy. In practice, considerable leeway is required to formulate the inerrancy hypothesis coherently" (p. 88).

In spite of these important observations, the book has some serious problems. I wish it had been written differently. First, materials often seem disjointed and disorganized. Barnhart does not tell us why he is writing the book or what he hopes to accomplish. He gives little historical background as a context for understanding the present crisis. What is the SBC? How did it reach this point? What is the thesis of the book?

Second, the book includes numerous references to other aspects of right wing evangelicalism in America without clear reference as to how this impacts the SBC controversy. In the middle of the first chapter, for example, there is a discussion of Dallas Seminary professor Norman Geisler and his views on creationism. The materials are interesting but bear no relationship to the rest of the chapter. Such digressions on the

New Religious Political Right occur throughout the book and contribute to the disorganization. This makes it difficult to follow the direction of Barnhart's thought and intent.

Third, much of the material is presented with little qualification or background information. Thus only those who already have a working knowledge of the complex events will be able to follow the details presented in the text. For instance, there is a reference to an "interchange" between "Fisher Humphery" (his name is Humphreys) and Houston judge Paul Pressler, a leader of the Fundamentalist group. Humphreys is accused of ducking one of Pressler's questions. Yet we are never told who Humphreys is (he teaches theology at New Orleans Seminary) or why his supposed equivocation is significant. (See pages 85-86.) This approach to people and events occurs throughout the book. In fact, certain passages seem more like hallway conversations at conferences and meetings. Perhaps greater documentation and broader use of recent articles and papers on the controversy would have helped clarify the various positions and persons cited.

The book is a potpourri of personalities and stories. Barnhart discusses Presler, Patterson, Dilday, Honeycutt, Rogers, J. Frank Norris, James Robison, William Powell, A. T. Robertson, W. T. Conner, Dale Moody, Glenn Hinson, et al.

There are also some interesting

revelations. Barnhart recounts a proposal from Paige Patterson and Richard Land of Criswell Seminary for "turning three of the six Southern Baptist seminaries into inerrancy schools." The three other seminaries "would then be free to go their own way. . . "(p. 104). Negative designation giving would keep funds from going to unacceptable seminaries.

It is an interesting proposal and may reflect the future of whatever remains intact in the "new" SBC.

On the whole, however, the book would have been enhanced by more careful organization, expanded documentation, and less attention to what might be considered side issues. Greater attention might also have been given to the context of events and personalities.

These are problems which seriously affect what might have been an otherwise helpful and timely study.

Bill J. Leonard

Ultimate Questions: A Theological Primer, By Clyde F. Crews. New York: Paulist Press. 169 pp. $6.95.

"O my soul, be prepared for the coming of the Stranger. Be prepared for him who knows how to ask questions."—T. S. Eliot

Knowingly or unknowingly, directly or indirectly, all human beings ask questions about life and death, meaning and purpose, pain and hope, character and morality. Father Clyde Crews, chairman of the Religion Department at Bellarmine College, surveys those "ultimate questions" as reflected in the great ideas of western literature, philosophy, art, and religion. In part, the book was written for use in the Bellarmine College curriculum in the belief that "when men and women have come to grips with questions such as these, and have achieved some measure of carefully considered response, that they begin to advance toward educated maturity." Yet the work need not be limited strictly to a college-student constituency. It is a valuable "primer" which enhances continuing self-development and serves as a guide for additional studies in the history of human thought.

Ultimate questions, Crews believes, are those which concern the very foundations of our lives and our continuing search for meaning. They are timeless issues which have received varying responses from the best interpreters throughout human history. Crews is particularly concerned with the "modern" dilemma created by the scientific revolution and the loss of certitude characterized in Matthew Arnold's classic "Dover Beach": "for the world which seems to lie before us, like a land of dreams . . . hath really neither joy, nor love, nor certitude, nor peace, nor help for pain . . . " The book surveys various "answers" to that dilemma evident in such literaries as Shakespeare, Dostoevsky, Emily Dickinson, and Thornton Wilder; in social scientists the likes of Rollo May; and

524

in the work of Darwin, Marx and Freud, whose ideas shook the foundations of traditional authority. Turning to religion, Crews provides an excellent summary of the varied religious responses evident in modern society. He then examines the basic "themes" of the great world faiths, East and West. With that, the book focuses on the nature of Christian faith and its contribution to the quest for ultimates. The chapters on Christianity reflect Crews' broad knowledge of the Christian heritage, Catholic and Protestant, and affirms those common ideals which transcend the church's sectarian divisions. The book presents a fine survey of complex concepts without technical jargon or superficial "God-talk." It reveals the continuing significance of the "humanities" in modern life and is helpful guide for the student, the pilgrim, and the seeker.

Bill J. Leonard

Jesus Today, by Gerald O'Collins, S.J. New York: Paulist Press, 1986. $4.95. 74 pp.

Written in conversational style, *Jesus Today* is based on lectures that O'Collins, Dean of the Theology Faculty of the Gregorian University in Rome, gave to mark the seventy-fifth anniversary of the Melbourne College of Divinity in July and August 1985. Accordingly, the author explores the contours of Christology in the Australian context vis-a-vis its philosophy, history, and eschatology. Attuned to modern scholarship's sensitivity about the role of personal experience in theological construction, O'Collins offers some proposals for a local-style approach to Christology. First, Christology must correlate the general human condition (with its death, absurdity, and hatred) with the life of Jesus of Nazareth; second, Christology must always be anchored in the paschal mystery; third, Christology must respond to the question, "Who do you say that I am?" in relevant space and time specificity. Australia's history, geography, culturally and religiously diverse population should all be taken into account.

This brief book is by no means a fully developed Christology, but a suggestive outline for those who would take up the challenge of theological construction for Australian Christianity. To that end, it is a helpful offering.

Molly Marshall-Green

Karl Barth, A Theological Legacy, by Eberhard Jüngel. Trans. by Garrett E. Paul. Philadelphia: Westminster, 1986. 168 pp. $13.95. ISBN 0-664-24031-3

It is most fitting that a selection of Jüngel's influential interpretations of important dimensions of Barth's theology appeared in the year celebrating the centennial of Barth's birth. Ably translated by Garrett E. Paul of Gustavus Adolphus College, these essays represent the major por-

tion of the German collection published in 1982. Jüngel, a professor of Dogmatics and Philosophy of Religion in the Protestant theological faculty at the University of Tubingen, first became known to many American readers for his definitive book on Barth's doctrine of the Trinity. Readers appreciative of his insightful analysis in that book will not be disappointed with this one. As in his earlier studies of Barth, Jüngle's aim is to avoid either an uncritical acceptance or rejection of Barth's theology. In the spirit of Barth's hermeneutic, the author leads us into a careful reading of Barth's theology with a view to understanding the latter's real concern by becoming engaged with his "subject matter," that is the God of the Gospel, attested in the Word of God, and revealed most fully in Jesus Christ.

The first essay, "Barth's Life and Work," provides a helpful overview with a focus on the *Church Dogmatics* while also assessing his place in contemporary theology. The second essay, "Barth's Theological Beginnings," is the longest. In it Jüngel leads his readers into the theological revolution associated with the origins of Barth's theology as he confronted the "revolution of God." The period covered dates from Barth's earliest publication in 1909 and concentrates on the genesis of major emphases associated with the so-called "dialectical" theology of the first and second editions of Barth's commentary on Romans published in 1919 and 1922 respectively. In contrast to the thesis of Marquardt and others arguing that Barth's early theology is to be understood as an outgrowth of his socialism, Jüngle shows convincingly that Marquardt's thesis is onesided. Jüngel sums up the relationship of the theological and political dimension of Barth's perspective thus: "Simply put, for Barth, the political is surely a predicate of theology, but theology is never a predicate of the political" (p. 104).

In "Gospel and Law: The Relationship of Dogmatics to Ethics," Jüngel unpacks the major elements of Barth's controversial view showing why his reversal of the usual Lutheran order, Law and Gospel, is critical to Barth's entire theology. The final essay, "The Royal Man," is an assessment of Barth's Christology relating to his depiction of Jesus Christ as the "Royal Man," and his significance for understanding humanity and human dignity. Jüngel's "Tribute" spoken at Barth's funeral introduces the entire collection. Among other things, Jüngel said: "His entire life and thought as a whole announced that "God" is a cheerful word" (p. 21).

In a time of cheap slogans and the quick fix in church and theology, Jüngel is a reliable guide to Barth's theological pilgrimage. My only regret is that the publishers did not include Jüngel's important essay examining Barth's understanding of analogy and its role in his theology. Nevertheless, there is much to inspire reflection and action here and

the footnotes and bibliography are helpful in pointing us to the sources.

David L. Mueller

A Karl Barth Reader, ed. by R.J. Erler and R. Marquard. Ed. and trans. by Geoffrey W. Bromiley. Grand Rapids: Eerdmans, 1986. 114 pp. $6.95.

This selection of brief excerpts from Barth's literary productions in sermons, lectures, letters, and parts of the *Church Dogmatics* was published in German to mark the centennial of his birth in 1986. Those to whom Barth is just a name, those put off by his voluminous writings, those always intending to discover something about Barth's interpretation of the gospel but who never did so, and those who don't think they agree with what they have heard others say about Barth--all will find something challenging in his witness to the truth of God made known in Jesus Christ. Instead of finding an austere proponent of a static theology fixed in concrete, Barth locates the sum of the gospel and has theology in Paul's witness to the abundance of the grace of God: "My grace is sufficient for thee" (2 Cor. 12:9).

The editors are to be commended for capturing in an insightful way something of the essence of Barth's theology of grace. In so doing, the reader is carried on a pilgrimage with Barth as excerpts from his writings are clustered mainly in chronological sequence around such decisive topics as: "The Theological Axiom," "The Crisis of All Powers," "Faith by the Decision of Jesus Christ," "The Gift of Freedom," "The Church as Watchman," "Pastoral Care," "Overcoming Evil," and "Humanity Before God."

One may find it necessary to disagree with Barth at points, but even then one will be challenged to examine more deeply the nature of the gospel. The final selection is a statement from a lecture Barth was preparing just before he died. He wrote: "The last word I have to say . . . is not a concept but a name. Jesus Christ. He is grace and he is the ultimate one beyond world and church and even theology. We cannot lay hold of him. But we have to do with him. And my own concern in my long life has been increasingly to explore this name and to say, 'In him.' There is no salvation but in this name. In him is grace. In him is the spur to work, warfare, and fellowship. In him is all that I have attempted in my life in weakness and folly. It is there in him" (p. 114)

Read it! It will do you good.

David L. Mueller

Confessions of A Theologian, by Carl F. H. Henry. Waco: Word Books, 1986. 407 pp. $14.95

It is fitting that Carl F. H. Henry has written his autobiography illumi-nating his pilgrimage to the present. Born in New York City in 1913 of industrious German immigrants who provided him no Christian nurture, Henry experienced a life-changing conversion as a young and promising newspaper reporter and editor at nineteen years of age. This change of direction led a gifted writer with an inquisitive mind to seek university and theological education. At Wheaton College and Northern Baptist Theological Seminary, Henry's Christian convictions and vision began to take shape. After receiving his doctorate in theology from Northern, Henry received a Ph.D. from Boston University with a dissertation on the thought of the Baptist theologian, A. H. Strong.

Among the catalytic events in Henry's long career was his appointment as the first Dean of newly established Fuller Theological Seminary in 1947. Through writing and lecturing, teaching and preaching, Henry established himself as one of the leaders of the growing Protestant evangelical movement. In addition, he had been active in the National Association of Evangelicals founded in 1942. His leadership among evangelicals was firmly established by his appointment as the first editor of *Christianity Today* serving from 1956-1968.

Throughout his adult life, Henry championed an evangelical christianity committed to the lordship of Jesus Christ and a strong evangelistic outreach. Billy Graham, a long time friend, shared much of the former's vision and theological perspective. A prolific writer, Henry developed and advocated a robust evangelical theology marked by a high view of biblical authority and a theory of Scriptural inerrancy. He also argued rigorously for a propositional view of revelation. This brought him into a sustained critique of liberal theology on the left and also into conflict with neo-orthodoxy. The latter is faulted for failing to adopt a theory of biblical inerrancy and a propositional view of revelation. Henry's consistent development of these views led to his publication of *God, Revelation and Authority* in six volumes from 1976-1982. Undoubtedly, this publication is among the most significant statements of American evangelical theology in the last half of the twentieth century. This must be said whether or not one agrees with the positions Henry espouses.

Reading Henry's autobiography catapults the reader into the world of evangelicals and to a lesser degree into that of its detractors. Encounters with evangelicals of all persuasions and the likes of T. F. Torrance, Barth, Bultmann, Brunner, and others are recounted in these pages. Looking back on a long career of teaching at Northern, Gordon Conwell, Fuller, Eastern Baptist Theological Seminary, and Trinity, Henry is probably more knowledgeable about evangelicals than virtually anyone else. His arresting final chapter, "The Evangelical Prospect in America," I found to be a sober assessment. He chides evangelicals for addiction to numbers, the cult of per-

528

sonalities, lack of rigorous scholarship, and a theologically informed engagement and critique of rampant secularism in American culture. He finds contemporary evanglicalism in need of radical reformation and renewal if it is to exert much influence in the last years of this century. He cautions evangelicals who malign their theological opponents—including evangelicals—with whom they disagree. He warns: "Christian integrity is nullified if spokesmen for scriptural inerrancy combine it with perverse misjudgment and distortion of others' views" (p. 390).

Henry tells his own story well. And in doing so, he helps the reader understand how his theology developed. In the main, Henry's purpose is not to argue his theological viewpoint in telling his story. It is largely presupposed rather than argued. In order to debate Henry, one must do so on the basis of his theological writing. Whether one agrees with him or not, it is clear that he is an impressive expositor of one form of evangelical theology in the last half of the twentieth century.

David L. Mueller

What is Christianity?, by Adolf von Harnack. Trans. by Thomas Bailey Saunders. Introduction by Rudolf Bultmann. Philadelphia: Fortress, 1986. 301 pp. $17.50. ISBN 0-8006-3201-x

The editors of Fortress Press are to be congratulated for reprinting this famous work and including it in the new series of "Fortress Texts in Modern Theology." First delivered by Harnack as university lectures with the title, *Das Wesen des Christentums,* or "The Essence of Christianity," in 1899-1900 and first published in German in 1900, the book became a best seller. In it Harnack, the great historian of dogma and exponent of liberal protestant theology, sets forth a "short and plain statement of the Gospel and its history." Intended as a popular presentation of his understanding of the gospel expressed in the "leading features of Jesus' message," and "in relation to certain problems," and in terms of the "Gospel in History," Harnack's treatment made publishing history.

This reprint of the first American edition of 1957 includes Bultmann's insightful introduction to the book and its significance. He recalls that the book went through fourteen printings and translations into many languages by 1927. "At the beginning of our century it exerted an extraordinary influence not only on the rising generation of theologians but also on the educated classes generally" (p. vii). It is noteworthy that it was Harnack's interpretation of the Gospel, and particularly this book, which became distasteful to Harnack's student, Karl Barth. Yet Bultmann notes that Barth always insisted that Christians must listen to modern as well as ancient teachers in the church. Viewed in this light, Harnack's analysis of the Gospel represents the distillation of some of his

historical research and his liberal theological conclusions.

Anyone wishing to comprehend the power of the liberal view of Jesus and his message must grapple with Harnack and this book. Furthermore, it helps illumine the course of liberal theology in the late 19th century and to see how it came to flower in one of its most famous advocates. No one can understand either Protestant liberalism or the course of modern theological movements following it which affirmed or opposed it without knowledge of this book.

This is a welcome publication in what promises to be a most helpful series of influential texts in modern theology no longer in print. A likeness of Harnack (d. 1930) graces the back cover.

David Mueller

Theologians Under Hitler, by Robert P. Erickson. New Haven: Yale University Press, 1985. 245 pp. No price given.

Most graduates of a seminary are acquainted with the name of Gerhard Kittel as the editor of the first five volumes of the classic reference work, *Theological Dictionary of the New Testament.* Most do not know that he also joined the Nazi party as member no. 3,243,036. Nor is it widely known that the French authorities imprisoned Kittel, first in the Tuebingen castle prison and then in the Balingen internment camp, from May 1945 to October 1946 because of his writings on the Jewish question. He would never teach again at the university and was denied his pension. He died in 1948 at the age of 59 in humiliation and poverty.

The names of Paul Athaus, a leading Luther scholar and Professor of Systematic Theology at Erlangen, and Emmanuel Hirsch, a Professor of Philosophy and Dean of theological faculty at Goettingen, are not as will known; but both (and Hirsch to his dying day) were political supporters of Hitler. During the heyday of the Third Reich, Hirsch was known as the prince among theologians in Germany. This book asks and tries to answer the question, "why?" How could responsible, devout Christian theologians support a movement that history has judged to be the embodiment of evil? Unlike others who have castigated Hitler's professors unmercifully, Erickson provides an informative, well researched, well balanced, and sympathetic explanation for the cases of three renowned supporters of Hitler: Kittel, Althaus and Hirsch.

In the first chapter, the author presents an excellent summary of the social change in Germany after the First World War and of the crisis for faith created by developments in theological scholarship. Then he presents his disturbing thesis. These men were reacting to the crisis of modernity (today, we would call it secular humanism). In the Weimar Republic, Germans were faced with economic, sociological, political, and intellectual upheaval. Old German Christian values seemed to be eroding; the spiritual future of the German *Volk* seemed to hang in the balance. Erickson contends that Kittel, Althaus, and Hirsch were "well-meaning, intelligent, and respectable" individuals who saw Hitler as one who would not only stem the tide of moral erosion in Germany but also enable the German *Volk* to meet its date with destiny. What is disturbing about this thesis is that these men were not monsters but conservative, pious, patriotic theologians who sought to protect their country from the dangers of the liberal intellectuals and the political left. It was a *Weltanschauungskampf* ("battle of world views"), and they thought Hitler would drive out the unclean spirit from the midst of the nation. The nation, however, wound up with seven more demons far more evil than the first.

What is also disturbing is the suggestion that the reason that Barth, Tillich and Bonhoeffer reacted, in the judgment of history, more heroically to Hitler was not because they had more courage, a deeper faith or a better theology. They simply had different backgrounds and had lived in different environments. Barth was Swiss and would hardly be enamored with German nationalism. Tillich was involved in the religious socialism in the 1920's. Bonhoeffer had an English family tie and had served a church in London during the 1930's and had also lived for a while in New York. Kittel, Althaus and Hirsch, on the other hand, had more provincial backgrounds and were reared in deeply partiotic, conservative families.

The case of Kittel is dealt with first and is the most incriminating. He was a specialist in Jewish backgrounds. In 1933 he joined the Nazi party and was a major figure in Walter Frank's Research Section on the Jewish Question, in spite of his later disclaimers. He contributed a number of papers to the cause. In a speech on this issue ("Die Juedenfrage," 1933), he rejected the solution of exterminating the Jews for the less than human reason that it had simply not worked in the past and would not work now. Zionism was not a solution because most Jews were communists and would not work hard enough to make a go of it in Palestine, and it would also create extreme hostility among the Arabs. Assimilation of the Jews would only lead to further decadence in Germany. The best solution, he thought, was for Jews to assume "Guest Status"--denying them normal civil rights, alloting them positions in the professions in proportion to their population and banning mixed marriages. In his self-serving defense after the war (*Meine Verteidigung*), Kittel would claim that he was not like the "vulgar anti-semites," he had based his position on sound biblical scholarship. God's judgment on the people for their disobedience required them to accept the role of alien, and pious Jews would recognize and affirm this. Kittel acknowledged that this would cause hardship for many but maintained that Christianity does not require that one be sentimental or soft. The author shows that Kittel was not an evil man. In his defense he could cite a number of personal kindnesses to Jews. He did take an evil stance but thought that he was illuminating things from the Word of God in the service of God's church.

Althaus was for less culpable than Kittel and is described as a mediator, but a mediator well within the Nazi orbit. Hirsch, the most brilliant and feisty of the three, was firmly committed to the Nazi renewal movement throughout his academic career and after his retirement (in order to evade the denazification proceedings) at the end of the war.

What went wrong with these theologians (and multitudes of other German Christians)? After reading this account, it is my conclusion that they confused Christianity with German Christianity. They were more captive to German culture and German nationalism than they were to the Word of God. But one should read this thought provoking book and draw one's own conclusions. The purpose, of course, is so that we might learn and avoid the pitfalls that ensnared so many German Christians.

David Garland

France and England in North America, 2 volumes, by Francis Parkman. New York: The Library of America, 1983. Vol. I, 1504 pp.; Vol. II, 1620 pp. $30.00

The Library of America represents an effort to publish great works of American literature, history and philosophy in "handsome, durable" volumes. The series includes all the works of Melville, Hawthorne, James, Emerson, and Thoreau, among others. The project is funded in part by the Ford Foundation and the National Endowment for the Humanities. These two volumes by Francis Parkman were written over several decades beginning in 1841 when Parkman was a Harvard sophomore. This monumental work traces the early explorations of the American continent by the great European powers. Parkman himself was a fine student of the American past. His book, *The Oregon Trail*, is another classic account of later explorations.

These are great books which tell the story of early America with a literary flair. There are stories of individual explorers—Jean Ribaut, Champlain and LaSalle—Jesuit intrigues, Indian wars, and accounts of daily life.

Volume II describes the conflicts between the British and the French in Canada, leading to the subsequent conquest of the country by the British. Stories also trace the growth of the American colonies and the appearance of such leaders as Franklin and Washington on the way to the Revolution.

This is fascinating reading with careful detail to explorers and explorations, political machinations, and above all the New World experience. A bit more introductory material to Parkman and the work might have enhanced the materials. Nonetheless, it is a worthy addition to a series of American classics.

Bill J. Leonard

Ecumenism Striving for Unity and Diversity, by Mark D. Lowery. Mystic, Connecticut: Twenty-third Publications, 1985. 181 pp. $9.95.
All These Lutherans, by Todd W. Nichol. Minneapolis: Augsburg Publishing House, 1986. 126 pp.
And Are We Yet Alive? The Future of the United Methodist Church, by Richard B. Wilke. Nashville: Abingdon Press, 1986. 124 pp. $6.95.

Mark D. Lowery teaches religion at Catholic Memorial High School in Waukesha, Wisconsin. This book was developed under the auspices of the Ecumenical and Interfaith Commission of the Archdiocese of Milwaukee. It is a study guide to major denominations and an introduction to the ecumenical movement. The work begins with chapters on the ecumenical perspective and the ecumenical movement. After a brief survey of issues in early Christian history the author turns to summaries of specific traditions and denominational groups. These include the Orthodox, Lutheran, Anglican, Presbyterian and Methodist traditions. Another catch-all chapter includes "the Evangelicals"--Baptists, Nazarenes, Pentecostals and Fundamentalists. Each chapter concludes with questions for facilitating group discussion. The book is a helpful introduction to the basic denominational beliefs and ecumenical possibilities. The chapter on Evangelicals, however, is much too superficial and general. Lowery might better have called this the Free Church Tradition.

All These Lutherans traces the road to merger by three historic Lutheran traditions which will soon become the Evangelical Lutheran Church. These groups include the Lutheran Church in America, the American Lutheran Church, and the Association of Evangelical Lutheran Churches.

Chapters sketch the history of each group, discuss significant leaders, and sketch earlier mergers—there were many. The Association of Evangelical Lutheran Churches, you may recall, began out of the schism with the Missouri Synod Lutheran Church. It is a good, organized history on the way to a new day for Lutherans in America.

And Are We Yet Alive? is a response to the continuing numerical decline and accompanying identity crisis within the United Methodist Church. The author, Richard B. Wilke, is bishop of the Arkansas area of the United Methodist Church. In what is no doubt a controversial assessment, Wilke calls on the church to rethink its organization and its approach to evangelism. He calls for longer pastorates, suggests that Methodists are not nearly so "methodical" as their name implies, and insists that the church must develop an evangelical response to the present day as earlier Methodists did for theirs. In a sense, he combines Methodist heritage with elements of the contemporary church growth movement. He suggests, insightfully, that contemporary churches may invert evangelism, assimilating persons into church community before they are converted. He writes that modern persons are often suspicious of institutions, and "people want to know that religion is real before they are ready to believe" (p. 70).

Whatever United Methodists may think about Bishop Wilke's analysis of their denominational situation, his book is a perceptive response to modernity and a reaffirmation of the church's evangelical task. It is a quest for "doing evangelism" beyond old stereotypes and new hype. United Methodists are not the only ones who should read this brief but important book.

Bill J. Leonard

Martin Luther: An Introduction to His Life and Work, by Bernard Lohse. Trans. by Robert C. Schultz. Philadelphia: Fortress Press 1986. 270 pp. ISBN 0-8006-0764-3

In 1933, during the 400th anniversary celebration of Luther's birth, Karl Barth wrote: "What else was Luther than a teacher of the Christian church whom one can hardly celebrate in any other way but to listen to him?" (*Theologische Existenz heute* 4, p. 11). In fact, however, it is surprisingly difficult to get back to the "real" Luther through all of the varied, conflicting images and stereotypes of him. This volumes is intended to introduce Luther to the non-specialist by surveying his life, writings, theology, and historical impact. Originally published in German in 1980, this book takes into account recent developments in Luther scholarship, including the ecumenical reappraisals stemming from the work of Joseph Lortz and his students.

Lohse presents the material in the style of an academic syllabus, with a brief analysis devoted to each of the major points of focus. This allows the beginning student to wade into the ocean of Lutheriana without drowning after a few steps. The final chapter lists the major editions, scholarly journals, and special aids to the study of Luther. Professor Lohse, who teaches church history and historical theology at Hamburg University, is to be commended for making available this important reference work, as is Robert C. Schultz whose felicitous translation has helped to bring Luther to the New World--again.

Timothy George

Collected Works of Erasmus, vols. 26 and 27: *Literary and Educational Writings*, vols. 5 and 6, ed. by A. H. T. Levi. Toronto: University of Toronto Press, 1986. 638 pp. $95.00.

With the appearance of these two volumes the University of Toronto Press has now published sixteen of the projected sixty-plus volumes of the Collected Works of Erasmus. Included here are some of Erasmus' most famous works along with several of his lesser known treatises.

The Praise of Folly is presented in a translation which earlier appeared in the Penguin Classics edition of this celebrated piece. Originally drafted as a personal tribute to Thomas More—the Latin title is a play on More's name: *Encomium Moriae*—the finished product became a controversial satire of contemporary religious complacency and superstition. Michael J. Heath argues persuasively for Erasmian authorship of the satirical dialogue, *Julius Excluded from Heaven*, in which the recently deceased pope, Julius II, is denied admission to heaven by St. Peter. Two other documents in this set, the *Panegyric for Archduke Philip of Austria* and *The Education of a Christian Prince* (dedicated to the future Charles V, Holy Roman Emperor), present Erasmus' ideal of political life and Christian statecraft. Another, *A Complaint of Peace*, is Erasmus' most sustained argument against war and violence. He vigorously excoriates fellow Christians who take up the sword against one another: "How can you call on a common father if you are drawing a sword to thrust in your brother's vitals?" However, unlike most of the Anabaptists later, Erasmus stopped short of consistent pacifism for he allowed that force might have to be used against the invading Turks should efforts at peaceful persuasion fail. A final treatise, *The Ciceronian: The Ideal Latin Style*, is a more rarified discussion of proper Latinity directed against certain Italian classical scholars who tried to "out Cicero Cicero" in their insistence on rigid conformity to his Latin style.

As we have come to expect from this series, these volumes are a monument to Erasmus in the clarity of the translations, the judicious erudition of the annotations, and the invariably high quality of the printed text. In addition to the editor, the translators, and the publisher, the Social Sciences and Humanities Research Council of Canada, is to be commended for supporting this expensive but laudable endeavor.

Timothy George

Symbol and Empowerment: Paul Tillich's Post-Theistic System, by Richard Grigg. Macon, GA: Mercer University Press, 1985. 151 pp. 14.50.

In this condensed and tightly-argued book, Richard Grigg offers a fresh perspective on the thought of Paul Tillich. He points out that while Tillich has been enormously influential, he has had few disciples, in large part due to Tillich's use of nineteenth century idealistic language. Grigg wants to show that viewing Tillich's thought via the phenomenon of empowerment will not only elucidate the import of his work but will make it more widely accessible. In addition, Grigg believes that Tillich's post-theistic theology offers a foundation for a world theology, a theology that would reveal the interconnections and unity between the various world religions.

Beginning with a perceptive phenomenological description of empowerment, Grigg argues for religious empowerment as that which enables one to have faith or courage in the face of the stresses and strains in the ontological conditions of being. In this as at other points, he reveals mastery of Tillich's complex system as well as mastery of the massive secondary literature Tillich's thought has spawned. A creative aspect of this section is the way Grigg shows how empowerment is mediated through symbols.

At this point Grigg makes an unfruitful turn. He argues that symbolic language must be capable of translation into literal language, or it is non-cognitive. Thus, God-talk can refer in the sense of denying the application of terms to God (the *via negativa*), or it can refer to the way God relates to us, that is, the way humans experience God's effects. Besides negative or relational terms, which are used literally, he believes that religious symbols can non-cognitively represent or "stand in" for God. In other words, they do not tell us anything about God, but they open up the possibility of experiencing God's empowerment. Admittedly, such a conception is consistent with some lines of Tillich's thought, where Tillich argues for a post-theistic "God beyond God," in fact, a God that transcends all subject-object and other creaturely distinctions. One can hardly use literal language of such a God. However, recent work on the cognitive efficacy of metaphor opens up the possibility of speaking about the unique being of God. This conception of metaphor resonates with Tillich's view of symbol as enabling us to speak about levels of reality impossible to speak about otherwise. Although Grigg carefully argues his point, he omits even the option of this metaphorical choice, which in my eyes is more promising and adequate to religious experience.

In connection with this discussion of symbol, Grigg makes a novel and helpful distinction concerning Tillich's notorious method of correlation. Grigg argues that sometimes Tillich is speaking of an apologetic correlation in which religious answers are related to specific cultural questions. At other times, Tillich implies a more profound relation between religious answers and universal questions arising from ontological structures, which Grigg calls a hermeneutical correlation. The need for empowerment arising from these universal human questions provides the meaning for Tillich's non-cognitive, representative symbols. These symbols do not de-

scribe God, even in an analogous sense; they stand for the empowerment experienced in response to universal human problems—problems of human finitude, estrangement, and ambiguity.

Grigg urges that Tillich's thought when seen from the perspective of empowerment provides a foundation for relating world religions. World religions can be seen as focusing on various types of empowerment, all of which are rooted in the ineffable source of empowerment, the divine. While agreeing that empowerment illuminates relationships among religions, I think one can say more, and most religions want to say more, about the source of empowerment than simply that, God is what we call the source of empowerment. In fact, I find it difficult to see how causal terms such as "source" or "ground" can be justified on Grigg's terms. Does "ground" say anything about God? Or does it say only something about human beings? It certainly is not a literal term, as Grigg himself recognizes, but is it completely "empty" as an assertion about God? Tillich himself did not seem to think so.

Grigg points out toward the end of his book that Tillich was really not an idealist. That is true, and this fact suggests that what makes Tillich difficult for many is his forbidding ontology—not his idealistic language. Significantly, Grigg continues to utilize Tillich's ontology. One could even make the case that Tillich's ontology does more to elucidate Grigg's understanding of empowerment than his notion of empowerment does to elucidate Tillich's ontology. While this is a provocative and challenging book, to be recommended for Tillich enthusiasts, my suspicion is that someone already wary of Tillich will not be converted by simply changing the perspective but nothing else.

Danny R. Stiver

The Intellect and Beyond, by Oliver R. Barclay. Grand Rapids: Academic Books, 1985. 157 pages. Paperback. $6.95.

This is a popular and practical book full of down-to-earth interpretations of the relation of Christian faith to culture. Olive Barclay is the former general secretary of the Universities and Colleges Christian Fellowship (formerly Inter-Varsity Fellowship) in the United Kingdom and writes out of a Reformed position. The title suggests a theological book. In reality, it is more practically oriented than theologically, containing advice concerning family, work, and government.

The primary point is that the whole of the Christian's life is shaped by what he or she thinks; thinking is a practical and essential Christian activity. Every Christian is called to develop an authentically Christian outlook on issues, an outlook that genuinely shapes one's responses. The great value of the book lies in

Barclay's perceptive criticisms of the abdication of thought on the one hand and of an overemphasis on thoughts the other hand. Despite his own tendency towards a propositional and static view of revelation, he argues that Scripture is not a complete system of truths but an open network of truths. Thus no comprehensive and precise doctrinal system is possible, although doctrinal systems are helpful. He strenuously resists attempts to make Scripture secondary to any system, however the system may have been rooted in Scripture.

Concerning ethics, he winds his way between situationalism at one extreme and legalism at the other. In his words, "Love has a shape." However, Scripture primarily offers principles that require wisdom to be concretely applied. In philosophy, he affirms the value of philosophical systems, but as in the case of doctrine, he reminds that such systems are always partial. For a Christian, they must be judged by Scripture and not replace Scripture.

With such an understanding, he offers balanced advice in the areas of anthropology, family, and culture. For example, with regard to culture, he urges critical affirmation, heavily emphasizing Romans 13. An anti-urban, romanticist glorification of nature is not necessarily a more Christian attitude than one that allows full participation in modern life and government. Yet always, a Christian outlook will be a critical one.

In general, he provides perspicacious insights on how one can think and live as a Christian in the modern world. At times, he glosses over the difficulty of determining just what the basic principles of Scripture really are but counters this tendency with his polemic against any complete world-view in Scripture. Laypeople especially should find this a readable and helpful book.

Danny Stiver

The Church in the World, by Robert E. Webber. Grand Rapids: Zondervan, 1986. 278 pp. $11.95.

Should the church live in opposition to, in tension with, or attempt to transform the world, and, if so, by what strategies and toward what goals? Webber, associate professor at Wheaton College, provides biblical, historical and theological data needed by contemporary evangelicals to deal constructively with that question. The place to begin, he says, is to recognize the powers of evil in the world confronting the power of God in Christ and the life of the church. Without an understanding of the reality and power of evil, the church may fall victim to misplaced faith in world structures. Political or economic alliances may be entered that become idolatrous. The tension between church and world is placed in historical perspective by examining various approaches, roughly corresponding to Niebuhr's typology in *Christ and Culture*. The most biblical (and Christian) approach, says Web-

ber, is the transformationist, informed by the early church and the Anabaptist vision. The effort is neither to Christianize the powers nor to allow the secularization of social structures.

Evangelical interests in social issues found expression through evangelists such as Wesley, Whitfield, and Finney who addressed the abolition of slavery, prison reform, and concern for workers and the poor.

Contemporary efforts to relate to social issues are explored by examining The World Council of Churches, The Catholic Response, The Religious Right, and the World Evangelical Fellowship. He argues that the Religious Right is an effort to Christianize the world following the Constantinian model. Their lack of support for religious liberty and their triumphalistic imperialism are threats to pluralism, domestic tranquility, and world peace. He says bluntly that it fails to have a vision of the church and world that is truly "biblical."

Webber's own sympathies lie with the evangelical approach, the foundations and rationale for which he has carefully laid throughout the book. The power of evil in the world requires aggressive Christian involvement; the church and world are different but related. Christ is Lord over the church which is to live as *Christus Victor* seeking to overcome the power of Satan; it also is to live eschatologically, proclaiming

Christ's sovereignty over all creation.

Few treatments so thoroughly or insightfully pull such an enormous amount of material together in so readable a fashion. This is a good book—one that will bring the light of biblical and historical perspectives to bear upon current efforts to relate Christian convictions to the world of political realities.

Paul D. Simmons

The Politics of Liberation, by John M. Swomley, Jr. Elgin, IL: The Brethren Press, 1984. 111 pp. $7.95.

Liberation approaches to politics are frequently misunderstood and/or misrepresented by conservative Christians in America. Suspicion, anger, and resistance are predictable consequences. John Swomley, Professor of Social Ethics at the St. Paul School of Theology in Kansas City, here provides a brief but highly readable treatment of liberation politics that may help bridge the information/understanding gap. A fuller treatment can be found in Swomley's *Liberation Ethics* (Macmillan, 1972).

Biblical foundations are given that provide a framework for Judaeo-Christian support for and involvement in liberationist politics. Swomley contrasts Christian (liberation) approaches to those of political realism and Marxism. He rejects utopian idealism and opts for non-violent strategies as basic to Christian political involvement.

Swomley insightfully deals with Christian perspectives on politics and the biblical view of the role of government and the use of power. The debate about ideology is also helpfully unraveled.

Brevity is both the beauty and the bane of the book. Many themes are touched upon in this positive statement of Christian liberation politics but often without sufficient amplification. Discussion groups will find this a tantalizing and provocative challenge, of course. An informed reader will find it an insightful and sympathetic statement of an important theological and political phenomenon.

Paul D. Simmons

Renaissance and Reformation, by William R. Estep. Grand Rapids: Eerdmans, 1986. 331 pp. $19.95.

Among Baptist scholars few, if any, have contributed as much to our understanding of the Reformation as William R. Estep, Distinguished Professor of Church History at Southwestern Baptist Theological Seminary in Ft. Worth. Best known for his scholarly labors on the Radical Reformation (e.g. his popular survey, *The Anabaptist Story* and his valuable source book, *Anabaptist Beginnings, 1523-1533)*, Professor Estep has now given us a new synthesis and overview of both the Renaissance and Reformation movements.

The grouping together of the Renaissance and the Reformation is common practice, as the proliferation of "Ren/Ref" courses in college and university curricula indicates. Often, however, the pairing of these two dynamic movements of renewal and change reflects a perspective which treats them either as polar opposites (cf. Van Gelder's *The Two Reformations of the Sixteenth Century*, 1961) or as two phases of the same phenomenon. While Estep leans more to the latter than the former, he recognizes that the two movements cannot simply be equated. Thus, while he lauds the genuine spirituality and scholarly contributions of Erasmus, Estep quite correctly points out that the great Christian humanist never attained the sense either of the gravity of sin or of the triumph of grace which characterized the experience of Luther. Still, the reform of church and society in the sixteenth century cannot be understood apart from the recovery of biblical and patristic sources made possible through the Renaissance revival of learning. Estep provides a useful service by showing both the continuity and the discontinuity between these interrelated movements.

Perhaps the strongest chapters of the book, not surprisingly, are devoted to the Anabaptists. Estep places the emergence of Anabaptism in the context of the Zwinglian Reformation, discounting the old theory

(recently renewed) of their origin in the violent peasant uprisings associated with Thomas Müntzer. One might have hoped for more attention to the diverse theologies articulated by the Anabaptists, but there is an admirable summary of Balthasar Hubmaier's religious thought. The chapter on "Calvin and the City of Refuge" emphasizes the international importance of the Reformed tradition. The treatment of Calvin is balanced and free of caricature, despite the fact that the reformer of Geneva—one senses—may be less congenial to the author than some of the other figures he deals with. The volume is rounded off by a chapter on the English Reformation and another one on "Conflict and Change" which carries the story of the Reformation into Spain, the Netherlands, and Scotland.

This volume has many features to commend it to the general reader: breadth of coverage, interpretive narrative which incorporates recent scholarly debate but does not get lost in a rehearsal of the details, and aptly chosen maps and illustrations. Estep writes with clarity and precision. He also has the ability of a master historian to make the past come alive—whether he is describing Boccaccio's peccadillos, Felix Manz's execution, or St. Teresa of Avila's ecstatic visions. No doubt this book will become a standard text for those who desire a coherent overview of that period of transition between medieval civilization and modern culture. It is fortunate that such a study has been written by one who sees in this period, not a mere maze of movements and ideologies, but rather a resource and challenge for the church today.

Timothy George

Christian Theology, by Millard J. Erickson, vol. 3. Grand Rapids: Baker Book House, 1985. 430 pp. (vol. 3), 1247 pp. (3 vols. in 1 vol.). $19.95 (vol. 3).

The third volume of Millard Erickson's *Christian Theology* has been out one year now. The first two volumes were widely acclaimed, and this third volume was worth the wait. The three volumes are sequentially paged, and as I write this, a one volume edition is already in bookstores. The three volumes are serially dedicated to Baptist Bernard Ramm, Methodist William Hordern, and Lutheran Wolfhart Pannenberg, who, as teachers and scholars, have contributed to Erickson's development as a theologian. These three volumes are destined to be widely used in university and seminary classrooms. They will serve as the first theology studied by thousands of men and women preparing for church-related vocations in evangelical schools. Erickson's three volumes will replace the multiple texts now used in the last years of an era which has not believed in the possibility of a systematic theology that is genuinely biblical. Erickson's work is a monument to the rise of strong evangelical scholarship which affirms the unity

of the Bible and that a true systematic expression of theology is a possibility.

This volume covers pneumatology, soteriology, ecclesiology, and eschatology. Erickson's previous volumes have been grounded in sound biblical exposition. My concern, after reading the first two volumes, was that in his effort to prepare a text most evangelicals could use, he would not have a clearly defined Free Church ecclesiology. My fears were unfounded. This volume continues the sound biblical exposition of the first two volumes and, out of that, a balanced baptistic ecclesiology.

The weakest part of the book is the section on the Holy Spirit. While the material he presents is, in the main, very good, it is too brief. The doctrine is not adequately covered even for an introduction. He straight-forwardly addresses the matter of spiritual gifts, but he does not deal adequately with the baptism in the Spirit, the filling of the Spirit, or the fruit of the Spirit.

The most helpful chapter in his discussion of salvation is that concerning election. He takes a modified Calvinistic position. Salvation is the restoration of man to a proper relationship with God, achieved only by the death of Jesus Christ for our sins. His ecclesiology is strongly toward the local congregation, and he insists that each individual assembly in a specific place is never regarded as only a part of the whole church. Rather, "the whole is found in each place" (p. 1033). He opts for congregational form of government. Baptism is "an act of faith and a testimony that one has been united with what Christ has done" (p. 1101). He defends believer's baptism by immersion. The Lord's Supper is a time of relationship and communion with Christ in which he is made objectively present by the Holy Spirit. Erickson has a fine section on the evangelistic and missionary functions of the church. His section on eschatology contains a good introduction to the history and contemporary views of the doctrine.

All in all, this work is an excellent completion to what was begun in the first two volumes. Not only are these volumes useful for students, but they could serve as a refresher course and preaching resource for pastors.

Charles L. Chaney
President
Southwest Baptist University
Bolivar, Missouri

Jesus According to a Woman, (rev. and enlarged), by Rachel Conrad Wahlberg. New York: Paulist Press, 1986. $4.95. 104 pp.

A collection of nine encounters between Jesus and women, this slim volume can function both a summons to devotion and penetrating new light on these Gospel texts. Looking at Jesus' interactions with women, the author argues that he treated women "with intimacy, high regard and naturalness" (p. 3). These encounters (which should inform our understanding of the character of women and Jesus' approbation of them) have too long been ignored.

A lay theologian, Rachel Conrad Wahlberg is the author of *Jesus and the Freed Woman* (Paulist Press, 1975) and numerous articles for religious magazines and books. Her writing is fresh and insightful, honed through extensive dialogue in an adult Bible class in her church. Even before the magisterial works of Schüssler Fiorenza, *In Memory of Her* and Letty Russell, *Feminist Interpretation of the Bible*, Wahlberg was forming her ideas about the marginalization of women in the church's tradition and biblical material and theological application (the first edition was written in 1975).

Indeed, she argues these New Testament women, i.e., Mary Magdalene, the "Uppity Woman" of Mark 7:24-30, the "Audacious Woman" of Luke 8:43-48, and especially the "Women Preachers" of John 4:4-42 and Luke 24:1-24, are integral to the story and actions of Jesus and the early Church. Wahlberg offers us a closer look at materials with which the church has grown comfortably familiar—too comfortable to hear the radicality of the Kingdom's demands as Jesus voiced them.

Molly Marshall-Green

Women-Church, Theology and Practice of Feminist Liturgical Communities, by Rosemary Radford Ruether. San Francisco: Harper and Row, 1985. $16.95. 320 pp.

542

Rosemary Radford Ruether is an internationally recognized writer and lecturer on feminism and religion. She is currently Professor of Theology at Garrett Evangelical Theological Seminary. Among her recent works on feminist liberation theology are *Sexism and God-Talk* and *Womenguides*. In addition, she has just completed co-editing the acclaimed three-volume documentary history *Women and Religion in America*.

This book is written because "women in contemporary churches are suffering from linguistic deprivation and eucharistic famine" (p. 4), according to the author. It offers a historical and theological contextualizing of the emerging alternative movement of "women-church" and a collection of liturgies to be used in worship in "feminist exodus communities." These are intentional communities of faith and worship that "guide one through death to the old symbolic order of patriarchy to rebirth into new community of being and living" (p. 3). Included are liturgies to celebrate the puberty of a young woman or birth of a child as well as rites of healing for a raped or battered woman. The critical passages of the lives of women are noted in creative ways that allow the experience of women to be acknowledged in the worshipping community.

Ruether suggests that this movement is contributing to a revival of religion in Europe and North America which have awakened to the im-

poverishment of radical secularization. This religious expression differs from the fundamentalist and liberation theological movements in that it displays a much more ambivalent relationship to biblical origins. Ruether's anthology does not advocate total abandonment of participation in existing churchly existing structures, but it recognizes the desperate need for ancillary communities of reference that nurture and support the liberation of women from oppressive patriarchal religion.

I would wish that such a movement had not been mandated by the recalcitrance of existing institutional churches. Realistically, for many, a new hearing of the word of life will become possible only through such bold ventures. This book marks Ruether's own movement toward a much more dialectical relationship to the Christian tradition. Many will follow.

Molly Marshall-Green

Sophia: The Future of Feminist Spirituality, by Susan Cody, Marian Ronan, and Hal Taussig. San Francisco: Harper and Row, 1986. 103 pp. $14.95.

Finding adequate symbols to express the feminine in the experience of God remains one of the grave yet exciting challenges for contemporary spirituality. Symbols not sufficently rooted in early Christian, especially biblical, tradition will not solve the dilemma experienced by the deeply devout who want to stay within the pale of Christian orthodoxy. Here is where Sophia of the Hebrew and Christian Wisdom literature steps in as a strong candidate, though not one without limitations, for Christianity nipped growth of Sophialogy in the bud very early and western Christians have not yet done much to rectify that.

The thesis of this joint effort to give Sophia her due is that, starting with the Bible, Sophia "can be developed into a powerful integrating figure for feminist spirituality." In Hebrew scriptures Sophia appeared in a surprising array of images as creator, wisdom, teacher, lover, tree or plant, and law. In relationship to God she participates in creation. judgment, and ruling. In Christian scriptures Christology quickly subsumed Sophialogy, Jesus himself being depicted as Sophia. Early Christians manifested a real reticence about her as gnostic Christianity took her into its arms and cultivated the image in extreme ways. In post-Biblical writings, consequently, Sophia faded farther and farther into the background; although eastern Christians did give occasional notice, as a result of hellenistic influence, they misplaced the Biblical perspective.

The authors of this slim volume think Sophia-talk highly profitable for feminist spirituality if proper connections are made. If I understand their proposal, Sophia would serve as a mediator between God and human-

kind in much the same way Christ has done for centuries. The authors, of course, do not propose to dispense with the Christ symbol but simply to enrich it with one especially attractive to women. For women Sophia would represent power, assertiveness, and nature. Unfinished aspects of the Sophia imagery, however, would have to be elaborated. Like Christ, Sophia would experience suffering and death and struggle.

Persons who reject development in theology will probably dismiss the idea without a hearing. Those who recognize development as axiomatic and are not scared away by gnostic associations, however, will find in the book a solid case for rethinking the place of Sophia. Surely no issue merits more urgent attention than that of the feminine in experience of God.

E. Glenn Hinson

Sisters of the Spirit: Three Black Women's Autobiographies of the Nineteenth Century, ed. with introduction by William L. Andrews. Bloomington: Indiana University Press, 1986. 245 pp. $29.50 ISBN 0-253-35260-6.

This book is part of a new series of studies in North American religion published by Indiana University Press. Catherine L. Albanese and Stephen J. Stein, series editors, are particularly concerned to publish sources in the history of minority and ethnic groups in the American

544

experience. This work, edited by William L. Andrews, Professor of English at the University of Wisconsin-Madison, is a valuable contribution to Black and Women's studies in American religion. The "sisters" in this volume are three black women preachers whose spiritual autobiographies provide insight into the spirituality and feminism of the 19th century black church. The women, Jarena Lee, Zilpha Elaw, and Julia Foote, were preachers of the gospel who struggled with God, call, and church establishments in their own unique ways. Lee, a preacher in the A.M.E. (African Methodist Episcopal) church, wrote her "life and religious experience" in 1836. In it she describes her conversion, her call to preach, and some of the difficulties she encountered as a female preacher of the gospel.

Zilpha Elaw's *Memoirs*, published in 1846, detail her continuing religious experience, marriage, and extensive travels as a preacher. (She preached in England and America and risked her life on preaching missions into slave territory.)

Julia Foote's *A Brand Plucked from the Fire* was published in 1879. It includes accounts of her early life, conversion, religious experience ("heavenly visitations"), "indignities on account of color," and her own reflections on the nature of the spiritual life.

This is an excellent collection of primary source materials which details the struggle of three articulate black female preachers for liberation from racial and sexual prejudice. It is a timely resource for students of American religion and for those women who continue the struggle.

Bill J. Leonard

A History of the Church of England: 1945-1980, by Paul A. Welsby. Oxford: Oxford University press, 1984. 300 pp. No price given.

Canon Welsby adopts a tripartite division for his study of the three and half decades of post World War II history surveyed in this most useful monograph. The divisions were 1945-59, the Sixties, and the Seventies, and he allotts virtually equal coverage to each of these eras. Three archbishops, Geoffrey Fisher (1945-61), Michael Ramsey (1961-75), and Donald Coggan (1975-79), occupied the primatial see of Canterbury during this time. In addition to these three, the narrative opens with reference to the almost universally lamented death of William Temple but surmised that he would not likely have continued to be effective as head of the English Church in the post-war world. The book closes with the appointment of Robert Runcie as Coggan's successor.

Welsby has produced an admirable survey dealing with contemporary history, a task in itself not without certain pitfalls. However, the author appears to have escaped most of these. When greater perspective on twentieth century history is attained, some of the precise delineations and events which he saw as watersheds may lose some of their present force. Even so, he is about as objective and critical as one could reasonably be given his proximity to the era under review as well as his close involvement with the post-war Church. He deals most credibly with the strengths and foibles of the three archbishops. Welsby acknowledged Fisher's flair for administration, but was properly critical of him both in office and in retirement. He quotes with seeming approval the observation that "the historian of the Church of England may yet recognize that the worst misfortune to befall the leadership at the end of the war was less the premature death of William Temple than his succession by Fisher of London and not by Bell of Chichester" (p. 9). Fisher receives stringent treatment for meticulous personal attention to the long wearisome task of revision of Canon Law to the neglect of more pressing issues. Welsby noted that Dean Matthews of St. Paul's compared this "to a man who occupied himself in rearranging the furniture when the house was on fire." (p. 42). Coggan too is faulted by Welsby for inability to delegate.

A host of important secondary figures of the Anglican Church come into view in this monograph, but the author does not bring them to life with the same flourish as he does other movements and issues within the church. There is a sense in which this shortcoming can be said to be a corrective to a considerable amount

546

of past Anglican historiography.

Skillful relating of the English Church to the crowded stage of twentieth century history and culture is one of the hallmarks of this study. At times the author shows genuine perceptiveness as an interpreter of contemporary history. To a lesser degree does he exploit historical continuity with the past, though occasionally some choice morsels are offered from post Reformation history. This imbalance stems in part from an undergirding thesis of the writer, namely the sharpness of the historical break which World War II triggered. In the thinking of many historians, World War I may ultimately prove more definitive.

Few developments in Anglicanism following the Second World War are not fitted into this kaleidoscopic picture. Obviously with such leaving of no stones unturned some things receive only cursory treatment. This is true of post war biblical theology in Britain even among Anglicans, to say nothing of such non-Anglicans as C. H. Dodd and Vincent Taylor. Some detail is given to the emergence of radical theology beginning with *The Rise of Christianity* by Bishop E. W. Barnes of Birmingham (1947). Welsby is more sympathetic to John Robinson, *Honest to God*. Lay popularizes of theology such as T. S. Eliot, C. S. Lewis, and Dorothy L. Sayers are momentarily noted. Indeed, Welsby maintained that the position of influence attained by the laity in the Church of England since 1945 was one of the most salient features of the entire period. Perhaps he would say that still another was the rapid growth of the Church in liturgical practice rather than in mere theory, which it had always been.

Much of the material in this volume will be known to many of its readers; nevertheless, the author brings considerable post-war history into a sharp focus. One learns something of the geographical changes in the dioceses, cathedral construction such as Coventry and Liverpool, the training of older men for the priesthood, the waxing and waning of Canterbury's relations with Rome, attitudes toward divorce, abortion, situation ethics, and homosexuality. Violence in North Ireland and South Africa are discussed. The growing self confidence of the evangelicals within the Anglican structure, particularly under the leadership of John Stott, ordination of women, the charismatic movement, views on evangelism, and numerous other topics offer varying degrees of interest and information. As for literary style, it is simple, almost always adequate, but neither inspired, imaginative, nor elevated. Footnotes are well done; there is a limited but useful modern bibliography and a good index. The paper and print are superior. This book deserves very wide reading in England, and even in America by those who are interested in the spiritual and intellectual environment of the last half of the current century. Many of the book's ideas transcend the island of Britain and the realm of theology with universal significance. Oxford University Press is to be commended for its publication.

William Allen Poe
Bethlehem Baptist Church
Winnfield, Louisiana

The Triumph of the Meek: Why Early Christianity Succeeded, by Michael Walsh. San Francisco: Harper & Row, 1986. 256 pp. $17.95. ISBN 0-06-069254-5

Laypersons and novices in the study of church history will welcome this popular history of Christianity to the time of Constantine. Written in a smooth, flowing style, the book puzzles over the intriguing judgment of Roman Catholic modernist Alfred Loisy that "Jesus preached the kingdom of God and the Church was what came." Protestants, of course, would not dispute this conclusion, but it is striking to hear a Jesuit scholar, currently Librarian at Heythrop College in London, substantiate it, for the statement resulted in Loisy's excommunication from the Church in 1907.

Although writing in a popular style, Father Walsh incorporates a remarkable amount of critical discussion, especially in connection with earliest Christianity. He has enhanced his narrative with fine color plates, maps, chronological table, and bibliography. A few corrections of historical fact would enhance the value of an otherwise excellent piece of work. Paul, for instance, did not split with Barnabas over meals with non-Jews but over Barnabas' nephew John Mark (p. 98). Excavations at Masada fail to confirm Josephus' claim that 960 persons committed suicide rather than submit to the Romans (pp. 108, 110). Priscilla is not "always" mentioned before Aquila but only two out of three times (p. 116).

E. Glenn Hinson

Apocalpse of the Word: The Life and Message of George Fox, by Douglas Gwyn. Richmond, IN: Friends United Press, 1986. ISBN 0-913408-91-3. 241 pp. $14.95.

Here is a cogent, smoothly written and finely crafted argument in favor of Lewis Benson's interpretation of the Quaker tradition as a product of New Testament apocalyptic. The author takes issue strongly with Rufus Jones' efforts to tie Quaker origins to the sixteenth century theosophist Jakob Boehme and the fourteenth century German and Dutch mystics, and from thence to the mainstream of human religious counsciousness. He shows greater appreciation for Geoffrey Nuttall's and Hugh Barbour's explanation of Quaker origins in the context of seventeenth century Puritanism in England. Yet he places even this theory under critical judgment for "reductionism" in viewing Quakerism too much in a Protestant frame.

Against these interpretations Douglas Gwyn ascribes to Fox a rad-

ical return to prophetic Christology. Although he grew up in the Puritan milieu, he departed sharply from the Puritans by reason of his vivid conviction that "Christ is come to teach his people himself." From about age nineteen on Fox wrestled with a pervasive sense of gloom until his own Pauline-like experience lifted it. This "conversion" brought with it a whole array of implications viv-a-vis both church and society.

Whereas Puritans looked upon the Bible as their sole source of the Word of God, Fox turned to the risen Christ—variously referred to as the Light, Seed, Spirit, etc.—for the revlation of judgment and righteousness. His unwillingness to ascribe final authority to scriptures brought him into conflict with Puritans such as Richard Baxter and Baptists such as John Bunyan. The more radical implications of his christology precipitated even fiercer reaction from the established church and the state, for they entailed not only criticisms of both but revolutionary efforts to implement a new order. For scriptural guidance Fox turned chiefly to the book of Revelation, the one portion of scripture cited extensively in his writings.

Apocalypse of the Word is a persuasive approach. The author, I think, dismisses Rufus Jones' interpretation somewhat glibly when he disallows possible acquaintance of Fox with medieval mystical ideas. Fox himself didn't have to read such writings to experience some exposure to them, for the Puritans self-consciously saturated their own thinking with the mystics' as a way of reviving heart religion and achieving a further reformation. Brilliant person that he was, Fox couldn't have escaped some direct if subtle impact. It would be interesting to see whether both Fox and the mystics did not use some of the same scriptural texts in much the same way. The Puritans, as is well known, resorted to the same scriptures Gwyn has found pivotal for "the man in leather breeches."

All of this is said to caution against constructing simple keys to the unlocking of an exceedingly complex religious movement in an enigmatic era. Fox and the early Quakers are by no means done an injustice, but one of the notable interpreters has been short-shrifted. Truth can be found in all three approaches.

E. Glenn Hinson

American Christianity, A Case Study Approach, ed. by Ronald C. White, Jr., Louis B. Weeks, and Garth Rosell. Grand Rapids: Eerdmans, 1986. $11.95. 188 pp. ISBN 0-8028-0241-9.

This book contains twenty case studies in church history for introducing students to crucial issues in American religion. The editors include Ronald C. White, Jr., Director of Continuing Education and Lecturer in Church History at Princeton Seminary; Louis Weeks, Professor of Historical Theology and Dean at Louisville Presbyterian Seminary; and Garth Rosell, Vice-President and Professor of Church History at Gordon-Conwell Seminary. They have enlisted the help of numerous scholars from various religious traditions.

The volume introduces us to the use of the case study method in teaching Christian history and provides suggestions for implementing the practice in the classroom.

Cases extend from the early period of colonization to the present day. They include such occasions as the trial of Anne Hutchinson, the Puritan dissident; Cotton Mather and the Salem Witch Trials; Jonathan Edwards and the Awakening; John Woolman and slavery; the Kentucky Revival; Susan B. Anthony and Women's rights, Martin Luther King and Civil Rights, and other significant historical issues.

The cases provide excellent summaries of historical situations. Conclusions are left open-ended for continued analysis by students and teachers. The book is a valuable resource for teaching church history and guiding students in theological problem solving. Highly recommended.

Bill J. Leonard

IV. Ministry

Encouragers: The Sunday School Worker's Counseling Ministry, by James E. Taulman. Nashville: Broadman Press, 1986. 96 pages. $4.95.

The author writes from a background of pastoral and editorial ministry. He presently serves as Design Editor, Bible Book Series, in the Sunday School Department of the Baptist Sunday School Board. He previously served as a pastor in Ohio and Kentucky. His training includes Clinical Pastoral Education following his seminary training at Southern Baptist Seminary.

Encouragers is a primer manual for "front line ministers" who teach Sunday School classes. The author gives direction for a variety of settings where lay counseling can contribute to Christian ministry. He defines this kind of counseling as encouragement, using models from Jesus and the New Testament as a basis. Counseling, as envisioned by Taulman, can be done in a number of episodical settings and thus render effective ministry.

Two chapters contain twelve suggestions for doing lay counseling. Some of these are of the common sense variety but would be needed by persons unsure of themselves in attempting lay counseling. Perhaps the most useful chapter is the one focusing on counseling children where the author helps lay readers

know what is safe and helpful to do with children. The last two chapters are a listing of "dos and don'ts" about visiting sick, the grieving, and making referrals.

It is a book which pastors of small churches and ministers of education could well have knowledge of in order to refer to lay persons who want some guidance in their attempts to help fellow Christians. The book could have been strengthened by giving more of the "why" of the guidance suggested, but for uninitiated lay persons it is a valuable resource.

Ernest White

This People, This Parish by Robert K. Hudnut. Grand Rapids: Zondervan, 1986. 192 pages. $7.95.

Robert Hudnut is pastor of the Winnetka Presbyterian Church of Chicago. This is his ninth book. Princeton University was the place of his education. He has served Presbyterian churches in New York, Minnesota, and Illinois.

This People, This Parish is a series of very short reflections on the author's ministry and his enjoyment of his life in the church. The chapter titles end ". . . in this Parish." the eleven chapters follow this order: God, Jesus, The Holy Spirit, The Bible, Worship, Sermons, Love, Differences, Illness, Death, and The Pastor. However, the chapters do not reflect really different themes in the vignettes. The chapter titles are more dividers than subjects.

The book is devotional and expresses the author's experience of the encounter of God and human life. The pattern and content of the vignettes soon become somewhat repetitious and redundant except as different experiences are used. The book might have more value as a daily devotional reading of the vignettes than a book to be read straight through.

It is a minister's attempt to express his fulfillment in the many facets of ministry and his love for the people with whom he has worked and lived as pastor. The spirit of the book surpasses the format.

Ernest White

Our Eucharistic Prayers in Worship, Preaching and Study, by Raymond Moloney, S. J. Wilmington, Delaware: Michael Glaiser, 1985. No. 14 in Theology and Life Series. 165 pp. $7.95.

When Vatican II committed the Roman church to a vernacular liturgy, it opened up certain problems of translation which made the provision of alternates to the Roman canon inevitable. Consequently, there are four Eucharistic Prayers now officially approved for use and possibly others will be sanctioned as time goes on.

Raymond Moloney, S. J., is a member of the staff of Milltown Institute in Dublin, Ireland, where for a number of years he lectured on liturgy to students of University College. This book, originating in those lectures, is written to help seminarians, teachers of religion, and interested laity into needed understandings of the theology and spirituality of these four liturgical prayers.

The prayers are presented in an order that comes closest to the probable order of their historical development, beginning with the prayer modeled on the ancient canon of Hippolytes (c. 216 A.D.) and moving through the prayer based on the Eastern anaphora and that of the Roman canon to a modern composition growing out of the Second Vatican Council. Each prayer is systematically set forth first with a general introduction, then by parallel presentation of the texts in English and Latin, followed by extensive notes.

Unlike Baptists and other Free Church folk, the Roman Church had placed great importance upon a traditional and oft-repeated spoken liturgy's making real the worship of the people. Though God's Spirit is free to work apart from formal liturgy, none can deny that Spirit's working effectively through highly structured liturgical worship. But familiarity with liturgical prayer is one of the prior conditions of praying it deeply. Moloney's central purpose is to heighten as well as deepen that familiarity. Worship leaders in other traditions may learn a valuable lesson here. We must patiently teach the words and ways of meaningful corporate worship until they are almost second nature. Then, as C. S. Lewis has put it: ". . .the perfect church service would be one we were almost unaware of; our attention would have been on God. . . " (Letters to Malcom, p. 7).

Hugh T. McElrath

Women and Worship: A Guide to Nonsexist Hymns, Prayers, and Liturgies. (Rev. Ed.), by Sharon and Thomas Neufer Emswiler. San Francisco: Harper and Row, 1984. $6.95. 144 pp.

This small, practical volume was first released in 1974 and proved so helpful and timely, a revised edition has been offered. The authors, co-directors of the Wesley Foundation at Illinois State University, are ordained United Methodist ministers. *Women and Worship* provides applicable and theological sound guidelines for those wishing to develop creative and meaningful nonsexist worship. Further, it can function as an index to many resources concerning use of language, faithfulness to scripture, and the church's hymnody. The appendices, including a listing of nonsexist hymns, guide-

lines for language, and extensive bibliography, are particularly helpful.

The Emswilers write with theological sensitivity, concerned more for the significance of the church's worship than for iconoclastic disruption of traditional forms (although the latter must occur that Christ's liberating presence might be fully experienced by all). The overarching thesis of the book is that correction of sexist religious language which is "so painfully offensive . . . to women who are struggling to discover their unique humanness in a male-dominated world" (p. xiv) must occur. Perhaps the most significant contribution of the book (ch. 3) is its assertion that the basic biblical witness calls for the equality and unique worth of all persons. The church today is called to enact that witness in its worship.

Molly Marshall-Green

The Divine Formula, by Erik Routley. Princeton: Prestige Publications, 1986. 172 pp. $11.95.

As I reviewed what was billed as Routley's last book, *Christian Hymns Observed*, for the Summer 1986 issue of *Review and Expositor*, I grieved inwardly that there would be no more wit and wisdom from this brilliant pastor, teacher, and hymnologist. How delighted I am to have been wrong! The present book was found in manuscript among Routley's papers at his untimely death. It is a fitting summa, however brief, drawing together his insights as preacher, liturgist, scholar, and fervent believer in a work more stimulating—if that is possible—than any of his earlier deservedly popular writings. It is the culmination of a series of books in which he explored the relationships between theology, aesthetics, and worship: *The Church and Music* (1950), *Church Music and Theology* (1958), *Into a Far Country* (1962), and *Words, Music, and the Church* (1968). This volume reflects shifts in his role, from pastor to teacher, and in locale, from England to the United States.

This latter change, first to Princeton University and then to Westminster Choir College, gave Routley a closer view to church music as practiced in various ways in the United States. It made him more understanding, if no less critical, of the often shallow employment of the vast resources enjoyed by American churches.

Routley's "formula" is for the interaction of believer and God which is the goal of Christian worship. It is examined from the role of worship planners and leaders. Simply outlined, it contains these elements: creation, communication, self-renunciation, and liberation. The tasks of various ministers in worship are brought together by the author's own experience and by his gift for addressing each special interest and ability, challenging these, and relating them one to another.

This is a book packed with radical Christian insight—radical not because it is provocative (which it certainly is), but because it is Christian. The author points unashamedly to the strengths and weaknesses of preaching, liturgy, and music as practiced in many parts of the western church. He challenges communicators of the Gospel to examine both method and motive. He asserts that the purpose of our proclamation is not to make hearers dependent on the proclaimer, but to send them away (and to others) with the Spirit in their hearts. He finds the human constraint, over-qualification, and guarantee of the Gospel diametrically opposed to the risk taught by the Gospel. Driving home this last point, he borrows a damning phrase from Edward Muir's "The Incarnate One" to describe what often occurs in worship which has become propositional: "The Word made word."

In keeping with the concepts espoused, Routley offers suggestions for the public reading of scripture, for the language of prayer in corporate worship, and for the design of liturgy which draws attention not to itself but to God. He comments on preaching to the converted (which, as he notes, is the task to which most pastors are called) and evangelism (much of which he finds self-defeating because of weaknesses in communication).

We who are professional proclaimers are called to consider our Christian maturity in light of scriptural principles. There are chapters on the

"Temptations" of organizers, preachers, and liturgists. In addressing these topics Routley displays a broad knowledge and view of scripture, illustrated by just the right examples. This sweeping grasp of theology made personal by the intensity of insight is reminiscent of another Britisher who came to call Americans to a more exacting practice of the gospel: Eric Rust. The brief expositions scattered throughout this book are penetrating and make the book valuable from that standpoint alone.

The format of this book is unusual. Though organized in conventional chapters, each paragraph is numbered. This provides a ready means of cross-reference, as the various topics are intertwined through the book. It also serves to make the index more useful.

As usual, Routley can be represented better by quotation than by summary: "The communications of art change people . . . in a sense in which the giving of information does not." "The temptation to please, when it is a temptation to control the reaction of the receiver of the message, is a corrupting influence because it is an intrusion of the work of the Holy Spirit." "Liberation is not what is claimed, but what is given." "The active principle of a living tradition is risk." "The things which destroy liturgy . . . are at bottom selfishness, lack of interest in people and a desire personally to shine." "Liturgy has lost its nature when it becomes entertainment for a passive

audience." "Imagination must be allowed to live freely with dogma; faith with reason." "If reason informs the Church's speech, and if its purpose is the liberation of hearers, then beauty will come." "The mystery of faith is not an enslavement but a liberation."

In this book, Routley combines the joy, the energy, the creativity, the understanding, and the faith which he found in scriptural worship, which he practiced, and to which we are all called. If he is correct—and I believe him to be at many points—our failure in worship is not that we have missed the mark, but that we have missed the point. We are in great need of more thought and direction such as is here provided. This book is a must for leaders of public worship. No minister will fail to be chastened, challenged, and encouraged by this stimulating work.

Paul A. Richardson

Music in the Romantic Period: An Anthology with Commentary, by F. E. Kirby. New York: Schirmer Books, 1986. 1000 pp. $21.95.

This annotated collection of scores includes 58 works by 25 of the better-known composers of the nineteenth century. These pieces are grouped by genre under five broad headings: "The Early Phase in Germany and Austria," "The Early Phase in France and Italy," "The Middle Phase in Germany and Austria, " "The Middle and Late Phases in Italy and France," and "The Late Phase in Germany and Austria." This grouping is both convenient and logical, following the pattern used in many texts, such as Rey Longyear's *Nineteenth-Century Romanticism in Music*. Each item is preceded by comments which give insight into the nature and structure of the individual work and help to place it in the context of both the composer's output and the broader development of style. The works included are "mainstream" examples, recordings of which should be available in any reputable library or record shop.

Each of the sections of the book is begun with a short summary of the concepts by which the following pieces are related. The work as a whole opens with an essay revised from *Piano Quarterly* which is as thorough and clear summation of what constitutes romantic music as one can expect in eight pages. Two very useful appendices provide lists of scholarly editions of the complete works of major nineteenth-century composers and of significant secondary sources in English.

Two aspects of this work are particularly commendable. First, the notes are both perceptive and brief, while carrying sufficient documentation to aid students wishing to do further exploration of background material. Second, frequent references are made to scores available in other anthologies. This unselfish feature will also be a great help to students.

This collection fills the gap in the series of volumes made available by Schirmer Books, between Kirby's *Music in the Classic Period* and *Music of the Twentieth Century*, by Bryan R. Simms. It is an improvement in content, commentary, and resources over Kirby's earlier book.

The book does have some minor weaknesses. Kirby's commentary is not always easy to follow. This will be a barrier to some persons facing these ideas for the first time. There are a few notable lapses in expression which should have been spotted by an editor ("Brahm's," p. ix; "association . . . are," p. 306). Missing are examples of song outside the core of Lieder, works of any genre from England or the United States, and representatives of church music. Such are the limitations faced with any anthology which tries to represent the vast span of literature from this period. Kirby notes the necessity of supplementing what is available here and focuses on the main currents of stylistic development.

This volume is a valuable source for historical or analytical study. It may be used profitably in the classroom or by an individual. Its combination of breadth, insight, and direction for further study commends it to anyone desiring to understand better the elements of romantic style embodied in the music of the nineteenth century.

Paul A. Richardson

A Primer for Preachers, by Ian Pitt-Watson. Grand Rapids: Baker Book House, 1986. 112 pp. $5.95. ISBN 0-9010-7096-1

Ian Pitt-Watson states in the introduction that he has used "primer" to describe his book because of its double meaning, a first stage or beginner and "a small charge used to trigger a much larger detonation." The book succeeds on both counts. First, with amazing succinctness he has addressed the fundamentals of preaching. Secondly, the book has some zingers that stimulate thought but demand further exploration than is found in the content.

The author treats preaching as a subspecies of biblical theology. He follows what seems to be a popular path today of setting rhetoric up as a straw man, concluding that "Homiletics employs communication skills but owes obedience to biblical theology." I hold a high view of rhetoric but would not take issue with that statement nor do I know any theologian-homiletician who would. Writers who find it necessary to attack rhetoric are not hearing the same preaching I am. For the most part what I hear is neither theologically sound nor rhetorically effective. I am often troubled by good biblical exegetes and theologians who don't know or care enough about rhetoric to communicate their theology.

The author is certainly correct in asserting the superior importance of content over technique. Few, if any,

would argue against the proposition that the end of preaching is to communicate the Word of God. He uses a broad definition of "expository" in his assertion that "biblical preaching and expository preaching are synonymous." His practical working out of the preaching task leads one away from the traditional more limited definition of expository preaching. "To be biblical," he writes, "a sermon must be rooted in the particularities of a passage of Scripture, in the immediate and wider context of the passage and in the cosmic sweep of the Christian gospel as a whole." By his definition all preaching in which a biblical text is dominant is expository preaching. Professor Pitt-Watson stresses the narrative character of the Bible and the desirability of a narrative approach to preaching. He writes of preaching as the intersection of the Biblical story and the human story and concludes, "Above all, preaching is the remembering and retelling of how our stories are being gathered into his (God's)."

The author's concern about misplaced emphasis on "how" did not inhibit the writing of excellent chapters on "Organic Unity" and "Language and Delivery." The final chapter on "Biblical Truth and Biblical Preaching" is one of those "primers" that should set the reader to a great deal of thought. He contends for a functional understanding of truth as opposed to a propositional one. In the best tradition of classical rhetoric he calls for proclamation that combines appeals to reason and feeling that will produce action. "The truth we preach," he insists, "must be a truth not just felt, but also thought and done."

This book is well worth the very reasonable price. It provides an excellent base for further study for some and a stimulating refresher course for others.

Raymond Bailey

Walking Straight in a Crooked World, by Don M. Aycock. Nashville: Broadman Press, 1987. 127 pp. $3.95. ISBN 0-8054-5043-3.

Don Aycock adds another in a series of books of and about preaching. Aycock writes with warmth in a conversational style that engages the reader emotionally as well as intellectually. He has written a lot of himself into this collection of meditations on Galations 5:22. Interwoven with personal recollections are anecdotes and quotations drawn from such diverse sources as the "All in the Family" television program, classical writers such as Francis de Sales and St. Teresa, and modern literature of authors like Arthur Miller and Flannery O'Conner.

"To 'walk' in the spirit means to live in, trust in, and act on what you believe as the truth of God," writes Aycock in the epilogue. The meditations that have preceded the epilogue provide vivid examples of how this is done in the contemporary everyday world. The writer has provided in an

entertaining manner practical help for Christian living.

Preachers will undoubtedly discover useful illustrative material that can be used to enhance sermons on many subjects. Great benefit could be derived from simple recognition of the many places where sermon illustrations and support can be found.

Walking Straight in a Crooked World is easy and profitable reading.

Raymond Bailey

Religious Broadcasting Management Handbook, by Thomas C. Durfey and James A. Ferrier. Grand Rapids: Zondervan, 1986. 234 pages. $12.95. ISBN 0-310-39741-3

This book is exactly what it claims to be—a resource handbook for the manager of a Christian broadcasting unit. Written by two faculty members of Oral Roberts University, it presupposes that Christian broadcasting is an effective form of ministry and outlines how to go about doing it in as professional a manner as possible. A reader who has questions about the value of the electronic church and wants to weigh the issues involved before investing in equipment would be better advised to read Engel and Norton's *What's Gone Wrong with the Harvest* and Virginia Owens' *The Total Image* first. Those who already feel certain of the value of Christian broadcasting and want to know how to go about it really ought to read this book.

The authors have done a good job of personalizing the technical language of broadcasting without shying away from using it. While the engineering section will not turn the reader into an engineer, it does provide enough background and terminology to understand the basic questions, while revealing the need to enlist the aid of a fully trained video technician for any major project. The many pages of appendices alone indicate what a task it is to license and construct a transmitter. The authors suggest that this is only one route to gaining access to broadcasting time, and outline several others.

Another section deals with formats for Christian programming, and briefly outlines how several of the most-used formats emerged, i.e. the Christian talk show. Once again, this is an over-view, not an analysis. Someone wanting new program ideas would be better served by Chip Turner's *The Church Video Answerbook*. Still, the authors have provided enough information for a handbook for managers.

The rest of the book details day-to-day operations of a broadcasting ministry, from buying time to record keeping to dealing with volunteers. Strong emphasis is given to out-performing professional broadcasters, and to maintaining financial responsibility. My one regret is that no index was provided. A handbook of this kind would profit from that addition. This is a valuable practical resource for the Christian media minister.

Robert Don Hughes

Distant Fire, by Martin Bell. San Francisco: Harper & Row, 1986. 161 pp. $15.95.

Review of books like this one always wind up sounding trite. At least mine seem to. This is a book about the spiritual journey. It is best read out of sequence, as the author suggests. You read this book in segments, not at one sitting. Sometimes only a phrase or a paragraph is adequate for serious reflection. The author, Martin Bell, is an Episcopal priest, now a full-time writer. His earlier work, *The Way of the Wolf*, received wide acclaim as a guide for the spiritual life. *Distant Fire* is another such book, calling the pilgrim to recognize transcendence and grace, mystery and common humanity. God is the object of these meditations which are at once prayers and poetry. There are numerous "hard sayings." This God cannot be manipulated. This God is at once gentle and terrible, the "fierce shepherd" and the "interloper from beyond." Bell blends his own prayer/poetry with that of Holy Scripture, quoting the text without reference, convinced that "there must not be a separation of voices" (p. viii). These passages reflect theology, not dogma. Indeed, the author praises a God who is beyond dogma—who breaks through all human efforts to control Deity with dogmatism.

For Bell, we are a vulnerable people. God has made us vulnerable and became vulnerable with us while removed from us-DISTANT FIRE. Thus, "unprotected from those who work evil, scattered and purged by Yahweh, we live as nomads in the service of the Lord" (p. 132).

Think about it.

Bill J. Leonard

Guidelines for Mystical Prayer, by Ruth Burrows, Denville, N.Y.: Dimension Books, 1980. $5.95.

Ruth Burrows is a Carmelite Sister who is steeped in the thought of Teresa of Avila and St. John of the Cross. Her understanding of the Christian life transcends denominational boundaries, as do the saints who are her spiritual guides.

In a remarkably lucid book she affirms that the mystical way is not limited to an elite but is available to everyone who desires an expanding awareness of Christ-in-us. Mysticism has "nothing to do with 'experiences'," says Burrows. Rather, "The heart of mysticism is Jesus." Jesus is God seeking intimacy with us—silently and in our hearts. Spiritual growth begins in awareness that we cannot do it by ourselves, no matter

how hard we try. Confidence that God alone can infuse us with love reduces our task to merely wanting to love God. Even the desire is a gift from God. We have only one work to do: to be willing to be loved.

A major contribution of Burrows' work is the evidence she presents that minimizes the importance of mystical phenomena. Feelings such as absorption and ecstasy, feelings of union, and awareness of God are never to be used as a criterion of spirituality. The only sense in which religious experience may be said to be necessary in spirituality is as a "living wisdom, living involvement," but not as transient emotionality.

Concerning prayer, Burrows asserts that in prayer thinking is counter productive. You learn to pray without thinking or without paying attention to and being identified with thinking.

Prayer is of four kinds: (1) the prayer of activity: when most of our attention is focused on some task, like two lovers working together; (2) the prayer of attention: when our minds are engaged in some spiritual action, like lovers in conversation; (3) pure prayer: when lovers are being together , "just loving;" and (4) the prayer of ecstasy.

Burrows writes primarily to her Carmelite sisters and secondarily to committed Christians everywhere. She is honest about her limited perspective and narrow range of sources but she plumbs the data of her own experience profoundly.

She struggles with the paradoxical relation between the phenomenology of stages on the spiritual journey and the spiritually destructive consequences of being self-conscious about one's own stage of progress. The issue remains open and unresolved. As an emphasis on the danger of being overly self-conscious, her case is solid. Her demand to be oblivious to a stage while on a stage in which you are struggling to subordinate ego needs may be an impossible requirement.

A bit dubious is her assertion that no mystical state of consciousness that can be looked at and understood in natural terms is of God since all Divine graces are totally supernatural. Her insistence on the ordinariness of sainthood calls for consideration of the hypothesis that alternate states of consciousness are a universal human potential—no matter at what stage they may occur. Until the data is examined more closely in cross-cultural perspective, the claim that Christian experience is totally supernatural must be seen as another instance of the Christian superiority complex—an attitude that contradicts the requirement of detachment from the ego.

A fundamental challenge of Burrows' work is its consistent definition of Christian spirituality as the integration of a total person around the love of God in Christ, empowered by the Spirit. She leaves no room for works righteousness on the spiritual

560

journey. Her central vision is indeed a pearl of great price.

Edward E. Thornton

The Vigil of Prayer, by Nolan P. Howington. Nashville: Broadman, 1987. 95 pp. ISBN 0-8054-1505x

Nolan P. Howington is one of Southern Baptists' best popular writers. He is also an able theologian and preacher and all of these skills are reflected in *The Vigil of Prayer*. The book cover calls the contents "sermonic essays" and that is as good a description as any. Prayer is as subject often neglected in Baptist churches. The assumption that prayer is automatic in the life of a Christian seems to prevail. Experience teaches that it is a false assumption. This book is a splendid tool for addressing this serious deficiency. In a lucid, vigorous style the author instructs the reader on the purpose and practice of prayer.

The problems of doubt and guilt as obstacles to prayer and problems remedied by prayer are among those addressed. In the meditation entitled, "Christ at Mid-Life," Howington demonstrates how prayer is essential to the natural life cycle and its problems. The chapters you would expect such as thanksgiving and the model prayer are there but even they are treated with a freshness that opens anew the powerful therapy of continuing communion with God. The book could be read in a single sitting but is worthy of careful meditation and absorption that is possible only with a chapter a day.

Raymond Bailey

Managing Stress in Ministry, by William E. Hulme. New York: Harper and Row, 1985. 138 pp. $13.95.

Managing Stress in Ministry is a second generation book on stress for ministers. While Hulme uses the many modern health science research discoveries about stress and presents several in precise but clear form, he has integrated this material with biblical and theological wisdom so as to provide a more balanced approach to the dual tasks of understanding and coping with stress.

Although pastors are his focused audience, Hulme's insights are transferable to ministers in a variety of vocational roles. Of maximum help to ministers is his sensitive exploration of the reasons for ministerial stress. He carefully explores the "built-in" stressors of the ministerial vocation as well as analyzing the ever-present stressors of the twentieth century. An important serendipitous gift in this book is Hulme's insightful discussion of the ways in which current clergy job descriptions reflect the American cultural milieu rather than the basic biblical and theological mandates. The additional stress experienced by ministers at-

tempting to be faithful to biblical/theological models of ministry created by such tension introduced thoughtfully.

Hulme deals critically with those addicted to handling stress with either a "power of positive thinking" mode on the model of Norman Vincent Peale or the "possibility thinking" methodology of Robert Schuller. Such excessive focusing on reality-denying procedures "produces an illusionary perception of the world in which we live." Hulme's own "concept of the balanced life" is reality embracing and follows a four-point preventive program including: (1) prayer and meditation, (2) physical exercise, (3) social engagements, and (4) appropriate nutrition.

To this he adds the daily exercise of "freedom under God to take control of our lives." The three-step methodology to escape from external control is: (1) to reject passive acceptance to "stimulus-reaction bondage," (2) to renounce both any addition to an ambivalent or double-minded life style and the hidden satisfactions such a life style gives its practitioners, and (3) to "believe that this decision is not just our decision but also God's and to hear and to see him calling us to move in this direction."

Hulme has used his own characteristically unique method of applying major biblical themes to the general lifestyle task of being a minister in the 1980's. This is not a technical book on stress, but a book for ministers based upon the better technical materials. It is easy to read, relevant to the practice of ministry, and generally insightful. It is a valuable resource for the newly ordained minister and to seasoned veterans.

Walter C. Jackson III
Professor of Ministry

Pastor as Person: Maintaining Personal Integrity in the Choices and Challenges of Ministry, by Gary L. Highbaugh. Minneapolis: Augsburg Publishing House, 1984. 150 pp. No price given.

The book *Pastor as Person* is an introduction to ministry for seminary students while at the same time being a book capable of introducing mature pastors to themselves in ministry. Gary Highbaugh has made use of "true-to-life" situations of ministers as confessional models for reflection. These carefully chosen persons illustrate the kinds of situations, feelings, joys, and dilemmas experienced by busy pastors; but they also enable the author to illustrate his own theoretical model of a pastor as a whole person. Insights from anthropology, the behavioral sciences, philosophy, and theology are openly used in the process.

The four case studies introduce the pastor as a physical person, thinking person, feeling person, and relating person, and all four are used in the summary chapter, the pastor as a choosing person.

This is a well balanced contribution to the understanding of the life and work of a pastor. Its emphasis by precept and example of the integration of insight and information from several disciplines makes the book worthy reading by seminarians. It lends itself to dialogic classroom settings and pastor's peer group settings because of its clear presentation of several viewpoints in each major section, and because the author clearly defines his own selected "holistic" choice.

Any student of the ministry or minister in service may find assistance and encouragement for growth in this volume.

Walter C. Jackson III
Professor of Ministry

Loneliness and Spiritual Growth, by Samuel M. Natale. Birmingham, Alabama: Religious Education Press, 1986. 171 pages. $12.95.

What experience is unavoidable, universal, and little understood? Samuel Natale answers "Loneliness!" He then leads the reader to confront loneliness as the key subjective experience which drives persons to community. The overt audience for this volume is religious educators but pastors and pastoral care specialists will find much of benefit. Samuel Natale is a psychologist who teaches at Iona College in New York, counsels individuals, and consults with religious educators. His varied investments are obvious in this volume.

Natale balances his attention on the cognitive, behavioral, and affective dimensions of loneliness. He utilizes the life cycle as his organizing principle. That is, he examines the dimensions of loneliness in childhood, adolescence, adulthood, and old age. He provides excellent overviews of the major theorists and summarizes the empirical studies in the field. His bibliographies provide information necessary to those who want to delve deeper. In brief, Natale has packed much valuable information concerning a crucial human experience into a brief, easily read volume.

There are two weaknesses in this work. First, he takes advocates of religion to task for not attending to the problem of loneliness and for not writing clearly on the subject. He seems unaware of the currents in modern theology which understand the divisions between persons' need for community and driveness to isolation. While he is accurate that little has been written on the psychological and social dimensions of loneliness by religious educators and pastoral caregivers, he does not attend to the excellent Biblical and theological perspectives which are available. Thus, his attention to "spiritual growth" is without clear psychological or theological meaning.

A second weakness is the interventions for the lonely which he recom-

mends. He proposes that the religious educator lead group activities and individual skill building events which appear to require the skills and knowledge of a psychotherapist. These are not clearly tied to churches' ongoing tasks and methods. The pastoral care specialist will also be dissatisfied with his oversimplification of rather complex relational events.

Natale has written a book worthy of attention from religious educators and pastoral care specialists. However, creativity will be called for in moving beyond the excellent theoretical and research resources he provides to ministry applications.

Steven S. Ivy
Chief, Chaplain Service
V. A. Medical Center
Nashville, Tennessee

Strengthening Families, by Nicholas Hobbs and Associates. San Francisco: Jossey-Bass, 1984. 348 pages, $23.95.

Strengthening Families is based on the premise that educating and socializing children is a public trust of vital consequence to our nation. According to demographic trends, a time is rapidly approaching when children will be a scarce resource in our nation. Hobbs suggests that child care and parent education are two key instruments to meet community and national needs for rearing competent, effective adults.

Strengthening Families examines public policy in these two related areas.

The authors provide an exhaustive review of current child care and parent education policies and programs and recent demographic trends. Chapter Three provides perhaps the most valuable reading in the volume; the authors overview American social policy values and present their own value-analytic framework for assessing public policies. This framework would serve the family minister well in the critique of church as well as governmental policies and programs.

In the remaining chapters of the book, the authors examine and evaluate five major policy options for child care and parent education, using their framework. The book concludes with recommendations and suggestions for the future development of family policy. The authors present research which demonstrates that early educational experiences can make a difference in the lives of children, especially poor children, and that these effects last longer when parents are involved in the educational program. They argue that child care and parent education need to be moved out of the public welfare bureaucracy so that these services can be available to all and so that objectives can be expanded beyond relieving the welfare rolls. Finally, the authors conclude that public school systems offer the most appropriate vehicle for the gradual expan-

sion of services to all families who need and want them.

The real focus of *Strengthening Families* is not how to strengthen families, but, more specifically, how public policies can strengthen the role performance of parents and the socialization of children. There is much more to family life, of course, than parenting, which makes the book's title somewhat misleading. The authors have rightly and effectively, however, provided some long-needed attention to the tangle of issues surrounding family policy.

Diana S. Richmond Garland

Corporate Cultures: The Rites and Rituals of Corporate Life, by Terrance E. Deal and Allen A. Kennedy. Reading, MA: Addison-Wesley Publishing, 232 pp. $8.95.

Corporate Cultures is a book every serious church leader can read with profit. It reports the results of intensive field research into the life cycles of contemporary businesses. Deal, of Vanderbilt's Peabody College, and Kennedy, president of a microcomputer software company, constructed a research design fueled by their desire "to see what had made America's great companies not merely organizations, but successful, human institutions." More than seventy-five business organizations were included in the research sample, and the authors consulted regularly with colleagues in the academy and active business endeavors as the research conclusions were formulated.

Their discoveries are instructive for the understanding and successful operation of organizations of the marketplace. However, the discoveries of successful and unsuccessful business "cultures" and the ingredients making then successful or unsuccessful are applicable to the understanding and operation of religious institutions such as local churches, associations, conventions, boards, agencies, colleges, and seminaries.

Successful businesses were found to be those which: (1) respond realistically to their market environments; (2) possess clearly defined values held to be valuable by managers and workers alike; (3) possess and cultivate "heroes"—people with the "right stuff" who personify their culture's values—who as such provide tangible role models for employee imitation' (4) possess rituals, "the systematic and programmed routines of day-to-day life in the company"; (4) have symbolic actions in the form of play, rituals, and ceremonies focused on recognition, because, "without expressive events, any culture will die"; and (5) an internal communication network made up of storytellers, priests, whisperers, gossips, secretarial sources, spies, and cabals. The most successful businesses are aware of these ingredients and manage them well.

Relatively unsuccessful busi-

nesses have: (1) no clear values or beliefs on which the managers and workers agree nor do they have agreed-upon principles about how to succeed in business; (2) some may have such beliefs but "cannot agree among themselves on which are most important;" (3) a situation in which different sections of the company "have fundamentally different beliefs"; (4) "heroes of the culture (who) are destructive or disruptive and don't build upon any common understanding about what is important;" and (5) no rituals or where the ones possessed are disorganized "with the left hand and the right hand working at cross purposes."

This book does not treat ethical issues in any depth, nor is there an attempt to resolve the basically autocratic undertone of the suggested pattern of recommended business success. It is also most disappointing to have the authors state in the concluding chapter that the Roman Catholic Church is a "religious" example of a "successful business" enterprise like the "atomized organization" they predict to be the successful business pattern for the future. This statement was apparently make about the church without a semblance of the careful research given to the secular institutions.

This book is useful to ministers and theologians seeking to "listen-in" on the conversations of significant groups in the American culture, but clergy must make allowances for the fundamentally behavioral modification mindset of the authors. It is a delightfully written series of essays more useful for its design than for its addictively pragmatic conclusions.

Walter C. Jackson III
Professor of Ministry

Overcoming Resistance: Rational-Emotive Therapy with Difficult Clients, by Albert Ellis. New York: Springer Publishing Co., 1985. 228 pages. $21.00

Albert Ellis is known as a leading authority on cognitive behavior therapy. In this book, he applies his rational emotive therapy, one variation of cognitive behavioral approaches, with clients he labels "difficult." Difficult clients are defined as those who resist change. He attributes this resistance to personality traits, such as fear of discomfort, fear of disclosure and shame, and feelings of hopelessness. He describes "special" clients as those prone to be resistant to change. These include psychopaths, sociopaths, substance abusers, involuntary clients, elderly clients, mentally deficient clients, severely depressed clients, those who are willfully resistant, and those who are moralistic and dogmatic. The author treats some of these with no more than a three sentence paragraph. He appears to be implying that the approach for intervention he describes in the book has general applicability across these varying treatment contexts, and in fact, with virtually all the problems people experience in living.

566

Ellis insists that "human disturbance is contributed to by environmental pressures, including our childhood upbringing, but its most important and vital source is our innate tendency to indulge in crooked thinking" (p. 164). He has a single focus—helping people think more rationally. No doubt, such an approach can be very helpful, and telling people that they can change their lives by changing their thinking can be empowering. At the same time, it is far too simplistic. There is no room here for advocacy, or even for empowering clients to make changes in other systems beyond their own thought processes.

One group which Ellis considers "often impossible to reach" (p. 157) are clients he considers moralistic and dogmatic. Ellis himself appears quite dogmatic in his dismissal of any approach which is "unscientific" or irrational; he has little tolerance for religious value systems. He contends that if "people were consistently scientific and nonabsolutistic, they would rarely invent or subscribe to dogmatic *shoulds* and *musts*, would stay with their flexible wishes and preferences, and would thereby minimize or eliminate their emotional disturbances" (p. 36).

In short, this book hides rather than frames the potential of cognitive approaches as a resource for those who would help persons with their problems in living.

Diana S. Richmond Garland

Casebook of Marital Therapy, ed. by Alan S. Gurman. New York: The Guilford Press, 1985. 392 pages. $30.00.

Ministry with couples in crisis seldom occurs in the high-powered clinic settings pictured in much of the therapy literature, with teams who consult and support one another behind one-way mirrors or with video-taped replays of their work. Instead, we often face the needs of hurting people alone, with perhaps an occasional consultation. The most common models for our work are published case illustrations of particular theoretical approaches or edited videotape demonstrations of a single brilliant therapy session. Though we may learn much about theory and strategies for change this way, these models inadvertently ignore the painful and sometimes halting steps that change requires over time.

Gurman's *Casebook of Marital Therapy* provides a welcome corrective. The fourteen contributors to this volume come from a variety of schools of thought. Their focus is not theory so much as how theory interacts with the reality of a given couple's unique problems and strengths. The authors do not offer their most stellar work; these full-length case studies illustrate the "everyday ups and downs of clinical practice with couples" (p. xiv). The result will be comforting and enlightening to anyone who works with marriages. The couples whom these authors describe struggle with complex issues that cannot be distilled into one central complaint that is resolved by one powerful intervention. The problems include infidelity, jealously and distrust, problems with parents and children, failing health, alcoholism, intimacy and sexual problems, and escalating conflict. The therapists are sometimes confused, make mistakes, and struggle to find ways to help. They obviously care about their clients and ponder what to do and whether what they can do is enough. To illustrate, David Treadway concluded his chapter with feelings which many counselors may have also experienced: "I feel a bittersweet sense of sadness. I cared about George and Betsy. I even miss them. But they are neither family nor friends. I felt intensely engaged with the essence of their lives, and now they are gone. I hope they are doing well, but I do not know if they are" (p. 175).

Casebook of Marital Therapy makes for comforting as well as engaging reading for those who have committed themselves to helping couples in crisis.

Diana S. Richmond Garland

Crisis Intervention: A Handbook for Practice and Research, by Karl A. Slaikeu. Boston: Allyn and Bacon, Inc., 1984. 374 pp. $34.27.

Crisis Intervention is at once a basic introduction to the professional task of caring for persons in crisis and an encyclopedia of emotional health care information arranged to facilitate easy reader access.

Slaikeu writes with the no-nonsense style of a clinician. His material is organized with remarkable clarity, precision, and brevity. Basic crisis theory is divided into developmental and situational events. Interventions are arranged on the style of Gerald Caplan's work, *Principles of Preventive Psychiatry* in a consistent model of first order (psychological first aid), second order (multimodal therapy), and third order (preventive and research) strategies. Crisp charts portray interventions in memorable formats, and clinical illustrations point to the value and effectiveness of interventions.

The theories and research of Caplan, Frank, Havighurst, Lindemann, Erikson, von Bertalanffy, Bloom, Carkhuff, Gilligan, Boisen, Scheidmann, Selye, Levinson, and others are woven together with skill. Slaikeu is eclectic and non-dogmatic. He defines the roles and crisis intervention methodologies of clergy, attorneys, police officers, community health professionals, public educators, medical/paramedical practitioners, and general "on the job" crisis workers. Crisis care for persons who suffer traumas such as attempted suicide, death, bereavement, natural disasters, war, divorce, physical assault, mid-life crisis, aging, etc., is skillfully treated. Useful assistance in crisis counseling by telephone is also a major contribution of this book.

The final parts of the volume are focused on the presentation of a model for crisis intervention research. Three appendixes add sample questionnaire, and a glossary of techniques for crisis intervention.

The lengthy (40 page) bibliography is impressive, but would be more useful if it were annotated or at least divided according to a useful design. It would be more helpful to students if basic research items were so labeled, and infinitely more valuable to busy health-care practitioners if the popular works suited for reading by crisis victims were indicated.

Chapter Ten, "Crisis Intervention by Clergy" is a brief, but accurate "still photograph" of a minister's role in crisis intervention. Ministers are portrayed here as valued persons in society who, because of their unique social role are natural crisis counselors. Here Slaikeu sets the stage for the task of theological interpretation necessary to lift the human activities of therapeutic intervention to the level of Christian ministry; but ministry is not his goal. Thus, he only sets the stage for such theological reflection.

This excellent volume is, however, a treasure for a busy minister. It is well balanced in its use of materials from the health sciences and is clearly compatible with principles of ministry. A major weakness for clergy in this regard is the narrowly selected group of pastoral care resources. Its goal related to the role of the minister in human crisis, however, is to attempt to assist minister-readers "to develop a clearer identity of themselves as helpers, especially as they compare themselves with other mental health counselors and psychotherapists" (p. 181), a goal shared by seminary educators as well as local church ministers.

This book has a well deserved place on the minister's bookshelf next to some explicitly "pastoral" works.

Walter C. Jackson, III

Family Mediation Practice, by John Allen Lemmon. New York: The Free Press, 1985, 282 pp. $17.95.

Family Mediation Practice is a carefully written manual for professionals who deal with families in conflict. While focused primarily upon divorcing families and the multiple problems of such families, John Lemmon has provided a volume written as a primer for those reading their first book in the field. At the same time it is a book able to be studied profitably by practicing counselors. Family therapy, family law, and the joint skills of problem-solving and mediation are skillfully presented and integrated in a way helpful to anyone seeking to perform as a mediator for a potentially difficult divorce settlement.

The author also deals with other conflicting events arising at the most stressful or vulnerable moments of a person or family's life cycle. Adoption, pre-nuptial agreements, parent-child disputes, child abuse and neglect, juvenile court issues, step-patenting, unmarried cohabitants, eldercare, neighborhood quarrels, and other such issues are given the benefit of Lemmon's wisdom in this comprehensive introduction to family mediation.

A one-step-at-a-time method of mediation is presented with well selected illustrations making principles and theories come alive in practical ways. Some brief but useful guidelines for labor management disputes, family business conflicts, and other marketplace disruptions are also included.

This book is a valuable single-volume introduction to the art of mediation. It will be useful to pastors as a quick introduction to mediation theories, laws, and techniques as well as to pastoral counselors already familiar with much of the marriage and family theory and techniques on which mediation is based.

Within the text and appendices, the book contains outlined reports of three precedent-setting cases related to the family mediation process and a carefully delineated chapter on ethical codes and standards of Family Medicine, codes and standards to be followed carefully by family mediators.

This book is recommended as a personal library resource book for ministers as well as a primer for any minister interested in becoming a reasonably well-prepared mediator.

Walter C. Jackson, III
Professor of Ministry

Clive Staples Lewis: A Dramatic Life, by William Griffin. San Francisco: Harper & Row, 1986. 507 pp. $24.95. ISBN 006 2503 529

Photo albums are often irresistible temptations for the curious or the bored. Their arrangement is a matter of pure choice by the compiler. So it is with this biography of C. S. Lewis; Griffin has elected to use a strictly chronological approach to his presentation of Lewis' 'dramatic' life. From 1925 and his installation as a fellow of Magdalen College, through the Oxford years, to the Professorship at Magdelene College, Cambridge, and then the years following up to his death, the words present living photographs of this man so admired by many. The biography has the characteristic of a photograph album in that one can "dip in" at random and feel quite pleased with the resulting picture. It may, in truth, be the best approach to reading this work.

There is little new material contained therein, as Griffin acknowledges in his preface. He has relied heavily on past published works, especially the Green-Hooper biography, though materials from interviews and journals add a new flavor

to some familiar tales. This is not the definitive Lewis biography--the author expresses his hope that Walter Hooper will write that before another dozen years have passed--but it is a very important addition to the ever-growing collection of materials about Lewis. There is no lack of interest in either the man or his writings. Consequently, this book will likely find a large readership. Knowing that, and considering the rather high price, it is difficult to understand why greater care was not exercised to eliminate repetitive passages and frequent typesetting errors which resulted in misspellings and mismeanings. [One of the more humorous examples is a reference to a "steam of consciousness" writing style.] It may be cavilling to note such problems, but one hardly expects such things in a volume by a veteran editor.

Such things aside, the biography is good and enjoyable reading. There is much in it to recommend it to readers. The scope alone makes it rather exciting. A summary of the events of each year/chapter is provided in the Contents Listing, allowing browsing readers the luxury of choosing episodes about which they wish to read. The detailed index is especially useful when trying to determine how or when or where an individual or episode fits into the greater picture.

Just as a photo album is a record of a labor of love, so this biography is a record of labors of love: Lewis' loves in life--Christianity, books, his friends, and Griffin's love and admiration for that life and those loves. It serves well that purpose for which it is intended, a chronicling of Lewis' life. Readers who read Lewis will want to read this book.

Melody Mazuk

Forty Acres and a Goat, by Will D. Campbell. Atlanta: Peachtree Publishers, 1986. 281 pp. $14.95. ISBN 0-931948-97-5

At the time, it seemed like a good idea—what better way to observe the birthday of Martin Luther King, Jr., than by reading a memoir of his fellow civil rights "inside agitator," Will D. Campbell?

The 1977 publication of *Brother to a Dragonfly* thrust Campbell into a limelight shades different from any exposure he had previously experienced. The exposure was double: Campbell and his work, in this instance, writing, were introduced to an audience who had never before heard of this preacher of the South who is a Baptist but is not a Southern Baptist preacher (p. 148), and the lives and dreams of the people of the Movement found new life in his words. Suddenly, a younger generation of activists 'heard' a new telling of the Old Gospel story. Who read it and can forget the terse presentation (in 10 words or less) of the Gospel message? And here, in the Church of Forty Acres and a Goat, Campbell has his Gospel in "three rusty pieces of junk that no one else would have on their place" (pp 144-145). But that generation of readers has aged a decade, the vision has clouded a little, and for some, priorities have changed. The elegaic overtones of this memoir are unmistakable, but the thread of hope, however faint, still runs firm and true.

A cast of characters, animal and human, have their stories related by Campbell, and in the telling a message sometimes is pictured clearly. At other times, one is left to ponder the effect of the tale, and to try to pinpoint what it is Campbell is trying to say. Overall, that may well be the intent of these collected stories—a self-examination of the "whys" and "wherefores" of these past three decades. Campbell has helped us to take courage to respond by telling us that he has had many teachers through the years, including Jackson A' Goat, a principal player in this tale, and he has learned something from each one.

Where has the Movement gone? The reading of this book has been accompanied by news of marches in Cumming, GA., and Louisville, KY., marches to keep the dream alive. No, the Movement is not dead. It has changed; it has, at times, lost momentum; it is no longer front page news everyday. But it has not died.

"Say good-bye to Jackson." T. J. Eaves, Campbell's friend and chief protagonist in this writing, took his leave with those words. In a sense, these words reflect Campbell's attitude: to say good-bye to an era. Loyal readers will find much in these pages to think about. Readers new to Campbell would be well-advised to go back and read *Brother to a Dragonfly* first. Though not sequential, the books are inter-related and inter-dynamic.

Will Campbell grieves on these pages, and we grieve in the reading of them. On balance, it still seems like a good idea to have read this on Martin Luther King, Jr.'s birthday. It was not a celebration, it was a reminder.

Melody Mazuk

Scuffmarks on the Ceiling: Enjoying (and Surviving) Your Child's Early School Years, by Denise Turner. Waco, TX: Word Books, 1986. 182 pp. $9.95.

Denise Turner is convinced that children should be enjoyed as well as endured, "even in those early school years when they seem to be bounding off the wall, even when there are scuffmarks on the ceiling" (p. 14). With a style which resembles Erma Bombeck's, Turner looks at parenting with wit and wisdom. She feels parents have forgotten that raising children is fun. She deals with her subject of child-raising in a realistic rather than romantic manner. "Having a baby forces you not so much to toss away the dreams, but to infuse them with real life" (p. 16). She demonstrates how her role as a parent has become an opportunity for her growth. Turner does not intend for the book to present new theories of perfect parenting. Instead, through anecdotes, both borrowed and first-hand, she encourages parents to find ways to instill meaning into the often frustrating or irritating realities of living with children. Throughout the book, however, she includes gems of truth gleaned from those who may claim expertise in parenting.

Turner consistently reminds the reader that God is involved in parenting each child. Part of her growth as a parent includes accepting the truth that her daughter and son are as much God's children as they are hers. Her determination to enjoy her children pervades such topics as a child's stress, passing along values, and imagination and creativity. Perhaps her gift in this book is her ability to look at what actually happens when raising a child and to point out the meaning that is there. She refuses to let the frustrations of parenting cloud her view of the rewards, though she presents an accurate and amusing picture of how parenting is both.

Carol Younger
Free Lance Writer
Paoli, Indiana

A Penny's Worth of Minced Ham: Another Look at the Great Depression, by Robert Hastings. Carbondale, IL: Southern Illinois University Press, 1986. 100 pp. $8.95. ISBN 0-8093-1304-9.

Robert Hastings has lived in Illinois and served Illinois Baptists most of his professional life. For seventeen years he served as the highly respected editor of the *Illinois Baptists*, the state paper. Those who have heard him speak and read his writing know him as a master story teller. His *Tinyburg Tales* are modern parables rich in Christian instruction. This present work is a sequel to his *Nickel's Worth of Skim Milk* and like that work falls into the category of folk history.

"There lingers in each of us a yearning for neighborhood, that feeling of belonging, of home, of roots, of the familiar" (p. 87), writes Hastings. Because he is right about the universality of those feelings, most people will enjoy this nostalgic trip through the author's boyhood in Marion, Illinois, during the depression. The problem with works like this is that while they remind us of important human values and the strength of the human spirit, they tend to romanticize suffering. Hastings confesses that these are "idyllic boyhood memories" but affirms the lesson that "life is something deep and hidden, warm and touching, divorced form dollar signs and wed to simplicity" (p. 89). I fear that similar memories of the past have influenced the policies of another Illinois product who is currently President of the United States. I hope we can recapture the values without the grim human suffering of a collapsed economy. Hastings was far more perceptive than President Reagan in his analysis of racism in Illinois in the 1930's. The President has commented that as a boy he was unaware of a race problem. Hastings writes sensitively of subtle racism in classroom segregation and a stricter discipline for dark-skinned peers.

Most people will enjoy reading this work which is enhanced by well-chosen poignant photographs.

Raymond Bailey

Getting to Know God, by Karen Dockrey. Nashville: Broadman Press, 1984. 96 pp. $4.50.

At one time Southern culture was such that most young people acquired a general understanding of Christianity from a pedestrian perspective. At least, Southern Baptists assumed that youth had this basic understanding of Christian vocabulary and concepts. Perhaps the Christian South never existed. If it did, it certainly does not today. From the broader perspective, young people in America today can grow up ignorant of the simplest aspects of Christianity.

In *Getting to Know God*, Karen Dockrey addresses youth who have questions about Christianity. In "everyday language" the book summarizes "what most Christian's believe most of the time." Dockrey writes at the elementary level for the young person who knows little or nothing about Christianity. In so doing, she tackles the most complex doctrines of the faith without using a theological vocabulary.

The book incorporates a variety of devices to involve the young person in learning for themselves. Exercises, questions, and reference Bible verses pepper each chapter to help the reader answer their own questions. Brief case studies illustrate points and provide a context for understanding the Christian faith. From the hypostatic union to a Christian worship service, Dockrey aims at the practical meaning of Christianity for a young person. Written in terms of the dilemmas of adolescence which adults do not always take seriously, the book presents the problems of youth seriously in the context of Christian faith.

This book emerges from many years of experience in youth ministry. Dockrey presents a format that draws on that experience in dealing with the questions and concerns of youth. While her discussion allows for the boarder community of Christians, she writes unapologetically from a Baptist perspective which appears in her explanation of baptism and tithing.

While *Getting to Know God* was written with the individual in mind, Dockrey has enhanced its utility with a companion *Study Guide*. The *Study Guide* presents a plan for using *Getting to Know God* in a group setting for youth. The plan outlines ten one-hour sessions designed to involve the youth in the study. It discourages a lecture approach and encourages maximum youth participation as a dimension of learning.

Books Received

Sisters of the Spirit, ed by William L. Andrews. Bloomington: Indiana University Press, 1986. 232 pp. $29.50. ISBN 0-253-035260-6.

A Karl Barth Reader, by Karl Barth. Ed. by Rolf Joachim Erler and Reiner Marquand. Grand Rapids: Wm. B. Eerdmans, 1986. 116 pp. $6.95. ISBN 0-8028-0190-0.

Institutes of the Christian Religion: 1536 edition. Vol I & II by John Calrin. Grand Rapids: Wm. B. Eerdmans, 1986/(reprint) 582 pp. 676 pp. $25.00. ISBN 0-8028-2319-8.

Letters of St Cyprian, Vol 3, by G. W. Clarke. New York: Paulist Press, 1986. 123 pp. No price given. ISBN 0-8091-0369-9.

Preaching on Favorite Hymns, by Frank Colquhoun. London: Mowbrays, 1986. 138 pp. $4.75. ISBN 0-264-67054-X.

Humor in Preaching, by John W. Drakeford. Grand Rapids: Zondervan, 1986. 101 pp. $6.95. ISBN 0-310-20121-7.

Religious Broadcast Management Handbook, by Thomas C. Durfey and James A. Ferrier. Grand Rapids: Zondervan, 1986. 234 pp. $12.95. ISBN 0-310-39741-3.

Exodus, by John I. Durham. Word Biblical Commentary. Waco: Word, 1987. 501 pp. $25.95. ISBN 0-8499-0202-9.

Faith Development and Fowler, ed. by Craig Dykstra and Sharon Parks. Birmingham: Religious Education Press, 1986. 300 pp. $14.95. ISBN 0-89135-056-X.

A New Hearing: Living Options in Homilectic Method, by Richard L. Eslinger. Nashville: Abingdon, 1987. 189 pp. $10.95. ISBN 0-687-27693-4.

280 Paradoxes or Wondrous Sayings, ed. by Sebastian Franck and E. J. Furcha. New York: Edwin Mellen, 1986. 499 pp. $59.95. ISBN 0-89946-814-1.

Less Than Conquerors, by Douglas W. Frank. Grand Rapids: B. Eerdmans, 1986. 278 pp. $14.95. ISBN 0-8028-0228-1.

Bearing the Cross: Martin Luther King, Jr. and the Southern CLC, by David J. Garrow. New York: Wm. Morrow Co., 1986. 625 pp. $19.95. ISBN 0-688-04794-7.

Medieval Thought, by Michael Haren. New York: St. Martin's Press, 1985. 211 pp. $27.50. ISBN 0-312-52816-7.

What is Christianity, by Adolf Von Harnack. Philadelphia: Fortress, 1986. 301 pp. $17.50. ISBN 0-8006-3201-X. Reprint of 1957 edition.

Nag Hammadi, Gnosticism and Early Christianity, ed. by Charles W. Hedrick and Robert Hodgson, Jr. Peabody, MA: Hendrickson, 1986. 307 pp. No price given. ISBN 0-913573-16-7.

The Mormon Corporate Empire, by John Heinerman and Anson Shupe. Boston: Beacon, 1985. 258 pp. $19.95. ISBN 0-8070-0406-5.

Understanding Cults and New Religions, by Irving Hexham and Karla Poewe. Grand Rapids: Wm. B. Eerdmans, 1986. 166 pp. $8.95. ISBN 0-8028-0170-6.

Quakers in Conflict, by Larry H. Ingle. Knoxville: University of Tennessee Press, 1986. 299 pp. $29.95. ISBN 0-89-049-501-1.

The Thessalonian Correspondence, by Robert Jewett. Philadelphia: Fortress Press, 1986. 192 pp. $17.95. ISBN 0-8006-2111-5.

Karl Barth, A Theological Legacy, by Eberhard Jungel. Philadelphia Westminster, 1986. 138 pp. $13.95. ISBN 0-664-24031-3.

Mt. Athos, by Kadas Sortiris. New Rochelle, NY: Aristide D. Caratzas, 1979. 128 pp. $20.00 ISBN 0-89241-369-7.

Family Resources: The Hidden Partner in Family Therapy, ed. by Mark A. Karpel. New York: Guilford, 1986. 469 pp. $37.50. ISBN 0-89862-069-4.

Servants of Satan: The Age of the Witch Hunts, by Joseph Klaits. Bloomington: Indiana University Press, 1985. 176 pp. $18.95. ISBN 0-253-35182-0.

Adventism in America, ed. by Gary Land. Grand Rapids: Wm. B. Eerdmans, 1986. 230 pp. $14.95. ISBN 0-8028-0237-0.

Child Welfare: A Source Book of Knowledge and Practice, ed. by Frank Maidman. Edison, NJ: Child Welfare League of America, 1986. 384 pp. $24.95. ISBN 0-87868-236-8.

Mark: Evangelist and Theologian, by Ralph P. Martin. Grand Rapids: Zondervan, 1982. 226 pp. $8.95. ISBN 0-310-28801-0.

The Baptist Heritage: Four Centuries of Baptist Witness, by H. Leon McBeth. Nashville: Broadman, 1987. 822 pp. $24.95. ISBN 0-8054-6569-3.

The Christian Home in Victorian America, 1840-1900, by Colleen Mc. Dannell. Bloomington: Indiana University Press, 1986. 155 pp. $25.00. ISBN 0-253-31376-7.

Death and Life: An American Theology, by Arthur C. McGill. Philadelohia: Fortress, 1987. 107 pp. $7.95. ISBN 0-8006-1927-7.

Partners in Peacemaking: Family Workshop Models Guidebook for Leaders, ed. by James McGinnis. St. Louis: Institute for Peace & Justice, 1984. 170 pp. $37.00.

How Karl Barth Changed My Mind, ed. by Donald K. McKim. Grand Rapids: Wm. B. Eerdmans, 1986. 181 pp. $9.95. ISBN 0-8028-0099-8.

Palladius - Dialogue on the Life of St. John Chysostom, ed. by Robert T. Meyer. 151 pp. $16.95. ISBN 0-8091-0358-3.

Image as Insight: Visual Understanding in Western Christianity and Secular Culture, by Margaret R. Miles. New York: Beacon, 1985. 154 pp. $27.95. ISBN 0-8070-1006-5.

Black Pioneers in a White Denomination, by Mark D. Morrison-Reed. Boston: Beacon, 1984. 182 pp. $9.95. ISBN 0-8070-1601-2.

Why Preach? Why Listen?, by William Muehl. Philadelphia: Fortress, 1986. 95 pp. $4.95. ISBN 0-8006-1928-5.

Christ and the Decree, by Richard A. Muller. Durham, NC: Labyrinth Press, 1986. 182 pp. $30.00. ISBN 0-939464-39-X.

The Just Demands of the Poor, by Marie Augusta Neal. Ramsey, NJ: Paulist Press, 1987. 142 pp. $8.95. ISBN 0-8091-2845-4.

Between Faith: Criticism, Evangicals, Scholarship: The Bible in North America, by Mark A. Noll. San Francisco: Harper & Row, 1986. 198 pp. $19.95. ISBN 0-06-066302-2.

John Colet's Commentary on First Corinthians, by Bernard O' Kelly, and Catherine A.L. Jarrott. Binghamton, NY: Center for Medieval & Early Renissance Studies, 1986. 271 pp. $20.00. ISBN 0-86698-056-3.

Calvin's O. T. Commentaries, by T. H. L. Parker. Edinburgh: T & T Clark, 1986. 244 pp. No price given. ISBN 0-567-09365-4.

The Gospel According to Matthew, by Daniel Patte. Philadelphia: Fortress 1987. 405 pp. $19.95. ISBN 0-8006-1978-1.

The Assembly of the Lord, by Robert S. Paul. Edinburg: T & T Clark, 1985. 545 pp. $32.95. ISBN 0-567-09341-7.

A Primer for Preachers, by Ian Pitt-Watson. Grand Rapids: Baker Book House, 1986. 107 pp. $5.95.

The Christian Problem: A Jewish View, by Stuart E. Rosenberg. New York: Hippocrene Books, 1986. 219 pp. $15.95. ISBN 0-87052-284-1.

Worldly Saints: The Puritans as They Really Were, by Leland Ryken. Grand Rapids: Zondervan, 1986. 221 pp. $14.95. ISBN 0-310-32500-5.

A Bell Ringing in the Empty Sky, ed. by Sy Safransky. Chapel Hill, NC: 1986. 514 pp. $12.95. ISBN 0-917320-24-7.

The Shaker Spiritual Narrative, by Diane Sasson. Knoxville: Tennessee Press, 1986. 219 pp. No price given. ISBN 0-87049-392-2.

Advances in Therapies for Children, by Charles E. Schafer, Howard L. Millman, Steven M. Sichel, Jane Riegelbaupt Zwilling. San Francisco: Jossey Bass, 1986. 430 pp. $27.95. ISBN 1-55542-010-9.

The Liturgy of the Hours, by Dominic F. Scotto. Petersham, MA: St. Bede Publications, 1986. 165 pp. $9.95. ISBN 8-932506-48-8.

Taking the World in for Repairs, by Richard Selzer. New York: William Morrow, 1986. 239 pp. $15.95. ISBN 0-688-06489-2.

Born to Die: Deciding the Fate of Critically Ill Newborns, By Earl E. Shelp. New York: Free Press, 1986. 206 pp. $19.95. ISBN 0-02-929110-D.

C. S. Lewis: Through the Shadowlands, by Brian Sibley. Old Tappan, NJ: Fleming Revell, 1985. 181 pp. $10.95. ISBN 08007-1509-8.

God's Word and Our Words: Basic Homiletics, Ronald E. Sleeth. Atlanta: John Knox, 1986. 125 pp. $7.95. ISBN 0-8042-1577-4.

Texas Baptist Leadership: Social Christianity 1900-1980, by John W. Storey. College Station, TX: Texas A & M Press, 1986. 224 pp. $22.50. ISBN 0-89096-251-0.

Theology Beyond Christendom: Essays on the Centenary of the Birth of Karl Barth, ed. by John Thompson. Pittsburg: Pickwick Press, 1986. 350 pp. $36.00.

New Hymns for the Lectionary, by Thomas H. Troeger and Carol Doran. New York: Oxford University Press, 1986. Ill pp. $7.95. ISBN 0-19-385729-4.

Protestantism and Progress, by Ernest Troeltsch. Philadelphia: Fortress, 1986. 109 pp. $8.95. ISBN 0-80016-3200-1.

Father Divine, by Robert Weisbrot. New York: Beacon, 1983. 223 pp. $19.95. ISBN 0-8070-0901-6.

And Are We Yet Alive?, by Richard B. Wilke. Nashville: Abingdon, 1986. 124 pp. $6.95. ISBN 0-687-01382-8.

Church and State in American History, 2nd ed., by John F. Wilson and Donald Drakeman. Boston: Beacon, 1987. 303 pp. $9.95. ISBN 0-8070-0409-X.

BOOKS REVIEWED